CHAMPAGNE

EXTRA CUVÉE   RÉSERVE 1914

Pol Roger & Co

Epernay

CHAMPAGNE

CHAMPAGNE

How the World's Most Glamorous Wine
Triumphed Over War and Hard Times

Don and Petie Kladstrup

WILLIAM MORROW
An Imprint of HarperCollins*Publishers*

HarperCollins books may be purchased for educational, business, or sales promotional use. For information please write: Special Markets Department, HarperCollins Publishers, 10 East 53rd Street, New York, NY 10022.

FIRST EDITION

Designed by Betty Lew
Frontispiece courtesy of Christian Pol-Roger

Printed on acid-free paper

Library of Congress Cataloging-in-Publication Data

Kladstrup, Don.
    Champagne: how the world's most glamorous wine triumphed over war and hard times / by Don and Petie Kladstrup.
        p. cm.
    ISBN-13: 978-0-06-073792-4 (acid-free paper)
    ISBN-10: 0-06-073792-1
    1. Champagne (Wine)—History. I. Kladstrup, Petie. II. Title.

TP555.K58 2005
641.2'224—dc22   2005050613

05 06 07 08 09 DIX/RRD 10 9 8 7 6 5 4 3 2 1

To the
GROWERS AND MAKERS
of
champagne
whose sufferings and sacrifices
gave birth to
a wine that has brought
joy to the entire
world

Gentlemen, in the little moment
that remains to us
between the crisis and the catastrophe,
we may as well drink a glass of champagne.

—PAUL CLAUDEL, FRENCH POET AND AMBASSADOR
TO THE UNITED STATES

CONTENTS

Contents

CHAMPAGNE

This Hallowed Soil

It had been described to us as one of the loveliest places in Champagne. Cross a little stream and go through a scruffy wood, we were told, and you will find yourself in a lovely clearing. It sounded like a perfect spot for a picnic. So we armed ourselves with a slice of pâté, a hunk of cheese, and a fresh baguette and set off. Oh yes, we also had a bottle of chilled champagne.

The morning mists were rising as we approached our destination. In the distance, we could hear the church bells of the tiny farming village of La Cheppe. It was just after nine. Only two hours earlier, we had been in Paris. Now, as we parked our car and made our way through some small woods, we felt as if we had been transported into another world.

Before us lay the ancient campsite of Attila the Hun. For a moment, we were taken aback. It was not the pretty little spot we had envisioned but rather a vast oval plain, about a half mile across and surrounded by earthen ramparts. The site was completely empty, like a fallow field. Nothing moved except a trio of deer that bolted out of sight when they spotted us.

Here, in this tranquil setting, on September 21, A.D. 451, Attila the Hun, the warrior chieftain of legendary cruelty, assembled his army of seven hundred thousand men and exhorted them, "One more blow and you will be masters of the entire world." The answering roar of approval must have struck fear into the hearts of their foes, the Gauls, Visigoths, and Franks who had joined forces with Rome to confront this ominous peril from the East.

What followed was one of the bloodiest battles in history. In one day alone, more than two hundred thousand men were slaughtered, their broken bodies scattered on the hillsides and fields of Champagne. Attila and his army fled. Before the battle, he had vowed that wherever his "horse shall tread, nothing shall ever grow again." [1]

He was wrong. The ramparts which circled the campsite were now thick with brush, alder, and ash trees. On the ground underneath, red currant and guelder rose competed for what was left of the sunlight.

We made our way up a heavily rooted path to the top of the ramparts and began walking, dodging branches and brambles while trying to imagine what it had been like on that day so long ago. What an incongruous setting for a picnic, we thought. Then again, what better place to try to reconcile le champagne, the wine that is the symbol of friendship and celebration, with la Champagne, a region that has been drenched with more blood than perhaps any other place on earth.

Consider this: the Hundred Years' War, the Thirty Years' War, a series of religious wars, a vicious civil war called the Fronde, the Napoleonic wars, the Wars of Spanish Succession—nearly all were fought primarily in Champagne. Even before those wars, Champagne had been plundered by wild tribes from the East such as the Teutoni, Cimbri, Vandals, and Goths. After them came the Romans who, by 52 B.C., managed to conquer all of Gaul and incorporate it, along with Champagne, into their empire. "From time immemorial," one historian said, "Champagne has suffered an overdose of invasions."

Fortunately, the Romans exerted a more civilizing influence than their predecessors. They planted the first vineyards and quarried limestone for building temples and roads. The quarries they left behind would be rediscovered centuries later and turned into the huge crayères that today are used for storing and aging champagne.

The Romans also brought their own laws, one of which spelled out punishment for anyone who attacked or damaged a neighbor's vineyard. It was a law the Franks would incorporate into their Salic Law generations later.

Not even the Romans, however, could control Mother Nature. When Mount Vesuvius erupted in A.D. 79, it destroyed not only Pompeii but also buried Rome's best vineyards. Overnight, wine became scarce throughout the Empire, so Emperor Domitian ordered that huge tracts of land used for growing cereals be turned into vineyards. Now instead of a wine shortage, the Romans were faced with a bread shortage.

To deal with that crisis, the emperor decreed that all of Champagne's vineyards be uprooted and converted into fields of grain. With Roman legions garrisoned on their soil, the Champenois had no choice but to comply.

Two centuries would pass before another emperor—appropriately, one who was the son of a gardener—revoked the decree. Emperor Probus not only gave permission for the people of Champagne to plant vines again, but he also sent Roman legionnaires to help.

We pondered all of this as we made our way around the ramparts of Attila's camp. It took us about two hours to complete the circle. Exhausted, famished, and thirsty, we could hardly wait to unpack our picnic.

As we spread our blanket and opened our bottle of champagne, everything began to feel right. Le champagne, which is masculine in the French language, seemed to be the ideal complement to the harsh environment of la Champagne, the province, which is feminine. A perfect couple, we thought, inseparable and joined in a union of strength, gaiety, and elegance.

Nothing about champagne, however, is simple or straightforward; its story overflows with irony. It gives the Champenois what one writer called "a taste for contradiction."[2] It takes poor soil to make good champagne; black grapes are used to make white wine; a blind man saw stars; the man credited with putting bubbles in champagne actually worked most of his life to keep them out.

The greatest irony of all, however, is that Champagne, site of some of mankind's bitterest battles, should be the birthplace of a wine the entire world equates with good times and friendship.

Those ironies are partly responsible for the aura of mystery and romance surrounding champagne. What is it about champagne?

Just saying the word is like waving a magic wand: people begin to smile, relax, and even fantasize. Certainly no other wine has lent itself to so much poetry, art, and hyperbole. Casanova considered it "essential equipment for seduction." Coco Chanel said she drank champagne on only two occasions, when she was in love and when she wasn't. Lily Bollinger, one of the grandes dames of Champagne, went further. "I drink champagne when I am happy and when I am sad. Sometimes I drink it when alone. In company I consider it compulsory. I sip a little if I'm hungry. Otherwise I don't touch it—unless I'm thirsty of course."

Everyone, it seems, has a favorite time for champagne. Patrick Forbes, the great champagne expert and historian, said he preferred it at 11:30 in the morning, when his palate was still fresh and he could taste every nuance and savor every bubble. When we asked Philippe Bourguignon, one of the world's great sommeliers, what he considered the best time for drinking it, he replied, "When I finish mowing the lawn." In the 1948 film *Letter from an Unknown Woman,* Joan Fontaine dreamily says to Louis Jourdan, "Champagne tastes much better after midnight, don't you agree?"

Then there was Oscar Wilde, who, upon arriving in France, told customs agents, "I have nothing to declare but my genius." Of champagne, he said, "Only the unimaginative can fail to find a reason for drinking champagne."

For ages, champagne has been used for celebrating weddings, baptisms, launching ships, spraying crowds at car rallies, and ringing in the New Year. It's been a tradition for so long that an English poet suggested that even Adam may have celebrated with it. In his poem "The First New Year's Eve," Thomas Augustine Daly wrote:

The man, the One and Only One—
First Gentleman on earth—
Said: "How about a little fun?
Come! Let us have some mirth!

"To some swell Night Club we must roam,"
Said he, "and drink champagne,"
But she said: "We can say at home,
And still be raising Cain."³

Health benefits have long been ascribed to champagne. In the 1930s the French medical community asserted that it was effective in fighting depression and warding off infectious diseases such as typhoid and cholera. Fifty years earlier, Germany's Iron Chancellor, Otto von Bismarck, a victim of chronic flatulence, claimed that champagne helped him "chase the winds." Winston Churchill said it "made his wits more nimble." He also used it to rally his colleagues during World War I. "Remember, gentlemen," he said, "it's not just France we are fighting for, it's Champagne!"

But that was hardly the first time champagne had played a pivotal role in the history of the world. During the Great Schism when there was a pope in Rome and one in France, the Holy Roman Emperor, King Wenceslas of Bohemia, went to Reims to discuss ending the split with Charles VI. The emperor, however, became so inebriated after drinking too much champagne, that he couldn't stand up to get to the meeting. After this condition persisted for several days, the French king finally sent two of his royal dukes to carry Wenceslas to the meeting. Wenceslas, however, was still in such a drunken state that he signed every paper

Charles put in front of him without reading them. As a result, the pope remained in Avignon, in his "Babylonian Captivity," and the Schism continued.[4]

Given that background, one might be tempted to dismiss champagne as something frivolous and unimportant. After all, what's to be made of a wine that goes by such names as bubbly, fizz, and even giggle water? The truth is, champagne is as serious and complex a wine as has ever been created. It's also the most difficult to make, something we quickly realized when we were invited to a dégustation (tasting) by Claude Taittinger, president and director-general of Taittinger Champagne.

Claude, as he does each year, had called together what he labeled "a closed circle" of friends including growers, producers, and others from the trade. Numbering around forty, they represented some of the finest palates in Champagne. The tasting involved about twenty new wines from the previous harvest, wines from different vineyards and villages that were to be blended in making Taittinger's 2004 vintage champagne, including his prestige mark, the Comtes de Champagne.

A bottle of champagne is rarely one wine; often it's a blend of as many as thirty or forty, the final product, or cuvée, being better than the individual wines themselves. "Blending," Taittinger said, "is a bit like being an artist. You don't know how many colors you are going to need when you begin the painting. You take a little red from here and some yellow from there. Sometimes you need to make the red lighter and the yellow darker to get the feeling that you want to convey."

We had been to tastings before, but never one like this, and we felt more than a little intimidated. The setting, in Reims, was the ancient home of the counts of Champagne, who ruled the province in the Middle Ages. One of the counts was Thibault IV, who introduced the ancestor of the chardonnay grape to Champagne when he returned from the Crusades.

The tasting, to use Taittinger's description, was like "a High Mass, a chance to restate, in a majestic setting, our commitment to a particular concept of champagne."

Two long tables had been set up, each with several rows of glasses filled with white wine, most of which had only a hint of sparkle. Half of the wines were chardonnay, the rest were pinot noir.

As each was sampled, Taittinger asked for reactions. Unlike everyone else, we didn't know how to react. We had tasted lots of champagne over the years but never by its individual parts. The nuances were lost on us. After one sample, Taittinger called on Don for his impressions. There was a moment of panic as he floundered and fumbled for words. Finally, Don blurted, "I'm not really tasting anything!"

Taittinger graciously steered the discussion away from him, noting that it takes years of experience to describe wine and identify the subtle differences. "How do you identify more body here, more character there, even more soul, sometimes," he asked. "How do you pick out from a bouquet the subtle aromas of tea, aniseed, vanilla, peach, wheat, even Virginia tobacco or truffles? How do you seek the appropriate adjective from words like cajoling, enchanting, warm, profound, impertinent, serene, when the wines themselves have none of these pretensions?"

Needless to say, our goal in this book is not to try to answer Taittinger's questions. Our book is not about tasting or the technicalities of champagne-making. It's more of an homage, maybe even a love letter. It's the story of how a small community of people, living in a harsh environment and subjected to centuries of invasions, triumphed over one adversity after another to create the greatest effervescent wine in the world.

That story began a long time ago when a Frankish warlord named Clovis routed the Romans in the fifth century and carved out a kingdom around Reims. His kingdom, however, was soon invaded by another Germanic tribe. Defeat seemed inevitable until Clovis's fiancée, a Christian, stepped forward and urged him to appeal to her God for help. Clovis, a pagan, was desperate and vowed that if her God granted him victory, he would become a Christian. Miraculously, his armies were imbued with new fighting spirit and put the enemy to flight.

Clovis kept his word. On Christmas day of 496, he and three thousand of his soldiers went to Reims to be baptized. The church was so crowded that the bishop, Saint Rémi, could not reach the holy oil to anoint Clovis. Fortuitously, a white dove appeared at that very moment and carried the vial of oil to the bishop.[5]

While the story has been embellished through the centuries, one thing is certain: a lavish banquet followed the baptism. The wine served was champagne or, to be more precise, the wine of Champagne. In those days, champagne was red, there were no bubbles, and it was often cloudy. The star-bright sparkling drink we enjoy today was still centuries away.

Nevertheless, champagne's fame as a celebratory drink had been established. From then on, nearly every king of France insisted on being crowned in Reims and celebrating afterward with champagne.

Crisis and conflict, however, were never far away. In the tenth century, Reims suffered four sieges in sixty years while Épernay was pillaged half a dozen times and all of its vineyards burned. Next came the Crusades, which drained Champagne of its able-bodied men; and after that, the Black Plague, which halved Europe's population in the fourteenth century.

The following centuries witnessed one bloody war after another, but each time, le champagne and la Champagne somehow survived.

In World War I, they almost did not. Of all the terrible moments in Champagne's long history, none was more catastrophic than World War I. It was Champagne's darkest hour.

Ironically, however, it was also the brightest, for at the very moment when all seemed lost, the people of Champagne found the strength and will to hold on. To appreciate what they went through, and how they miraculously survived, we realized that we had to gain a better understanding of the war itself.

The Great War, as the French call it, was a catastrophe that touched nearly every family in France. A young army captain, writing in his diary, described it best: "Will France be quick to forget her 1.5 million dead, her one million mutilated, her destroyed cities? Will weeping mothers suddenly dry their tears? Will orphans stop being orphans, widows being widows?" The young officer's name was Charles de Gaulle.[6]

His words moved us but left us with questions of our own. What makes World War I so different from other wars? Why is it that after so many generations the Great War still haunts us? Is it the testimony of soldiers who saw their comrades "laid open from the shoulders to the haunches like a carcass of meat in the butcher's window"?[7] Is it the powerful imagery of trench warfare, evoked by poets like James H. Knight-Adkin in "No Man's Land"?

> But No Man's Land is a goblin sight
> When patrols crawl over at dead o' night;
> Boche or British, Belgian or French,
> You dice with death when you cross the trench.

No death, perhaps, illustrated the senseless slaughter more than that of Prince Henri de Polignac, a career army officer whose family ran the champagne house of Pommery & Greno. "He was one of those rare people who knew the hour of his death," remembered his grandson, Prince Alain de Polignac.

Henri had been ordered to lead a charge out of the trenches into the face of German guns on a hill. When he radioed headquarters that it was impossible, that there was no territory to be gained and that his entire unit would be killed, he was told, "Those are your orders." The first wave was wiped out. Henri called headquarters again, pleading with them to change the orders. They refused. A second wave met with the same fate.

Now it was Henri's turn, but by then his radio was dead. Readying his men, he moved to the front of the line and gave the signal to charge. They were cut down just like the first two units. "My grandfather was one of the first killed," Prince Alain said, pointing with his forefinger to the center of his forehead to illustrate where he'd been shot. "The last man had barely fallen when a messenger on horseback rode up with orders to cancel the charge."

In Champagne, where the brunt of the Great War was fought, people talk about "the duty of memory." Only one village in all of France escaped without losing at least one of its citizens. This explains why, even in the tiniest of villages, there is a monument honoring those who were killed in the war. Every year, wreaths are laid and ceremonies are held.

Wherever we went, people kept returning to one theme: the extraordinary amount of blood that had been shed. "World War II," they would say. "Oh, it was terrible, but it was nothing compared to the Great War."

At Compiègne, the clearing in the woods where the Armistice was signed, we visited a small museum. Inside was a bank of stereoscopes, old viewing devices that turn photos into three-dimensional images, the sort of thing you used to find in your grandmother's parlor.

Although we'd grown up on television footage from Vietnam and were familiar with newsreels from World War II, we were unprepared for the pictures that leaped out at us: soldiers languishing in mud-filled trenches, others coated in chalky dust which turned them into ghostlike figures, towns and villages reduced to rubble, fields and vineyards crisscrossed by barbed wire and so cratered by artillery shells that they resembled a lunar landscape.

Then we saw the corpses. Some were piled high on the frozen ground and blanketed by snow; others lay where they fell, their comrades in arms, with blank expressions on their faces, standing helplessly by.

Next to the museum was an old railroad car. Inside was a long, dark mahogany table complete with chairs and nameplates. Everything was just as it had been on the eleventh hour of the eleventh day of the eleventh month of 1918, when the Allies accepted Germany's surrender. We looked on in silence and could almost feel the ghosts.

Then we met a living ghost. His name was Marcel Savonnet, and he was about to celebrate his one hundred and sixth birthday. Savonnet was the last poilu, the last Champenois to have fought in World War I. "Poilu" was what French soldiers called themselves, a word that means "shaggy ones," in reference to the unshaved, unkempt appearance that came from long months in the trenches. Like Samson, they claimed their long hair gave them strength.

The man we encountered, however, was more like an apparition, a fragile wisp of a man, barely five feet tall with head bent, moving slowly across the room with the aid of a walker. We met Savonnet at his home in Troyes, the ancient capital of Champagne. His living room was decorated with medals and citations.

Savonnet eased himself into an armchair, raised his head and began talking in a voice that was little more than a whisper. He was eighteen when he was sent to Verdun in 1917. "It was butchery," he said. "Every day death rained down, every day more bodies."

Often, Savonnet paused, and his eyes would slowly close. Then, just when we thought he'd fallen asleep, he would continue. "Today you can see the whole pattern of the war, the big picture, but we couldn't. Each soldier had his own little corner, his own narrow view of what was happening. We were isolated, and all we could think about was staying alive."

We saw that Savonnet was growing tired so we stood up to leave. His head came up one last time.

"Thank you for remembering us," he said. "Thank you for not forgetting."

Marcel Savonnet celebrated his one hundred and sixth birthday on March 22, 2004. It was a quiet celebration at home, with his family and with a few sips of champagne. A few months later, we called to see how he was doing. His son answered the phone. "My father left us on November 1," he said. "It was a quick end, but after such a life as he had . . ."

The younger Savonnet didn't finish. He didn't have to.

Finally, we began to understand. With Savonnet's death, we had not merely said good-bye to an old soldier; we had said farewell to one of the last links to an age that has disappeared.

It was a time, said historian Correlli Barnett, when people believed in a cause and were "ready to die, if need be, for King and Country, Kaiser and Fatherland, or La Patrie."[8] They lived by virtues such as comradeship, discipline, and courage, virtues that enabled them to triumph over great adversities.

Nowhere was this more true than in Champagne. As one champagne-maker told us, "It is a law of nature that the best products always grow under somewhat unsuitable circumstances, because they are forced to surpass themselves."

So it was with the Champenois, and World War I was their defining moment, the crucible in which champagne was forged. It was literally a trial by fire in which the champagne industry was nearly destroyed, when the courage and dedication of the Champenois were tested as never before.

That they met this test, along with so many others throughout the centuries, is what puts champagne in a class by itself. It's what gives champagne an almost mystical quality, an allure that has captured the hearts and imaginations of people throughout the world—and provided us the incentive and inspiration to try to explain how it all began.

CHAPTER 1

The Monarch and the Monk

They were born the same year and died the same year, and yet, they could not have been more different. One lived in absolute luxury, the other in abject poverty. One prided himself on his long, curly locks, the other shaved his head. One wore red high heels, the other simple sandals. One garbed himself in silk and velvet, the other in rough brown linen.

But Louis XIV and Dom Pérignon had one thing in common: both loved champagne, or, more precisely, the wine that would become champagne. Despite their differences, no two individuals did more to launch champagne on its path to fame and glory.

In the beginning, however, there was no such thing as champagne. Champagne was not a wine; it was a place, a region known mainly for fine, quality wool. If peasants had extra land, they sometimes planted vines and made wine to supplement their diets or earn extra income. Because that wine was so insignificant, it didn't even have a name. Instead, it was lumped in with other wines as "vins de l'Ile de France" or sometimes just "vins Français." Other times, it was labeled by the town or area it came from, such as "vins de Aÿ," "vins de la montagne," or "vins de la rivière." One thing it was never called was "champagne."

Also, it was red, but not dark red. It was pale, more onionskin in color, a variable pinkish brown which people described as oeil de perdrix, or partridge's eye.

More significant, there were no bubbles—not intentional ones, at least. Bubbles were considered a fault, something that ruined the wine and was to be avoided.

Although the Romans had begun planting vines and making wine in Champagne around 57 B.C., it wasn't until the eleventh century that anyone outside the region paid much attention. That was when the son of a vigneron from Châtillon-sur-Marne was elected to the papacy, assuming the name Urban II. The new Pope did much to promote the wines of his native land, letting it be known that he "preferred them to all others." [1] (It was an open secret in Rome that the best way to gain an audience with His Holiness was to arrive with a quantity of wine from Champagne.)

But there was something else the Pope did that enhanced the reputation of the region's wine even more: He launched the Crusades.

Champagne was a patchwork of warring fiefdoms whose leaders kept the province in constant turmoil. There was no central authority; some people were loyal to the king, others paid homage to the Duke of Burgundy, while still others owed their allegiance to the emperor of Germany. Some, who had bits of property scattered around the area, could find themselves paying homage to as many as five or six different overlords.

This tangle of allegiances led to so much upheaval and destruction that the Church was finally moved to appeal for a

"Truce of God," which forbade fighting during religious festivals, Holy Days, and on Sundays. Thus were weekends born.

Weekends, however, did little to bring an end to the turmoil. Rather than continue trying to restrain it, the Church opted to direct it for its own purposes.

In 1095 Pope Urban declared, "Let those who until now have been moved only to fight their fellow Christians now take up arms against the infidel." With those words, the First Crusade began. His call for a holy war struck a particularly responsive chord with his fellow Champenois, as warlords and others put aside differences and set off for Jerusalem, accompanied by their armies and retinues.

For the first time in generations, an atmosphere of calm descended over the region. Emptied of feuding factions, Champagne was transformed into an "island of peace," [a] capable of profiting from its location at the crossroads of Europe's two major trade routes. One ran east–west between the Frankish and Germanic kingdoms; the other extended from the North Sea to the Mediterranean. These routes made Champagne a natural center for commerce and helped spawn huge annual trade fairs, events that went on for weeks and attracted merchants from throughout the continent. There was lace from Holland, blankets from Belgium, furs from Russia, leather and gold from Italy, fine steel blades from Spain, oils from the Mediterranean, and wool and linen from France.

But not wine. The wines of Champagne were produced for local consumption and in such small quantities that even local needs often couldn't be met. Offering wine for sale or trade at fairs was out of the question. Merchants wanting wine to take home had to travel to Burgundy, a difficult journey that took at least a week.

By the 1200s, that began to change. Wool producers from Champagne, who made a bit of wine on the side, came up with a novel idea. To entice trade-fair visitors to buy their wool, they decided to provide free wine as well.

The promotions worked better than producers dared hope. Not only did they sell more wool, but they also began receiving orders for wine. Within a short time, wine had overtaken wool as the major product of the region. Although most buyers felt it necessary to "baptize" the wine before drinking it, diluting it with water because it was rather rough, they still found it agreeable. Best of all, it was cheaper than wine from Burgundy.

The Crusades, however, did more than provide a peaceful interlude in which Champagne could exploit its location at the crossroads of two trade routes. They also spurred the expansion of Champagne's vineyards. Because crusading was astronomically expensive, knights, nobles, and other landowners authorized peasants to plant more vines and make more wine to help finance their expedition. They also drew up wills. Hoping to ensure their salvation, the holy warriors stipulated that if they failed to return from the Holy Land, part of their property—including vineyards—would go to the Church. Many did not return, and the Church's landholdings increased dramatically.

The quality of Champagne's wines improved, too, for monks were the true oenologists of the day. They were committed to their vines and knew more about viticulture than anyone else. Wine was essential for celebrating Mass, treating the sick, and welcoming pilgrims as well as other travelers. More important, it was a financial mainstay for monasteries. Tithes were frequently paid with grapes and wine, which the monks could then sell or barter. In short, without vineyards, it's hard to imagine how monasteries could have functioned, or even existed.

The abbey of Hautvillers, perched on the southern slopes of the Montagne de Reims, was no exception. Founded in the seventh century, it had become renowned as a place with a mystical quality, a place lost in time. Shrouded in a bluish mist that often rose from the hillside, Hautvillers had an "extraordinary appeal for the faithful. Young men flocked there to become monks; old men came there to die." [3]

One woman came there as well. After she was dead.

Her name was Saint Helena. She was the mother of Constantine, the first Christian emperor of Rome. Helena had been buried in Rome in the fourth century, and was venerated for helping to save Jerusalem from the pagans and for finding the True Cross.

In 841, a monk from Hautvillers named Teutgise paid a visit to the Eternal City. He had been ill for many years, and had appealed to many saints for help, all to no avail. After praying at Saint Helena's shrine, however, he claimed to have been miraculously cured. For reasons that are unclear, Teutgise stole Saint Helena's mummified body from its mausoleum and spirited it back to Champagne, hoping that the sacred relics might be reburied at Hautvillers.

When the archbishop of Reims and the abbot of Hautvillers learned what he had done, they were horrified. Fearing the pope's wrath and scoffing at Teutgise's claims that the relics had miraculous powers, they refused to accept the body. Locals considered the matter a hoax. They, in fact, had far greater concerns. It had not rained for months, and vineyards were shriveling up. Don't worry, Teutgise said. If you fast for three days and pray to Saint Helena, the rains will come, and the drought will end. Deciding they had nothing to lose, the peasants agreed.

Three days later, the rains began falling. When other miracles followed, the archbishop and abbot reconsidered, dispatching a delegation to Rome. The pope, eager to avoid a scandal and happy to find a way to save face, declared that Saint Helena seemed very happy in her new French home and should not be disturbed. Vineyard workers, then in the midst of an abundant harvest, were overjoyed and vowed that from that day on, they would honor Saint Helena as their patron saint.

But not even the presence of a famous saint could save the abbey of Hautvillers from the afflictions that followed the Crusades. As crusaders returned home, Champagne again was plunged into violence. Throughout the fourteenth and fifteenth centuries, landless knights and ambitious lords fought for turf while bands of outlaws roamed the countryside, burning and pillaging. Entire towns and villages were abandoned. "There is not a recognizable track left," one person said. "There are no farms and, with the exception of a few bandits, no men."

The abbey of Hautvillers was sacked and burned to the ground at least four times. Even French troops sent to protect it had their way. "They drank six hundred casks of wine," said a farmer who lived nearby. "They cut down trees from the woods and burned the doors of the abbey. These are not dogs that the king has sent to guard his flock, but wolves."

By the end of the sixteenth century, nearly all of the monks at Hautvillers had fled. "It has been reduced to almost nothing," one of them said. "The few who remain cannot take care of it." [4]

In 1634 the abbot of Hautvillers admitted defeat and placed the monastery in the care of his brethren at Saint Vanne, an abbey in Verdun. For the next thirty years, the monks of Saint Vanne worked tirelessly to resurrect the property. Rubble needed clearing, buildings had to be rebuilt, fields and vineyards had to be replanted; but it was a torturously slow process.

By the 1660s it was clear to everyone that Hautvillers, the abbey that had become the resting place for a saint who had worked miracles, needed a miracle of its own. That miracle arrived in 1668, in the person of a young monk named Dom Pérignon.[5]

Dom Pierre Pérignon didn't have to become a monk. He could have lived a comfortable life, following in his father's footsteps as an official in the regional courts. As the eldest son, he would have been charged with managing the family's property, which included several vineyards around his birthplace of Sainte-Menehould, a picturesque village in eastern Champagne.

When Pierre was thirteen, his family sent him to a Jesuit school in nearby Châlons sur Marne. There he found his true calling. After five years of study, he announced that he wanted to become a monk and entered Saint Vanne, a monastery known for its rigorous holy life as well as its high intellectual standards. Prayer and total obedience were the order of the day. There were prescribed hours for meals, work, worship, sleep, and silence, all of which required incredible personal discipline and strict adherence to the Rule of Saint Benedict: "As idleness is the enemy of the soul, the brothers should be constantly occupied.

Manual labor is recommended, as it is during this time that the mind is inspired with its most fruitful thoughts." [6]

The cells in which the monks lived were minuscule; they were narrow and no more than nine feet in length. "It would have been surprising if Dom Pérignon had not felt like a bird in a cage or a foot in a too-tight shoe," [7] commented one historian. Nevertheless, he thrived, distinguishing himself by his deep religious convictions and devotion to hard work.

Dom Pérignon was thirty years old when the abbot of Saint Vanne appointed him as procureur, or business manager, of Hautvillers. The condition of the monastery was far different from what it had been years earlier, when another monk described it as "fit to delight every eye, satisfy every desire and charm every heart." Everything was in a state of decay. The church, hospital and storehouses were a wreck; living quarters were in shambles. Even worse were the vineyards. Dom Pérignon, whose responsibilities included being the abbey's cellarmaster, realized immediately that restoring Hautvillers to health depended on resurrecting its once-famous vineyards.

Those vineyards produced wine that had been celebrated in song as early as the thirteenth century. King Philippe-Auguste is said to have specifically ordered les vins d'Auviler for his royal table. They were also served at the coronations of Charles IV and Philippe VI a century later.

Restoring the vineyards was backbreaking work. Weeds and rocks needed clearing and brambles had to be cut away. New soil had to be hauled up from the valley below. Under Dom Pérignon's direction, vines of lesser quality were replaced with better ones. "Eliminate those that make nothing but common wine," he said. "Aim instead for quality that brings honor and profit."

Dom Pérignon has often been acclaimed as the person "who invented champagne." In truth, no one invented champagne; it invented itself. All wines start to bubble the moment grapes are pressed. Yeasts on the skin come into contact with the sugar in the juice, converting it to alcohol and carbonic gas, a process known as fermentation. In colder winegrowing regions like Champagne, the yeasts go into hibernation during the winter before all the sugar has been converted. In spring, they wake up and resume attacking the unconverted sugar, resulting in more alcohol and carbonic gas, the latter rising to the surface as bubbles.

In Dom Pérignon's time, no one knew about yeasts; they would remain a mystery for another two centuries until Louis Pasteur discovered them. Bubbles were considered a flaw, a vicious caprice of nature, and Dom Pérignon worked assiduously to eliminate them from his wines. Not only was fizzy wine unacceptable for Mass, it was unacceptable to the masses who were used to drinking still wines. Yet, because of Champagne's climate, fermentation was often a problem. Wine merchants warned customers, "Drink it before Easter, before spring when the weather warms and the wine starts to fizz again."

In the forty-seven years that Dom Pérignon served as cellar-master at Hautvillers, he never succeeded in totally eliminating bubbles from his wine. What he did accomplish was something much more important. He set down what some have called "the golden rules of winemaking," procedures that are still followed today. Among them: Use only the best grapes and discard those that are broken; prune vines hard in the early spring to avoid overproduction; harvest in the cool of the morning; press the grapes gently and keep the juices from each pressing separate.

At the time, these were radical ideas that ran counter to common practice. Most winegrowers grew as many grapes as they could. More grapes meant more wine and more money. Few realized, until Dom Pérignon came along, that limiting yields resulted in grapes of greater concentration, and that by picking early in the morning, one could make wines with more delicacy and finesse.

It was in blending, however, that Dom Pérignon showed his real genius. His ability to taste was legendary. He was blessed with a sensitive palate and a formidable wine memory. It was said that when workers brought him grapes from different vineyards and villages, he could tell "with frightening certainty"[8] where each grape came from. The real test was in assembling those grapes, deciding which to use and marrying them in such a way to create wines of perfect harmony and balance. In that, Dom Pérignon had no equal.

His talents were so extraordinary that it was not surprising certain myths would arise: that he possessed a secret recipe for making champagne; that he was blind; that after tasting sparkling champagne for the first time, he exclaimed, "I have tasted the stars!"

None of this is true. Yet, because of his wisdom, gifts of observation, very sure taste, and assiduous work, Dom Pérignon succeeded in making wine that was better than anyone else's. He was the first in Champagne to use corks for sealing bottles, which was far superior to wooden pegs wrapped with oil-soaked hemp, which most winemakers used. He also always strived to make wines that were natural with no foreign substances added.

They were "perfection married with simplicity," one contemporary said.

Many records were lost when Hautvillers was pillaged during the French Revolution, but if the few remaining documents are accurate, most of the wine that Dom Pérignon made was red, not white, and definitely not sparkling. In 1713, two years before the cellarmaster's death, an inventory was conducted of the wines at Hautvillers. It listed several hundred barrels of red wine, a smaller number of barrels of white wine, but absolutely *no* sparkling wine.

In addition, records from the abbey show that almost all of the vineyards it owned were planted with red grapes. There is also the overriding fact that most people at the time preferred red wine. Dom Pérignon was too good a businessman to have risked Hautvillers's fragile finances by trying to make much white wine or sparkling wine. What he *did* do was pave the way for such wines to be made. His advocacy of gentle pressing meant that the color from the grape skins was largely eliminated from the juice, resulting in wines that were no longer murky but instead distinguished by their clarity.

Only two letters written in Dom Pérignon's hand still exist. One of them accompanied a delivery of wine to the town manager of Épernay, and said, "Monsieur, I have given you twenty-six bottles of the best wine in the world."

He wasn't bragging, but merely stating a fact.

Louis XIV came into the world on September 5, 1638, about three months before Dom Pérignon. His arrival was greeted with rejoicing and a great deal of surprise, because his parents, Louis XIII and Anne of Austria, had been married for twenty-three years without having borne a child, and spent most of the time apart.[9]

The royal baby quickly called attention to himself. Within six months, he had worn out seven wet nurses. More painfully for the nurses, his teeth had come in early. The royal doctor decried the nurses for failing to produce enough milk and turning the infant into "a vampire."[10] Altogether, it was a bad omen, said the Swedish ambassador to the royal court. "France's neighbors should beware of such precocious voracity."[11]

Louis loved sports, gardening, and art. He liked dancing the ballet so he could show off his well-formed legs. He acquired a taste for feminine company but considered women "treacherous, stubborn, and indiscreet, objects to be used." When attending fairs or other public events, he relished going incognito. He hated tobacco, admired hearty eaters, and, while a stickler for etiquette, enjoyed food fights and tossing pellets of bread at women.

There was something else he loved, too: champagne. He had his first taste at his coronation in Reims when he was sixteen. The ceremony took place in Reims's great cathedral, where French kings were traditionally crowned. It was during the celebration that followed that he was introduced to the wines of Champagne. "Sire," said one of his vassals, "we offer you our wines, our pears, our gingerbreads, our biscuits, and our hearts." The teenaged king replied, "That, gentlemen, is the kind of speech I like."[12]

For the next fifty years, Louis XIV rarely drank anything but champagne. The entire royal court followed suit.

The Sun King's patronage marked the beginning of a prosperous time for winemakers in Champagne. Roads and canals were expanded, enabling producers to reach wider markets. Trade with other countries was increased, thanks, in part, to Louis's industrious finance minister, whose motto was "export or die."

Even the king's palace at Versailles served as a vehicle for promoting champagne. With its Hall of Mirrors, exquisite gardens and ever-present sun motif, the palace was an irresistible draw. Other rulers tried to imitate it; every noble in France lobbied for lodging there. It was just what the Sun King wanted: a magnificent edifice that displayed the greatness of France and reflected his personal glory. It was also a showcase for his own tastes.

Everything Louis did, and especially what he ate and drank, was followed avidly. His dinners were like theater performances, his courtiers standing and watching as the king dined alone. If the king liked a certain dish or beverage, everyone at Versailles knew about it instantly, and it would be on the table of the rich and titled almost immediately. So it was with champagne. Because it was Louis's favorite wine, it soon became everyone else's.

Eating and drinking were not casual matters in seventeenth-century France, especially when royal taste buds were involved. Everyone was desperate to please the king and make sure that whenever he traveled, he was served what he liked. On one occasion, it became a matter of life and death.

In the summer of 1669 the Sun King and his entourage paid an unexpected visit to the Prince de Condé at his château in Chantilly, just north of Paris. The prince had the best chef in

France, a certain Monsieur Vatel. Such was Vatel's reputation that he was expected to be able to provide for the unexpected, even if it involved two thousand sudden guests. Copious quantities of champagne were brought up from the prince's cellars while Vatel searched frantically for enough food. There was plenty of fish, he was told, so Vatel decided that would be his pièce de résistance.

Everything seemed to be in place with the king and the prince enjoying themselves when Vatel was informed that the fish had not arrived. He was distraught, utterly mortified; his reputation as the greatest chef was about to go up in smoke. Vatel left the kitchen, went to his living quarters and there, he threw himself on his sword.

His death was treated as a national tragedy, especially after it was learned that the fish *had* arrived, and it had all been a misunderstanding.[13]

In addition to champagne, Louis XIV had one other passion: war. During his seventy-two-year reign, there were only seven years of peace. "Peace tormented him," it was said, "so he sought to awake war."[14] He particularly loved sieges and launched wars against England, Austria, Spain, and the Netherlands. In one battle, Louis's love of champagne played a pivotal role.

It happened in 1676 as two armies—one commanded by the Sun King, the other by William of Orange—faced each other on the field of battle. The two armies had been engaged in a series of skirmishes for months, all aimed at settling the border between France and the Netherlands. The French clearly had the upper hand. They were better armed and outnumbered their foes forty-eight thousand to thirty-five thousand. Wherever they went, cities surrendered to them.

Not surprisingly, William of Orange was in a state of deep depression. He was out of money and getting no help from his allies. Now he was being forced into a battle he didn't want and knew he would surely lose. Cannons from the French side had begun firing. Rather than respond, William did nothing, hoping to postpone the inevitable.

Suddenly, the cannons fell silent, and a herald from the French camp appeared at William's tent. "His Majesty, the Sun King, is out of wine," the herald explained. "He begs for you to give me safe conduct through your lines so that I might fetch a supply of champagne for the royal table."[15] William agreed, but on the condition that the herald tell him what was happening in the enemy camp. The herald explained that the cannonade that had been heard was in celebration of a victory that the king's brother had just won elsewhere.

Then came an even bigger surprise. The herald unwittingly revealed that a war council had advised Louis against going into battle, and that the Sun King had agreed. William, who had been on the verge of surrendering, was giddy with relief and sent the herald on his way.

On his way back, William stopped the herald and said, "Give the king his champagne with my blessing, but also, give him a message. Tell him that had he chosen to attack, he most certainly would have won."

The Sun King regretted his decision not to fight for the rest of his life. His only consolation, perhaps, was the champagne that his emissary returned with.

But it was a consolation he would not enjoy for much longer.

A bitter tug of war was going on at Versailles between the king's official doctor and an ambitious rival named Guy-Crescent Fagon. The doctor, Antoine d'Aquin, was a staunch advocate of champagne, saying it was good for the Sun King's health and that the monarch should drink some with every meal. Fagon, who coveted d'Aquin's job, favored the wines of Burgundy. With help from Louis's mistress, he outmaneuvered d'Aquin and had himself appointed the royal doctor.

The king was plagued by a wide assortment of ailments, including migraines, gout, and gastric distress. His maladies commanded the attention of everyone. Everything from the color of his urine to the number of bowel movements he had daily was recorded in meticulous detail. One section of the king's medical journal even recorded the discovery of a live, six-inch-long worm in the royal stools.

An anal fistula elicited pages of commentary, and its lancing by a surgeon and three doctors kept the entire court up nights for news of the Sun King's condition. Louis was purged and bled frequently and treated with the "hot iron" to cauterize his jaw when teeth were removed.

Fagon attributed the king's health problems to champagne. "As a result," he declared, "I have decided that from now on, only Burgundy shall be served at the royal table." Louis accepted the doctor's advice, but it depressed him.

Fagon's decision, however, sent shock waves through Champagne. The Champenois felt insulted and claimed that their honor had been called into question.

It also aggravated a quarrel that had been going on between

Champagne and Burgundy since 1652. Both regions were making red wines and both were convinced that theirs was not only the best, but also the healthiest. They took pains to prove that with winemakers and merchants, paying medical students to present theses backing their point of view. The theses were used as advertising and distributed to customers.

After Fagon's assertion that Burgundy was better, the Faculty of Medicine in Reims set about refuting his claims. As proof, physicians cited the example of a vigneron named Piéton from Hautvillers, where Dom Pérignon's abbey was located. The vigneron married at age 110 and died when he was 118. They did not say if the marriage produced any offspring, but they did stress that this example proved, beyond question, that wine from Champagne was better for health and longevity.

Burgundy winegrowers were quick to respond. They summoned a physician named Jean-Baptiste de Salins, who was dean of the medical school in Beaune and one of the most respected physicians in France. He would, they hoped, prove Burgundy's superiority once and for all.

The setting was the auditorium of the Paris Faculty of Medicine. When Salins arrived, it was already jammed with doctors, reporters, Burgundians, and wary Champenois. As he approached the podium, a hushed silence fell over the crowd.

Salins began by pointing out that the courts of England, Germany, Denmark, and Italy drank only wines from Burgundy. He acknowledged that wines from Champagne were popular, but that, he said, was only because two of the king's ministers had vineyards there and were promoting them for personal profit. "Those wines have no strength, none of the vigor people used to call generosity," he said. "They are weak, half-hearted and watery; their color is changeable and unreliable, and they cannot withstand transport."[16]

Burgundy, he said, is robust, a rich red, the color of blood. He cited two examples where Burgundy was served, one at a festival in Venice and the other at a coronation in Poland. "The wines had to be transported a great distance," he said. "In both cases, they were in perfect condition when they arrived."

As Salins concluded his remarks, he looked up from his prepared text. "The wines of Burgundy," he declared, "have no equal and are good no matter what the season."

Cheers and jeers erupted from the audience. In one part of the auditorium, a fistfight broke out between citizens of the rival regions, forcing guards to be called to break up the scuffle.

Salins's speech was rushed into print and distributed throughout the country. The Champenois were reeling. They had not missed the doctor's not-so-subtle jabs about their wines' pale and variable color, or their annoying tendency to begin effervescing in the spring. It was like throwing oil on fire, and the war of words heated up.

Quickly, the Champenois picked a champion of their own who rebutted Salins point by point. Pierre Le Pescheur said Champagne's wines had become popular on merit alone, not because the court favored them. "And by the way," he added, "it's scurrilous to say that the ministers have vineyards in Champagne. They do not. They are in the wool business."

Le Pescheur accused the king's doctor of "sinister machinations" in persuading the monarch and his retainers to transfer their loyalties to Burgundy. "As soon as people get away from the court, most tell us they go back to champagne because there is no pleasure in drinking Burgundy."

Le Pescheur went on to describe how champagne had attracted a loyal following throughout Europe. The English, Germans, and Scandinavian countries had bought more wine from Champagne than from Burgundy "because it's better," he asserted. "Since we have learned the secret of making clear wines, one can, without risk, transport them to the ends of the earth. Poland and Venice are nothing," he sniffed. "We have sent our wines as far away as Persia, Siam, and Surinam and everyone has found the wines delicious even after those long voyages."

In conclusion, Le Pescheur cited a group known as l'Ordre des Coteaux, a fraternity of young noblemen with gourmet tastes who had done much to popularize the wines of Champagne, especially at Versailles. These were men who insisted on the finest of everything: veal from Normandy, partridges from the Auvergne, and wine only from the hillsides, or coteaux, of Champagne. Their most famous member was the Marquis de Saint-Evremond, who had fled to England to avoid imprisonment in the Bastille after writing a satirical letter about the monarchy. He had become an arbiter of fine taste there.

Saint-Evremond wrote another letter, which Le Pescheur quoted, noting that "For some time now, the wines of Burgundy have been losing their credit with people of truly fine taste. Those who appreciate the best should go as far as they have to, pay as much as necessary, to obtain wines from Champagne, for they are the real wines for all seasons."

By the time Le Pescheur's thesis was published in 1706, everyone wanted to become involved in the debate. Poets, playwrights, and other writers were all arguing in print for their favorite wines. In 1712, when a professor from a college in Champagne wrote an ode in Latin praising the local wines, the city of Reims rewarded him with huge quantities of champagne, along with a pension. That prompted even more writers to make wine the center of their works.

By the end of the year, Paris was awash in pamphlets, poems, theses, and other wine-quarrel-related polemics, most of them turned out by a printer named Thiboust who made so much money out of the war of words that he was able to retire.[17]

The battle between the two wine regions went on for nearly 130 years. At times, it raged so furiously that Burgundy and Champagne were at the brink of civil war. Finally, however, the conflict collapsed under the weight of words.

But there was one other factor that helped bring the quarrel to an end, one that was completely unexpected. Champagne-makers had finally begun learning how to harness bubbles. Not only that, a growing number of doctors, and not just in Champagne, was becoming convinced that the bubbles in champagne were good for health. Bubbles, they said, could cure malaria. With ramparts in Reims and other cities surrounded by stagnant moats, this was news that caught everyone's attention. Suddenly, sparkling wines became popular, especially among the titled and the wealthy.

As a result, there was nothing to fight about. Champagne and Burgundy were now making completely different wines. Instead of trying to make a red wine that would compete with Burgundy, the Champenois had embarked on an entirely new course. Burgundians, in turn, could now concentrate on making their wines without worrying about being undercut by champagne.

The war of words was finally over. "Happy is the nation that never knows any other kind of war," one writer said.

Neither Louis XIV nor Dom Pérignon would have been pleased about the way the war ended, for neither liked bubbles in their champagne. The cellarmaster of Hautvillers had struggled all his life to keep bubbles out, while the Sun King, in old age, had become conservative and staid, viewing bubbles as a symbol of the debauched lifestyle of his nephew, the Duc d'Orléans.

In the last years of his life, Louis XIV had been told to eat less and exercise less strenuously. The monarch was suffering from an increasing number of disorders, including one that his physician, Dr. Fagon, had diagnosed as sciatica. The Sun King was actually suffering from gangrene in the leg. "Just bathe it regularly in Burgundy wine," Fagon said. "It'll be all right." Louis XIV died in protracted agony at the age of seventy-six, just three days before his seventy-seventh birthday.

He left behind landmarks and laws that represented his political determination and his personal vision of grandeur, but, said historian René Gandilhon, "The sun of Louis XIV would have been deprived of at least one of its rays if a humble Benedictine monk had not, at that time, perfected the art of making champagne."[18]

Dom Pérignon died three weeks after Louis XIV. He never met his sovereign, even though there were times when they were only a few miles apart, but perhaps it is just as well. As Gandilhon noted, "There were too many battles inscribed on His Majesty's honors to please one who lived under the sign of peace."[19]

Thanks to Dom Pérignon's work at Hautvillers, the abbey, by then, was flourishing; the size of its vineyards had doubled. As a mark of respect for the cellarmaster and all he had accomplished, the monks of the monastery laid him to rest in a section of their church normally reserved for abbots.

"Never was there a man more talented in making wine," said his successor. He was "the guardian and teaching angel of the house," observed another monk, "a man who died in the full odor of sanctity and will be remembered gratefully by his holy brethren." [20]

CHAPTER 2

The Men in the Iron Masks

The hunting had been good; enough game was brought down to feed the entire court at Versailles for several days. The hunters were exhilarated, but they were even more thrilled by the thought of the lunch that would follow. Fresh oysters had been brought in that morning from the bay of Colchester on the English coast. A new wine was also being served, one that had taken the rich and titled by storm: sparkling champagne.

That was the image that flashed into the mind of Jean-François de Troy after receiving a commission from France's Directeur des Bâtiments du Roi, the superintendent of buildings, to create a painting for the Hunt Dining Room in les petits appartements of Versailles, where the king did his personal entertaining.

The scene was one de Troy knew well. He was no starving artist, but rather, a very successful one, who had spent much time around the king's court and been part of the social whirl that characterized the Siècle des Lumières (the Age of Enlightenment).

It was a period of intellectual and artistic renewal in France, and Jean-François de Troy was the perfect man for those glittering times. He was handsome, charming, and always impeccably dressed. Rarely was he ever seen without a beautiful woman on his arm. People commented on his witty and brilliant conversation, a commodity highly valued in eighteenth-century France.

De Troy's artistic training had come at the hands of his father, who, as head of the French Academy of Painters and Sculptors, enjoyed royal patronage, a key for opening doors and making contacts. But it was Jean-François's talent that commanded the royal court's attention.

When the Directeur des Bâtiments informed him in 1734 that Louis XV would like him to do a painting, de Troy understood immediately what the king was looking for. He was aware that Louis had always felt suffocated by the grandiose formality of his great-grandfather the Sun King. Louis preferred something more intimate, a place where he could escape the public glare and spend time with close friends, especially his mistress, Madame de Pompadour. That was why he set aside a special room at Versailles just for dining. It was the first time any room at the palace had been designated uniquely for such a purpose. De Troy's job was to help create the right atmosphere.

And what better way to do that, he thought, than to use champagne as a focal point of the painting, the centerpiece of a convivial meal. For de Troy, champagne symbolized the good life—gaiety, lively conversation, elegance—the very things the king hoped to evoke with his new dining room.

Working from his Paris studio, de Troy first rendered several sketches with charcoal on blue paper, then an esquisse, or rough version of the painting he planned to do. When he presented his ideas to the king's advisers, they were enthusiastic and authorized de Troy to proceed.

The result was *Le Déjeuner d'Huîtres* (the Oyster Lunch). It was the first time sparkling champagne had ever been depicted in a painting.

In a way, it is almost a snapshot: twelve gentilhommes are seated at an oval table covered in white linen, conversation abruptly stopping as they watch the cork shoot from a bottle of champagne toward the ceiling. Only by following their gaze can the cork be spotted, for the bouchon is nearly lost against a column. The man who opened the bottle seems to be the most enthralled. He's still holding the knife he used to cut the string that held the cork in place.

In the foreground, generous amounts of oysters spill out of baskets onto the floor while bottles of champagne are being chilled in an ice-filled rafraichîssoir. At each place setting is a small bowl with a cone-shaped glass slanting downward. Glasses of champagne were drunk in one gulp in those days, then turned over in a bowl to let the substantial amount of sediment thrown off by the champagne drain out. The next gulp of champagne was always served in a fresh glass.

Although the men supposedly have just returned from a hunt, they are dressed in clothes far too elegant for that; their garb is more in line with the magnificent decoration of the room and de Troy's appreciation for elegance. The only female presence is a lush statue of Amphitrite with her dolphin watching them from a niche in the wall. From the ceiling, a kind of in-house joke looks down on the group. It is a reversed image of one of de Troy's other paintings, *Zéphyr et Flore*.

Le Déjeuner d'Huîtres, however, was de Troy's tour de force, an exquisitely wrought, finely finished work that drew raves from the moment it was unveiled.

Nevertheless, there was one feature that no one may have noticed. Every person in the painting, from servant to master, has essentially the same face. Perhaps, as one art historian observed, it is because de Troy was no portraitist. Then again, maybe that's how he wanted it, how he planned it—to make sure champagne was the star of the show.[1]

In some ways, it was a miracle this show ever took place, that Louis XV ever became king. There were so many people ahead of him to succeed Louis XIV. One by one, however, in less than a year, all of them died. First was the Sun King's son, then his grandson, and afterward, his eldest great-grandson. Other family members, including Louis XV's mother, died as well, all succumbing to smallpox or the measles. The orphaned Louis survived only because his nurse spirited him away from the royal doctors, whose remedy for nearly every disease was a phlebotomy, or bleeding.

With only a fragile infant left as his heir, the bereaved and aging Sun King rewrote his will, stipulating that France, after his death, should be ruled by a Regency Council until Louis XV came of age. What worried the king was that his nephew Philippe, the Duc d'Orléans, would try to take over the throne. Philippe was debauched, a man who exhibited "unbridled tastes of the flesh" and in whom, it was said, "all the vices competed for first place."

But even an absolute monarch cannot control things from the grave. When the old king died in 1715, Philippe maneuvered to have the monarch's will overturned and himself appointed Regent, the effective ruler of France until Louis XV was old enough to assume his duties.[2]

Life at the royal court changed abruptly. Versailles was essentially closed down and everything transferred to Philippe's residence at the Palais Royal, in Paris. Five-year-old Louis XV, along with his nurses and tutors, was installed in the nearby Tuilleries Palace.

With the Duc d'Orléans at the helm, France, as one observer said, "embarked upon one of the most frivolous, extravagant, rip-roaring decades in its history." Although the intelligent and militarily astute Philippe devoted his days to work, nights were a different story. Fast young women, powdered dandies, rakes, and amorous abbots descended on the Palais Royal in droves for Philippe's candlelit suppers. His "petits soupers," however, were little more than orgies, and they made for riveting gossip. Philippe did nothing to discourage it. He even coined a new word to describe the men who joined him in his nightly revels: roués, "men so wicked," he said, "they deserve to be broken on the wheel," or roue.

According to one of his roués, the Duc du Richelieu, "The orgies never started until everyone was in that state of joy that champagne brings."[3] Most of the time, it was the women who opened the bottles. They delighted in the sexual symbolism of the explosion of froth when they cut the string and the cork flew out. Nor did the symbolism escape one of the licentious priests who kept company with the roués. He wrote:

Vois ce nectar charmant
Sauter sous ces beaux doigts
Et partir à l'instant.
Je crois bien que l'amour en ferait tout autant.[4]

See how the delightful nectar
Spurts beneath those pretty fingers
And runs away.
I hope love can do as well.

Before long, petits soupers had become one of the most popular forms of entertainment in France, and other countries were quick to copy. Nothing could have done more to boost the popularity of champagne, or enhance its reputation as a wine of gaiety and love.

In London, the British took it a "step" further. According to a local newspaper, "some bloods" were carousing with a celebrated fille de joie when one of them pulled off her shoe. "In an excess of gallantry, he filled it with champagne, and drank it off to her health. To carry the compliment further, he ordered the shoe itself to be dressed, fried in batter and mixed in a ragout, and served up for supper."[5]

By 1730, sparkling champagne had conquered the courts of Europe, with copious amounts being drunk in the palaces of London, Brussels, Vienna, and Madrid. In Berlin, Frederick the Great of Prussia raised a question that still puzzled everyone: what is it, exactly, that makes champagne sparkle? He tossed the question to experts at the Academy of Sciences, who said they would be delighted to investigate but that they could not afford to buy the necessary champagne for an experiment. When they asked Frederick if he would be willing to donate forty bottles from his cellar, he refused, saying he preferred to keep his ignorance rather than lose his champagne.[6]

Of all the royal courts, however, Russia's was probably the most susceptible to the sparkle of champagne. Peter the Great took four bottles to bed with him every night. His daughter, Czarina Elizabeth, became the first ruler to designate champagne as the official wine for toasts, replacing Tokay. Catherine the Great, whose sexual appetite was legendary, used champagne to "fortify" her young officers. She must have been especially pleased with one by the name of Razumovsky because he ordered one hundred thousand bottles of French wine each year, nearly seventeen thousand of which were sparkling champagne. The Czarina promoted him to the rank of field marshal.[7]

According to British wine authority Hugh Johnson, "No other wine, no other drink, had ever created, by its special qualities, a whole mood that almost amounted to a way of life."[8]

Yet, sparkling champagne constituted only a tiny percentage, less than two percent, of the wine being produced in Champagne. Most of what was still being made was cheap and red.

Champagne-makers shied away from sparkling wine because it was totally unpredictable. Sometimes it was flat and lacked effervescence. Other times it was "green and hard as a dog," as one producer described it when grapes failed to ripen.[9] If the wine rested too long in wooden casks, the bubbles could be too big, almost gloppy, a condition described as "yeux de crapauds" (toads' eyes). If dirt or bacteria got to it, the champagne might be oily and murky, or have the texture of a slimy worm.

One of Champagne's first wine merchants, Adam Bertin de Rocheret, flatly refused to have anything to do with sparkling champagne. When he received an order from the famous d'Artagnan, head of the king's musketeers, he refused to supply it, explaining, "It's an abominable beverage. Effervescence belongs to beer and whipped cream."[10]

But there was a more compelling reason why so many merchants and producers avoided sparkling champagne: it was dangerous. The buildup of carbonic gas, the very element that gave champagne its sparkle, was often so great that it caused bottles to explode. The process of fermentation was unknown. No one had heard of yeasts or carbonic gas; certainly no one knew how to control them. "These phenomena are so strange," observed one scientist, "that no one will ever be able to explain them. All these accidents are so varied and extraordinary that even the most experienced professional cannot foresee them or prevent them from happening."[11]

About all anyone knew was that their wine would start to "work" just after bottling, then go into hibernation during the winter. After "the March moon," when temperatures rose, the wine began to "fret" as it underwent what is now known as secondary fermentation. By summer, the wine could be "en furie," bubbling like a witch's cauldron, until bottles began exploding.

"Devil's wine," they called it, and no one dared enter a cellar without first donning an iron mask. These masks resembled a crude version of a baseball catcher's mask and were constructed with a heavy layer of protective grillage. Even with the masks, lost eyes and scarred hands marked those who worked among the bottles. At one firm alone, three men lost eyes from shards of flying glass.

Often, there would be a chain reaction with the heat from one exploding bottle setting off others. Cellarmasters sprayed cold water to keep temperatures down, but rarely did it do any good. "I started with six thousand bottles," said one champagne-maker. "By the end, only 120 were left." Another distraught producer, after seeing his hard work blow up in front of him, ran through his cellars with a club, whacking the remaining bottles and screaming, "Damn you then, go ahead and break."

So much champagne was spilled that cellars often resembled foamy swamps. Many producers began building their cellar floors at a slant so the juice could be drained out. At some houses, the froth was funneled into giant pots that workers took home for use in cooking. Usually, workers were also given the right to collect the broken glass, which they could sell as a kind of hazard pay.

Given the risks, many Champenois were startled when a young winegrower named Claude Moët said he was going to devote his business exclusively to sparkling champagne. Is he crazy? they wondered. Doesn't he know he stands to lose 20 to 90 percent of his bottles to breakage every year?

Moët was keenly aware of the problems but was convinced a new era was at hand. He believed what Dom Pérignon's successor, Dom Pierre, had said a short time earlier, that tastes were changing and that it would not be long before sparkling wine triumphed over the other wines of Champagne.

Moët's flair for salesmanship helped bring that about. He was one of the first to realize the importance of personal contact with customers, especially those with influence. In the 1730s he began making regular trips to the palace of Versailles. Within a short time, he had become one of the tiny handful of wine merchants accredited to the royal court.[12]

It helped that one of his ancestors fought at Joan of Arc's side in 1429. He was a Dutchman named LeClerc who aided in keeping the English at bay so Charles VII could be crowned. Standing at the head of the army near the gates of Reims, LeClerc shouted, "Het moet zoo zijn"—"It must be so"—as the Maid of Orléans ushered Charles into the cathedral.[13] His strong voice and even stronger sword arm were richly rewarded by the king. The cry also earned him a new name: Moët, which the king gave him to honor his determination.

That characteristic defined Claude Moët as well. By 1750, despite problems with breakage, he was producing fifty thousand bottles of sparkling champagne a year. It was an unheard-of quantity in a region that never produced more than three hundred thousand bottles in any one year during the eighteenth century.

On one of his trips to Versailles, Moët was introduced to a group of beautiful young women who were eager to try his champagne. They found it "deliciously feminine" and asked for more. One of those women was Madame de Pompadour, Louis XV's official mistress, who quickly became one of Moët's most loyal customers and made sure his sparkling champagne was served at every important function. "Champagne," she pronounced, "is the only wine that leaves a woman beautiful after drinking it."

Such aphorisms, casually tossed off, seemed to reflect an age when conversation was considered as much an art as painting or sculpting. According to writer Nancy Mitford, "Chat was the pastime of the age, cheerful, gossipy, joking chat, running on hour after idle hour, all night sometimes, and at this the Marquise [Pompadour] excelled."[14] Chat added vivacity to the dinner parties of Louis XV, affairs frequently held in the intimate atmosphere of the Hunt Dining Room, where the rigid etiquette of the court was relaxed and guests were encouraged to speak their minds. Politics, philosophy, food, sex—no topic was taboo for discussion.

Based on letters and other writings left behind, including extensive notes made by Madame de Pompadour's maid, who sat quietly, almost out of sight, in a corner or on a small balcony, one can easily imagine some of the conversation that took place.

LOUIS [raising a glass of champagne]: "We would like to propose a toast to the Duc de Richelieu for his victory at Mahon in Minorca."

POMPADOUR [smiling]: "The Duke seems to take a town in the same light-hearted way that he seduces a woman."

LOUIS: "Ah, but he said in his dispatches that besieging the town was boring because there were no women. His only consolation was food and drink."

POMPADOUR: "Well then, did he tell you about his cook? There was no butter or cream on the island so he made the most delicious sauce out of oil and eggs. The Duke adores it and calls it 'mahonaise.' "[15]

Soldiers, gardeners, and architects were frequent guests at the dinner parties, reflecting the king's special interests. Writers, however, were rarely in attendance because Louis felt intimidated. When they were invited, usually at the insistence of Madame de Pompadour, who was especially fond of Voltaire, they had to eat in another room. The king considered Voltaire

annoying and ill-mannered, but he did agree with a couplet he
wrote about champagne:

De ce vin frais l'écume pétillante
De nos Français est l'image brillante.

What Voltaire was saying was that the character of the French
is mirrored by the brilliant sparkle of champagne. Not "vin de
Champagne" as most then referred to it, just "champagne." It
was a distinction Madame de Pompadour was adamant about.
She was one of the first to realize that sparkling champagne was
unique and nothing like the other wines of Champagne.

The marquise had spent a good part of her life in Champagne.
Her father and brother had property there; the king even had a
special road built to make her journeys to Champagne faster and
more comfortable. She had seen how the wine of that province
had evolved, first as a celebrated still white and later as a popular
red when Louis XIV became king. Now, under Louis XV, it was
changing again.

One of his first acts was to set standards for sparkling champagne. Bottles which once came in all shapes and sizes now had
to be uniform and contain the same amount of champagne.
Corks had to be tied down with a "three-threaded string, well-
twisted and knotted in the form of a cross over the cork."

But the king's greatest contribution to champagne was freeing the business from its shackles. Prior to 1728, all wine, including champagne, had to be transported in wooden casks
because that was how it was taxed. For nonsparkling wines, this
was not a problem, but for champagne it was disastrous. Wood
destroyed its effervescence. Its porous nature allowed the gas to

escape, resulting in champagne that was flat. Champagne-makers petitioned the king, saying they could soon be out of business unless the law were changed. After lengthy deliberations, Louis said he was "pénétré de ces raisons" and would permit champagne—but only champagne—to be shipped in bottles.[16] The king's decision meant that for the first time, producers could begin exploiting champagne's commercial opportunities in earnest. As Louis himself acknowledged, "People who like champagne want it to have bubbles."

Bubbles, however, were something champagne-makers constantly wrestled with. Either there were too many, which led to exploding bottles, or there weren't enough, in which case the wine was flat. Producers went to unusual lengths to create at least a bit of sparkle. Some added alum, elderberries, various drugs, and even pigeon droppings to their champagne. The latter was something producers understandably tried to keep secret, even though a French chemist in Champagne testified that pigeon excrement "contained healthful properties for humans."

In the village of Aÿ, a certain champagne-maker claimed he possessed Dom Pérignon's "secret recipe," telling customers that by mixing in candied sugar, peaches, cinnamon and nutmeg, along with a dose of eau de vie, their champagne would be "delicate and fizzy."

There was, however, a more amusing and dramatic way of injecting bubbles into champagne. It was portrayed in Nicolas Lancret's *Le Déjeuner au Jambon,* another painting commissioned by Louis XV for the Hunt Dining Room. Hanging just a few feet away from the flying cork in de Troy's *Le Déjeuner d'Huîtres,* it could not have been a greater contrast. The painting is of a picnic, and a rather raucous one, for it seems the guests have already drunk too much. The host, looking disheveled, is standing up, pouring champagne from a great height into a glass held at knee-level, his goal being to increase the effervescence by making the wine foam up.

But it was de Troy's depiction of champagne with the "saute bouchon" (literally "cork jumper") that drew the most attention and led the painter to hope that his fondest dream was about to come true: to become First Painter to the King. When asked to do another painting in 1736, he felt sure that goal was within his grasp. But he was wrong. The coveted post went to another artist. As consolation, de Troy was later appointed director of the French Academy in Rome.

Much to his surprise, it turned out to be a glorious assignment, with the lifestyle he'd always yearned for. De Troy drew a princely salary and was granted the title of "prince" to go with it. It was a great honor for the artist because the Roman Academy had rarely elected a foreigner to be their prince. De Troy also had a gorgeous apartment, a box at the opera, and a beautiful mistress to share it with.

In some ways, it was a relief to be where he was, away from the petty jealousies of the artistic scene in France, and away from the changes friends said were unfolding there. Although France was still prosperous with the economy thriving, literacy doubling, and life expectancy rising, there were disconcerting signs. The monarchy had ossified. It seemed old-fashioned, out of step with the times. In addition, many had come to resent the king's attitude that the "entire public order emanates from me."

That resentment was often on display in coffeehouses, where writers and other intellectuals, the philosophes, gathered to hold forth on such topics as human reason and the rights of man. But they had to be careful. One slip could mean exile or imprisonment. When criticizing the frivolities and sexual escapades of the royal court, for example, figures like Voltaire, Rousseau, and Diderot often couched their attacks in fiction and allegory.

How different it was from the "chat," the freewheeling discussions that had taken place in the elegant salons de Troy remembered. Even his beloved champagne was not as popular as it had been, he was told. The price of it had soared until a single bottle now cost as much as the average person earned in four days.

More disturbing, from his standpoint, was that artistic tastes were changing, too. The light, elegant social scenes de Troy had painted were no longer in vogue. Classicism was replacing rococo. People were looking for works done in a more severe style, like the enormous canvases done by Jacques-Louis David.

In 1752 de Troy was informed that he was being replaced in Rome and should return home. It came as a crushing blow. He realized that if he went back, he would never fit in, that he'd be seen as out-of-date. It was the worst thing that could happen to a man who prided himself in being à la mode. Consequently, de Troy stalled, presenting the king with one excuse after another for why he couldn't leave.

One night, while attending the opera with his mistress, a messenger stepped into the box and whispered in de Troy's ear that his replacement had arrived. De Troy knew then there would be no more excuses.

When the opera finished, he escorted his mistress home,

then suffered a heart attack. Within a few hours, the seventy-three-year-old artist was dead.

The changes that so disturbed de Troy only accelerated. In 1757, just five years after de Troy's death, an unemployed domestic servant, armed with a knife, pushed past guards and wounded Louis XV. The assailant said he had been moved to act because of the misery of the people.

That misery was caused by a myriad of factors: a disastrous seven-year war with Britain that cost France most of its colonies; spiraling taxes; a series of poor harvests; soaring food prices; rising unemployment and crime; and a cattle plague that wiped out thousands of herds.

With Louis XV's death from smallpox in 1774 and the ascension to the throne by the immature Louis XVI, the monarchy, in the minds of most, became even more imperious and out of touch with reality. When the new king was questioned whether one of his edicts was constitutional, his answer was abrupt: "It is legal because I wish it." [17]

In Champagne, where, just a short time earlier, everything had gone from strength to strength, the picture suddenly turned bleak. With the American War of Independence in 1776, the British blocked shipping lanes to isolate their rebellious colony, and champagne sales dipped precipitously. That same year, because of extremely hot weather, breakage of bottles reached a record high, with losses well over 90 percent. Then, because of drought, came a series of terrible harvests. One year saw crops only one-twelfth the normal size. In the once-prosperous village of Oger, a local official noted that "the vigneron no longer possesses anything of his own and has been returned to being nothing more than a serf."

But it was bread, the staple of the French diet, that was the final straw, or crumb. Throughout Champagne, and in other parts of France as well, hungry peasants rose up in protest over grain shortages. In the summer of 1789 bread prices soared to their highest level ever. When people complained, Queen Marie-Antoinette issued her now-famous retort, "Let them eat cake."

On an overcast and muggy July 14, angry crowds in Paris attacked customs officials posted at the city gates, accusing them of preventing grain from getting in. Spurred on by radical orators like Camille Desmoulins crying "Aux armes!," mobs coursed through the streets, searching for weapons and gunpowder. In another part of the city, throngs overran the hated Bastille prison and freed its handful of prisoners.

"Is it a revolt then?" asked Louis XVI, when he heard the news. "No, Sire," came the response, "it's a revolution." [18]

The images are familiar: châteaux and churches in flames, nobles fleeing the country, tumbrils rolling through streets past jeering crowds, carrying aristocrats, priests, royal ministers, and ordinary people to the guillotine.

But there are other images that are not so well known, such as revolutionary tribunals that sipped champagne while sentencing people to death.[19] The radical editor Marat was murdered in his bath while waiting for a shipment of champagne which, as it turned out, had been drunk by customs officers. Desmoulins and another revolutionary, Georges Jacques Danton, shared a bottle of champagne from the village of Aÿ, singing "Vive l'Aÿ et la liberté," moments before they were hauled to the guillotine. Louis XVI and Marie-Antoinette were served champagne with last meals before being beheaded.

It was only by chance that the king and queen were apprehended while trying to flee the country. How their capture came about was something Voltaire would have appreciated, for as he once said, "History can turn on accidents."

This "accident" happened in Champagne as the royal family was trying to make its way to the German border. Near Châlons-sur-Marne, they came to a fork in the road. Although one path was shorter, it was bumpier and hillier, running along the Marne River and then across the Montagne de Reims. Louis opted for the longer route, gambling they could make better time on it because it was flatter and smoother.[20]

It passed through Sainte-Menehould, the birthplace of Dom Pérignon, and there their luck ran out. As the royal coach rolled by, Jean-Baptiste Drouet, a former dragoon who was the son of the local postmaster, looked up and thought there was something familiar about the profile of the man inside. Drouet reached into his pocket and pulled out a 50-livre Louis constitutionnel, a piece of money created in 1791 which circulated throughout the Revolution and until 1803. A quick glance confirmed what Drouet suspected: the profile on the piece matched the one in the carriage.

He followed the royal family to nearby Varennes and there sounded the alarm. Within minutes, the king and queen and their children were in custody. The following day, they were on their way back to Paris.

The demise of the ancien régime and its replacement by a Republic plunged France into a decade of political, social, and religious turmoil. Not only was France at war with itself, but it was at war with nearly every other country in Europe, suffering a series of dispiriting defeats at the hands of those seeking to take advantage of its weakened position.

On September 20, 1792, residents of Paris learned that Prussian and Austrian troops had crossed into Champagne with the intention of taking their city. Stirred by newfound patriotism and a sense of outrage, thousands of civilians put aside their political differences and rushed to Valmy, a small village six miles west of Sainte-Menehould, where they joined with the French Revolutionary Army to confront the foe. Compared to other battles, this one was not very bloody; about five hundred men were killed. Nor was it a protracted engagement. Within hours, the ragtag force of the French had turned back the combined forces of two of Europe's strongest armies.

The German writer Johann Wolfgang von Goethe, who was present at the battle, declared to his fellow Prussians afterward,

"This is the beginning of a new epoch in history, and you can claim to have witnessed it."[21]

It was a morale-booster of epic proportions for France. Valmy not only restored the country's confidence but also gave it a sense of national identity. A day after the battle, a constitutional convention in Paris proclaimed the First Republic, marking a formal end to the Bourbon dynasty. Gone was the cry, "Vive le roi!" Now it was "Vive la nation!"

But it was a nation that would be born in blood. With the long arm of the Terror seeking out anyone perceived to be an enemy of the Republic, France was convulsed by a wave of fear and incrimination that threatened to tear the new Republic apart. In just eighteen months, fifty thousand people were put to death on the guillotine.

It was chilling, and often surreal, as one victim after another was led to an elevated platform and forced to kneel, their neck stretched over a block before a weighted blade came crashing down. With each beheading, a deafening cheer rose from the masses watching the spectacle.

But those closest to the scaffold could hear another noise, one that came from those waiting their turn to mount the steps to the guillotine. According to the Marquise de Créquy, a wealthy aristocrat who managed to escape the blade, "bankers, nobles, and others were yelling to their jailers to bring them champagne."[22]

In Champagne, producers had to tread extra carefully because their clients were the very people being hunted. Champagne-makers stayed up nights changing names on bills, erasing titles from records, and substituting "citoyen" (citizen), the preferred form of address during the Revolutionary period.[23]

At the same time, champagne exports slowed to a trickle. So little champagne was getting to England that it was said to have been "doled out like drops of blood."

If there was any good news for champagne-makers, it was the removal of an insidious tax system that existed under the monarchy. Champagne had been taxed at every point, first, before it left the cellar, then again during shipment, and yet again when it reached its destination. By then, more than half its sales value had been lost to taxes.

Monasteries, however, had been exempt from these taxes. Such privileges had generated increasing resentment among peasant winegrowers. Not only did peasants have to pay taxes to the government, but they also had to tithe part of their crop to the Church. In addition, commoners were forbidden to sell their grapes until the monks and nobility had sold theirs. This system, which had been designed to help the poor, often did just the opposite by forcing small winegrowers into ruin. The result was that monks and other clergy became targets of revolutionary mobs.

With the founding of the First Republic, tithing along with the abusive tax system was abolished. Church property was nationalized and then sold off. Not only did this help pull the fledgling Republic back from the edge of bankruptcy, but it also changed the face of the country.

Church land had accounted for at least 10 percent of France's agricultural area, and half of that was in vines. In Champagne, the best vineyards had belonged to the Church. These were broken up into tiny parcels and sold at reasonable prices to vignerons.

As these small plots were gobbled up, the government announced it had decided to keep one vineyard intact, that of the monastery at Hautvillers where Dom Pérignon once worked. It was purchased by a champagne producer from Reims.

The gay gallantry and elegant social life of France's last Bourbon rulers helped put champagne in the spotlight, but it was against a far different backdrop that it gained a truly international stage. This backdrop involved wars, fiercely fought battles, and lengthy military occupations. Directing it all was a young Corsican officer named Napoleon Bonaparte.

It was no accident that Napoleon became a champion of champagne. He was born into a winemaking family, with his father having inherited a vineyard. His mother brought additional ones into the family as a part of her dowry. Napoleon's uncle often bragged that the Bonapartes never had to buy wine, olive oil, or bread because they had enough land to grow whatever they needed. The wine they made was Vitulo, a red that was Italian in style and rather good.

Napoleon's boyhood was a rough life of simple pleasures, riding a mule from his house up a steep hill to the family vineyards, where he and his brothers and sisters worked and played. He was a lively, mischievous child, a "quarrelsome imp," as Napoleon admitted some years later. His father nicknamed him "Hurricane."

But Napoleon's childhood was a short one. When he was nine years old, his parents sent him to study at the prestigious Royal Military Academy of Brienne, in Champagne. In the beginning, Napoleon hated it. Everything was different: the land, the people, and the way they talked. Other students made fun of his accent, and Napoleon pleaded with his parents to let him come home. The weather was miserable, too, he said. Winters were bitterly cold, a far cry from the warmth and sun of the Mediterranean.

But one thing was the same: there were vineyards. Vines surrounded the school, providing a tranquil setting for long walks and moments of solitude. Sometimes, when the weather was good, he would sit under a tree near the vineyards and read books such as *Jerusalem Delivered.* Eventually, Napoleon settled in and became deeply attached to his new home. He would later refer to Brienne as "my native land."

But Napoleon was not the easiest pupil. Instructors found him "taciturn, capricious, haughty, and extremely disposed to egoism." However, they also considered him "studious, good in math and geography, energetic in his answers, and full of unbounded aspirations."[24]

That was something that caught the attention of a young salesman who arrived in Brienne one day in hopes of persuading the academy's faculty to buy some of his champagne. Jean-Rémy Moët was the grandson of Claude Moët, who had popularized sparkling champagne at the court of Versailles. Only twenty-four, Moët had already traveled widely for his family's champagne firm. It was by chance that he and Napoleon were introduced, and Moët was immediately impressed with Napoleon's intensity and curiosity.

In many ways, they were complete opposites. Napoleon was just a young teenager and regarded by his classmates as something of a country hick. Moët was sophisticated, eleven years older than Napoleon, and knew the champagne business from top to bottom. And yet the two hit it off, perhaps recognizing the qualities they did share, such as ambition, determination, and a talent for managing detail.

When Moët left Brienne, he and Napoleon stayed in touch, with Jean-Rémy inviting the boy to visit him in Épernay. It was the beginning of a friendship that would last their entire lives.

In 1792, Jean-Rémy's father died unexpectedly, leaving him solely responsible for the House of Moët.[25] It could not have happened at a more difficult moment, for the Reign of Terror had just begun. Like other champagne producers, Jean-Rémy struggled to keep his business afloat, selling small amounts of champagne wherever and whenever he could. He had just begun exporting to America, and it was a market he did not want to lose. Moët had already acquired some important clients, among them George Washington, president of the United States. His first shipment to the United States had arrived just in time for a dinner party Washington gave on March 4, 1790. Washington's account books show that he paid sixty-six pence to have "six baskets of champagne" delivered from a boat to his residence. According to one of the guests, Senator Samuel Johnson of North Carolina, "the President and Mrs. Washington served some excellent champagne."[26]

But during the French Revolution and the wars that followed, Jean-Rémy was able to get only one more shipment of champagne to the United States, largely because of blockades by the British navy. Adding to his woes was the poor condition of the vineyards. They had been neglected after the clergy scattered, sitting untended while awaiting sale to new owners. Often, the buyers were people who had little knowledge of viticulture and no idea of how to take care of the vines. As a result, champagne producers like Jean-Rémy were hard-pressed to obtain an adequate supply of grapes.

Although this period posed enormous problems for people like Moët, they presented great opportunities for Napoleon, now a junior officer in the army. Because of his knowledge of wine, he was put in charge of confiscating the Church's famed vineyards of Clos du Vougeot, which were owned by the great Citeaux monastery in Burgundy.

His success at Citeaux brought him to the attention of the commanding general in Paris, who summoned him to put down a rebellion by royalist supporters. Napoleon accomplished that with a "whiff of grapeshot," as some described it. This earned him a promotion to general; he was just twenty-four. He was then given command of campaigns in northern Italy, where he succeeded in crushing the Austrian army. In 1798 Napoleon was dispatched to Egypt in an effort to check British advances in the Middle East. Unlike Italy, this campaign fared poorly and prompted his soldiers to question, in a song, why they were even there: "The water of the Nile is not champagne! So what are we doing on this campaign?"[27]

While things were going badly in Egypt, the situation in France, in some ways, was even worse. Fallout from the Revolution had left the country floundering, with monarchists clamoring for a restoration, the Terror still engendering fear and the Directoire, a corrupt, ineffectual body that was running the country, unsure which way to turn. Inevitably, they turned to Napoleon, appointing him First Consul, effectively making him France's ruler, in 1799. Five years later, he declared himself emperor.

Napoleon's ascendancy to power marked an era of genuine prosperity for Champagne. His appointment of Jean-Antoine Chaptal as minister of the interior was a master stroke. Chaptal was a brilliant chemist who had written *Traite sur la vigne,* a groundbreaking book that went beyond the local myths and traditions of winemaking to develop scientific techniques that could be applied to any vineyard. In his work, Chaptal described how vignerons could boost the alcoholic strength of their wine by adding sugar, a process that bears his name, chaptalisation. This proved especially important in Champagne, where grapes frequently failed to ripen because of the colder climate, resulting in champagne that was low in alcohol and highly acidic.

But obtaining sugar was a problem. It had to be shipped from sugar cane plantations in the Caribbean, making it a luxury few could afford. Now, to make matters worse, wars and blockades had completely cut off supplies.

Fortunately, Napoleon, whose interest in science and agriculture was extensive, remembered a scientist who, fifty years earlier, claimed that sugar could be refined from a certain kind of beet. Impossible, thought most people who considered it pure fantasy. Farmers refused to have anything to do with the idea. Napoleon, however, was convinced that the special variety would answer France's needs. He was determined to make the country self-sufficient and ordered his agriculture minister to investigate and then launch a program to encourage the planting of sugar beets.

The new and cheaper supply of sugar was a godsend for champagne-makers. No longer was their champagne "green and hard as a dog." Now it was sweet, and more and more people were clamoring for it.

As for Napoleon, he was abstemious. He ate little and drank even less. But there was one thing he did seek out. According to his secretary, "a single glass of champagne was enough to restore his strength and produce cheerfulness of spirit."

Before each of his military campaigns, Napoleon always made a point of passing through Épernay, stopping at the cellars of his friend Jean-Rémy Moët to pick up a supply of champagne. "In victory you deserve it, in defeat you need it," he said. Only one time did he fail to make his usual stop, and that was because he was in a rush. He was on his way to Waterloo.

Largely because of Napoleon's patronage, Jean-Rémy's champagne business had blossomed. Napoleon and his wife, the Empress Josephine, were frequent guests of Moët's. To make sure they felt at home and could be entertained in style, Jean-Rémy had a replica of the Trianon palace and its gardens at Versailles built on his property, calling in the famous miniaturist, Jean Isabey, to oversee the project.

Not surprisingly, other members of the Bonaparte family made their way to Jean-Rémy's as well, among them Napoleon's brother Jérôme. In 1811 Jérôme, who'd been made king of Westphalia by his brother, came to order six thousand bottles of champagne. At dinner that evening, Jérôme confessed he would have ordered twice as much champagne were he not afraid the Russians would drink it all.

"The Russians! . . . I don't understand you, Sire," replied Jean-Rémy.

"All right, I'll let you into a state secret. War with Russia has just been decided upon in my brother's cabinet. It's terrible, terrible. I see no hope of success."

"But, Sire . . ."

"Yes, I know what you're going to tell me: "The Emperor's genius overcomes all obstacles!' That's what everybody says. . . . I
hope I'm wrong. . . . Only time can tell." [28]

Jérôme was not wrong. Napoleon's venture into Russia the
following year ended in disaster with the loss of half a million
men and his Grande Armée in full retreat.

By January 1814 the armies of Russia, Prussia, and Austria
invaded Eastern France and headed toward Champagne. Realizing their commander's eagerness to get there, Prussian soldiers
wrote a verse in his honor:

> *Throw bridges over the Rhine.*
> *I must drink Champagne wine,*
> *It is at its best, straight from the nest,*
> *Soon it will all be mine.* [29]

With memories of Attila and other invading armies, the entire region was thrown into panic. Villages emptied as people
grabbed food and whatever else they could carry to take refuge in
the hills and forests. Enemy armies crisscrossed Champagne,
helping themselves to everything they could lay their hands on.
"The Prussians are insatiable," exclaimed one of Napoleon's
generals. "You cannot believe the amount of champagne they
drink."

At Jacquesson & Fils, a firm in Châlons-sur-Marne whose
cellars had so impressed Napoleon in 1810 that he awarded it
a gold medal, a contingent of Bavarian soldiers broke into
the caves but found they couldn't open the bottles. Adolphe
Jacquesson, one of Champagne's most ingenious pioneers,
had been experimenting with metal wires to hold corks in place

and had sealed most of his bottles that way. In frustration, the Bavarians simply broke the necks off and guzzled what they could.[30]

Napoleon, by this time, was fighting some of his most brilliant battles, but they were rear-guard actions aimed at limiting damage while his army retreated.

On March 17, 1814, with enemy forces breathing down his neck, Napoleon paid a last visit to Épernay, spending the night at the house Jean-Rémy had built for him. Sipping a bowl of consommé, Napoleon studied a map for a few minutes before turning to his friend and saying, "Well, France isn't in Russian hands yet, but if I should fail, within a month I shall either be dead or dethroned. So I want to reward you now for the admirable way you have built up your business and all you have done for our wines abroad." With that, Napoleon took his own Legion of Honor cross and pinned it onto Jean-Rémy.[31]

The emperor departed for Paris the next morning and abdicated a few days later. By then, Épernay and Reims were occupied cities.

Enormous fines and crushing requisitions were levied on the Champenois in retaliation for those Napoleon had imposed on countries he'd conquered. Cellars throughout Champagne were plundered, the worst being those of Moët, which saw six hundred thousand bottles emptied by Russian soldiers camped on the premises.

Moët, however, remained sanguine through the worst of it as he recalled an old French proverb: "Qui a bu, boira" (he who has drunk once will drink again). Jean-Rémy was convinced, as he told friends, that "All of those soldiers who are ruining me today will make my fortune tomorrow. I'm letting them drink all they want. They will be hooked for life and become my best salesmen when they go back to their own country."[32]

He was right. During the Revolution, champagne had proved that it did not take sides, and it was no different this time. Leaders from every country France had fought against were soon trooping through the cellars of every champagne house, tasting and buying. Among them were Czar Alexander of Russia, Franz II of Austria, King Frederick William III of Prussia, Prince William of Orange, and England's Duke of Wellington.

The most popular cellar was Jean-Rémy's. He had worried about what Napoleon's abdication and subsequent exile would mean for his business. Instead, he found that he had become "the most famous winemaker in the world," supplying champagne to every European court.

None of the victorious rulers seemed to be in a hurry to return home. As one champagne-maker said, "They came back to Champagne because they said they did not have time to taste champagne while they were busy fighting. They were curious about this new kind of wine that sparkled, so they returned."[33]

And were seduced.

CHAPTER 3

On the Top of Golden Hours

In times gone by, it was something of an event getting to a French provincial town. One's arrival was announced by the crack of a whip as a horse-drawn coach was driven with great flourish into the courtyard of a hotel. In those days, recalled Robert Tomes, "you were a traveler and everyone said they were charmed to see you." The owner and his wife, dressed in their best and wearing their sweetest smiles; the waiters with their napkins over their arms; the chambermaids giggling in the rear—all were there as you descended from the coach. Even the chef would come out to lift his white cotton cap in greeting.

For Tomes, a U.S. consular officer, the journey was a little different. He had been "shot out of the heart of Paris" aboard a high-speed train, arriving in Reims feeling "just like any other package being transported from place to place."

The year was 1865. In America, the Civil War was drawing to a close and Tomes had been sent to France to collect duty on champagne being exported to the United States. His "high-speed" trip of one hundred miles had taken more than four hours, the train puffing through vineyards and valleys at the remarkable speed of thirty miles an hour.

Tomes was unceremoniously dropped in front of the Hôtel Lion d'Or and kept waiting in the stark front hall until his patience was nearly exhausted. "I finally received a key, heavily weighted with brass chain and number, and was left, with a few confused words of direction, to find my way to the appointed bed chamber." [1]

Although it was sunny outside, the room, with its bare floorboards and decrepit furniture, was dark as a dungeon. When Tomes opened the faded drapes, he discovered why. Across a narrow street loomed the great Gothic Cathedral of Reims, where nearly every king of France had been crowned.

What struck Tomes was not how large the cathedral was but how small it made everything else look. It dominated the city and landscape for miles around and was the first thing Tomes saw when he awoke each morning.

"As time habituated me to the somber atmosphere of my room and my consciousness became fully awakened to the presence of my imposing neighbor opposite, I learned to appreciate the gloom in which I was shrouded, and would not have exchanged it for the brightest sunlight that ever shone."

The cathedral, whose first stone had been laid in 1212, was not only a religious statement but also a meditation on Champagne's history and its people. The intricate tracery and profusion of sculpted figures on the façade came together with such harmony and grace that it reminded Tomes of "petrified music." [2]

During his eighteen months in Champagne, Tomes recorded

his impressions in a small book, *The Champagne Country.* "It is impossible to walk in any part of the old town of Reims without remarking some specimen of ancient architecture. There are whole streets of peaked gables facing the road, and upper stories with arches below for the passage of the people, projecting over the sidewalks."

What makes Tomes's memoir so poignant is that he was describing a world that would soon vanish. In less than fifty years, the Reims he came to love—the crowded, narrow streets with their shops and cafes; the Promenade de Cours, where he went for leisurely strolls under its overarching foliage; and above all, the city's magnificent cathedral—would all be destroyed by German bombs.

Tomes's first impression of Reims, however, was less than flattering. He thought the city was dull and dirty. He was not impressed with the people, either. They have "a natural inaptitude [sic] for commerce" unlike, he added, the Germans, British, and Americans. "The Frenchman contents himself for the most part with adjusting a color, devising a pattern, inventing a toy, or peddling small wares. They make good shopkeepers." He noted that every successful champagne house was either owned or managed by a German. The only one that was exclusively in French hands went bankrupt, "and it was a common remark," said Tomes, "that it perished for want of a German."

As for people's manners, Tomes found their "bowing and scraping" and the "excessive uncovering" of their heads to be irritating. "There are no people in the world who take off their hats so often and spout so many complimentary phrases. To me, it is nothing more than a cheap substitute for real civility."

What surprised him as much as anything was that most of the people he met knew so little about the rest of the world, or so he thought. "Their ignorance of every other country but their own is sublime. The common Frenchman is so absorbed in the admiration of la belle France that he cannot admit the possibility of a rival."

They are also "deep drinkers and gross feeders," he complained. Tomes found their penchant for downing escargots to be disgusting. "The common slug or snail, the slimy wanderer of our gardens, is a choice article of their dainty diet. The ugly monster is sealed down within its shell by a thick paste composed of butter, hot spices, and flour, and being thus prevented from wriggling out, is thrown into a pot of boiling water. In a few moments, it is withdrawn, served up, and eaten with great gusto by its devourer, who, provided with a little two-pronged fork made for the purpose, draws out the snail deliberately from the convolutions of its shell, and holding it up, stretched out in all its ugly proportions, throws back his head and drops it into his gaping mouth."[3]

It was all a bit much for Tomes to digest at first. Reims was not like the busy port cities of the East Coast, and nothing like those in Japan that he'd gotten to know when he accompanied Commodore Matthew Perry on his mission to open that country to the West. Landlocked Reims was quieter, less cosmopolitan, less in a hurry, more comfortable in its own skin as the French like to say.

In time, though, Tomes began to feel more at home in his new surroundings. He began to see things differently, as he had with the cathedral. No longer did he look about and see only gloom and dreariness; instead there was something vibrant, a timeless quality that made everything resonate as much as it had in centuries gone by.

There was the Porte de Mars, a triumphal stone arch built by the Romans in 277 A.D. in honor of Julius Caesar, and the Maison des Musiciens, the house of musicians, regarded by archaeologists as an outstanding example of architecture of the fourteenth century. The city's library, he learned, contained thirty thousand volumes and one thousand rare manuscripts, many of which had been rescued from the monasteries of Reims when they were burned during the French Revolution. He also learned that it was only because of the monks at one of those monasteries that the world ever learned of Aesop's Fables. According to the head librarian, monks at the Monastery of Saint Remi unearthed the original manuscript, then copied and disseminated it to the public, making them the first publishers of the fables. Unfortunately, the original copy that the monks had worked from was destroyed when the monastery was burned in 1791.

Tomes's opinion of the Champenois changed, too. Instead of people who bowed and scraped and were unworldly, he now saw them as bright, sophisticated, and extremely outgoing. They are also "the most devoted of lovers and tenderest of parents."

Perhaps Tomes had merely been misled by an ancient French proverb: Quatre-vingt-dix-neuf moutons et un Champenois font cent bêtes (ninety-nine sheep and one inhabitant of Champagne make 100 beasts—or fools, depending on one's interpretation).[1] The origins of the proverb go back several centuries, to a time when the manufacturing of woolen cloth was a major part of Reims's economy. A tax had been imposed upon every flock of 100 sheep that entered the city. To avoid it, the peasants began bringing in only ninety-nine at a time. This vexed the feudal lord of the city, who decided to position himself at the main gate and collect the revenue himself. As each shepherd arrived with his ninety-nine animals, his lordship yelled out to his men-at-arms, "Make him pay! Quatre-vingt-dix-neuf moutons et un Champenois font cent bêtes."

But it was a visit to the city cemetery that would leave Tomes with one of his most lasting impressions. "There, such cheerful names as Heidsieck, Clicquot, Roederer, and Mumm stared at me from tombs of stone," he said. "I had never thought of those jolly names, so associated with gaiety, weddings, feasts, and merrymakings, being crowned with death's-heads and bloody bones. It seemed like a mockery of all good fellowship, and I shall never hereafter lift a foaming glass of champagne to my lips without thinking of the burial place at Reims."

That fall, a wine merchant invited Tomes to accompany him to the harvest in nearby Verzenay. Unlike his high-speed train trip from Paris to Reims, this one was made slowly, in a broken-down cart pulled by a docile old horse; all the good teams of horses were being used for the harvest. It was the eighth of September and, as it turned out, the hottest day of the year. To Tomes's immense relief, the merchant had brought along a hamper of his best champagne to accompany them on their eight-mile journey. As they made their way along a sun-baked chalk road, the two sipped iced champagne and exchanged idle chatter. Occasionally, Tomes would turn his head and stare in awe at Reims's cathedral, still visible as they neared the vineyards of Verzenay. From the opposite direction came horse-drawn wagons filled with barrels of juice from freshly pressed grapes. The barrels had been covered with tarpaulins and thick layers of green leaves to shield them from the hot sun.

The harvest of 1865 was one of the most glorious Champagne has ever known. Tomes remembered how "the soil had drunk deep of a plentiful moisture from the bounteous rains of spring" and how afterward the sun shone brightly every day. Not since 1811 had grapes ripened so beautifully or sugar levels been so high, enabling picking to begin three weeks early. "It is difficult for those who have not lived in a winegrowing country to conceive the animated happiness produced by a prosperous harvest," Tomes said. Winegrowers, he observed, are an "anxious race," never able to relax for fear the weather might suddenly change.

That year, though, the weather held. Grape prices were high and winegrowers were ecstatic. "It was," said Tomes, "as if every man had drawn a prize in a lottery."[5]

That wondrous harvest seemed to encapsulate everything that was happening in France. It was an era of unprecedented growth and prosperity. Baron Haussmann was transforming Paris from a slum-ridden city crumbling with age into a city of light, a grand metropolis of wide boulevards and gracious buildings designed to be a showcase of Napoleon III's Second Empire and the envy of the world.

French industry had been given a boost as well, its strength now greater than all the other countries of continental Europe combined. French colonies doubled, trade tripled, and the use of steam power quintupled. A newly modernized banking system enabled people to open savings accounts and obtain credit to start businesses. "The Empire means peace," declared Napoleon III.[6] In fact, it meant more than that:

> 'Twas the time when Europe was rejoiced
> France standing on the top of golden hours
> And human nature seeming born again.[7]

Although William Wordsworth wrote those words in the euphoria following the French Revolution, they were even more relevant now. People had money; there was a new dynamism and a sense of exhilaration, a feeling that anything was possible.

Nowhere was that more true than in Champagne, where the rattling of bottles on assembly lines, the incessant thud of corking machines, and the creaking of freight elevators filled the air as machines began taking over work traditionally done by hand. What had once been a cottage industry was now big business.

Hardly a day passed without some new breakthrough. A pharmacist named Jean-Baptiste François invented the sucre-oenométre, a device that measured the amount of sugar in wine and helped champagne-makers gauge how much sugar to use to produce a fermentation. Louis Pasteur's discovery of yeasts helped champagne-makers understand what fermentation really is, a reaction which, until then, had been regarded only as a "strange phenomenon" that often resulted in bottles of champagne suddenly bursting. In Châlons-sur-Marne, an enterprising champagne producer named Adolphe Jacquesson invented the bottle-washing machine. He also invented the wire muzzle, which replaced string that had previously been used to hold down corks. William Deutz "topped" him by developing the metal foil that covers the muzzle and cork.

One of the most significant breakthroughs was remuage, a process aimed at removing sediment from champagne. Removal of this deposit was a problem that had plagued champagne-makers from the time of Dom Pérignon. Usually, bottles were given a rousing shake in order to concentrate the sediment toward the bottle's shoulder. The wine would then be decanted into other bottles, leaving as much of the sediment behind as possible. Unfortunately, most of the bubbles were lost in the process. It was at the house of Veuve Clicquot-Ponsardin that a solution was finally found, a breakthrough that came as no surprise to anyone who knew Nicole-Barbe Clicquot-Ponsardin.

Nicole-Barbe was just twenty-seven and the mother of a three-year-old daughter when her husband died in 1806. He and her father-in-law had run the company, which was known at the time as Clicquot et Fils. Its activities were primarily banking and wool trading; making champagne was a sideline. Upon his son's sudden death from a fever, the elder Monsieur Clicquot announced he could not go on and was shutting down the business. Nicole-Barbe, however, said she would have none of it. Although she had played no role in the firm before, she persuaded her father-in-law to let her take over the company.

Her first move was to change its name to Veuve Clicquot-Ponsardin, "Veuve" meaning widow, a respected form of address that was common in France at that time. She also decided that the company's future rested with making champagne. Her iron will and keen business sense paid off. Within four months, Nicole-Barbe had turned the company around, accomplishing this by concentrating on continental European sales and ignoring England and America. She also paid close attention to what customers said, especially when there were complaints. Chief among them was that champagne was often cloudy, a condition caused by sediment in the bottles.

Legend has it that the diminutive Widow Clicquot, who stood no more than five feet tall, hauled her kitchen table down to the cellars and began experimenting. There may be some truth to it, but more likely, it was her cellarmaster, Antoine de Müller, who hit on the real answer. Müller cut holes in the table so that bottles could be inserted by their necks at a slant. The bottles would then be given a periodic twist and shake, gradually increasing their angle until they were practically standing on their heads and the sticky sediment had been nudged toward the cork. When the cork was pulled, the sediment shot out first, leaving most of the wine behind and most of its effervescence intact. The champagne could then be topped up, recorked and readied for shipment.[8]

Müller and Veuve Clicquot tried to keep their method a secret but word soon leaked out, transforming champagne-making and turning it into a genuine industry.

By the end of the 1860s, most people in Champagne believed they really were "standing on the top of golden hours." As one review gushed, "Champagne is not a wine, it is *the* wine." For the first time, the term "champagne" was included in the French dictionary. It was defined as "a wine produced by art" but something "more than a wine." The dictionary cautioned that champagne's "capricious nature must be treated with respect and humility for, in the wrong hands, its nature can be forced and reduced to nothing more than a means of making money."

Winemakers elsewhere tried to cash in on the champagne boom and make sparkling wines themselves. In Burgundy, there was a sparkling Nuits-St-Georges, a sparkling Montrachet, and a sparkling Romanée-Conti. In Bordeaux, there was a sparkling Sauternes. In the southern Rhône, one winemaker produced a sparkling Châteauneuf-du-Pape. Aside from their fizziness, however, they bore no resemblance to genuine champagne. "They are miserable parodies," one critic said.

Champagne had become unique. Now it had to become universal, and that required a reliable system of transport. Until the 1860s, producers had relied on the River Marne and a network of inadequate roads to get their champagne to market. Both means were slow and unreliable, especially the roads, which were so bumpy and poorly maintained that many bottles were broken before they reached their destinations.

All of that changed under Napoleon III. France embarked on a massive modernization plan aimed at transforming not only Paris but the entire country. The lynchpin was the construction of a comprehensive railway system, one that would kick-start business and heavy industry and get farmers to think beyond mere subsistence agriculture and to produce goods for the broader marketplace. Between 1852 and 1870, France's railway network grew sixfold. Tracks now linked Paris to every corner of the country, as well as to most of Europe.

For Champagne, it was a godsend. New markets became accessible and annual sales of champagne skyrocketed from a few hundred thousand bottles to twenty-five million. Champagne houses proliferated as well. At the turn of the century, only ten champagne firms existed. Now there were more than three hundred.

The arrival of trains and steam-driven machines heralded the advent of modern times for Champagne. And something else was happening, too.

Ever since the time of the first Napoleon, when France was carving out a continental empire, champagne houses had gradually been building small armies of salesmen, pointmen for the industry, who possessed a James Bond flair and a killer instinct for making a sale. They were dashing, daring, and when the occasion called for it, utterly devious. Long before the railroad, long before the days of mass marketing and modern advertising, these men traveled the world—even its battlefields—to promote and sell champagne.

"Wherever French troops were to be found—in Germany, Poland, Moravia—a Heidsieck, a Ruinart, a Jacquesson, or an agent of one of the other firms was never far behind," wrote Patrick Forbes, author of the classic work, *Champagne: The Wine, the Land and the People.* The Napoleonic Wars of 1804–14 provided fertile ground for selling champagne, he said. "As soon as the battle was won, up they would move their supplies for the victory celebration, and quickly establish a sales organization in the invaded territory."[9]

These men, however, were just as much at home dancing the night away at a fancy ball or entertaining customers in the finest Paris restaurants.

"They dine at Vefour," observed one buyer. "They have a horror of intemperance and only talk about their product in a very restrained way. They find it quite ordinary to be in the great literary salons, along the famous promenades, in the foyer of the

Opera, and after a conversation there with you they very delicately mention the virtues of sparkling champagne. They always end those conversations with an air that is almost innocent. 'Oh,' they quickly add, 'I will send you a case, no strings attached,' and as they say it they pull on their white gloves and button them, then begin talking about race horses or taking the waters at the spa." [10]

Despite the glamour, their jobs were not easy ones, observed Robert Tomes. "The traveler of a wine-house must not only have a strong head but a bold face, a voluble tongue, and an indiscriminate and inexhaustible sociability. He must never confess to a headache, he must be at home in every company, must always have a story to tell, never let the talk flag for a moment, and clink glasses miscellaneously with all the world." [11]

They also were incredibly creative. In 1811, for example, as Napoleon's armies were advancing on Moscow, Charles-Henri Heidsieck had an idea. Why not try to get to Moscow before Napoleon, in time to celebrate with the winners? The challenge was making himself noticed in a city that was preoccupied with war. The twenty-one-year-old Heidsieck decided to buy a magnificent white stallion and ride it all the way from Reims to Moscow, a distance of two thousand miles. His entry into the city caused a sensation. Trailed only by a servant and a packhorse loaded with samples of champagne, Heidsieck was besieged by people anxious to meet him and try his champagne. [12]

His exploit must have driven Louis Bohne crazy. Already a legendary agent for Veuve Clicquot, Bohne considered Russia his private bailiwick. He was personal friends with the czar and czarina and so close to the Russian Court that, on one occasion, he was slipped a secret which he immediately relayed to his home office: "The czarina is pregnant. What a blessing for us if she were to have a Prince! In this immense country, torrents of champagne would flow. Don't breathe a word about this in Reims. All our competitors would want to rush North!"[13]

Which, of course, they did. Sensing the enormous potential, Moët, Ruinart, Jacquesson, and Roederer all dispatched agents to Russia.

But Napoleon's invasion of Russia in the summer of 1812 made business both difficult and illegal. As the czar prepared to lead his army into battle, he also issued a decree banning imports of French wine in bottles—a deliberate slap at Napoleon, whose love of champagne and support of the industry were well known. Unlike still wines, which could be shipped in barrels, champagne could only be exported in bottles.

Louis Bohne was determined to circumvent the ban. His first move was to register Veuve Clicquot as a coffee importing company and smuggle champagne into the country by hiding the bottles in barrels of coffee beans. The limits of that ploy were soon apparent, however, for only so many bottles could be hidden in a barrel of coffee beans. Soon Bohne began hatching a bigger scheme.

He had become something of an expert at sneaking ships past Britain's naval blockade and getting champagne to Holland, Poland, and Germany. For Russia, he would need all those skills and more. Napoleon's invasion had proved a disaster, and in the wake of France's defeat, Champagne suddenly found itself under military occupation by Russian troops and their Prussian allies. Now, Bohne not only had to worry about skirting a naval blockade, he also had to figure out how to get his champagne out of Reims without the Russians and Prussians noticing.

Fortunately, the two armies were not getting along. The

Prussians, who were bivouacked in the countryside, were jealous that the Russians were ensconced in the more comfortable confines of Reims, where so many great champagne cellars were located. In a pique, the Prussian commander announced he and his men were going to march into Reims, demand tribute, and help themselves to a bit of champagne. The Russian general fired back, "I have received orders from the Czar himself not to exact any requisitions from this town. As for your insolent threat of sending troops to Reims, I have plenty of Cossacks here to receive them." The Prussians stayed where they were.

As the two allies continued bickering, Bohne quietly hired a Dutch vessel, the *Gebroeders,* and began moving a huge quantity of champagne toward Rouen, where the ship was docked. To distract the Russians, Bohne's boss, Madame Clicquot, opened her cellars and let them drink as much champagne as they wanted. It was a perfect ruse. No one paid any attention to what Bohne was doing, or noticed when he and the *Gebroeders* set sail from Rouen in early June with ten thousand bottles of champagne safely aboard. The ship was so packed that there was no room for a bed in Bohne's cabin. There were plenty of bedbugs, however, which Bohne said "were two inches long and drank half the blood from my body." [14]

A month later, after successfully skirting the blockade, Bohne and the *Gebroeders* sailed into the Prussian port of Königsberg, on the Russian border. But the czar had not yet lifted his ban on champagne and Bohne was becoming impatient. Eager to sell his cargo and return home, Bohne spread the word around Königsberg that all of his champagne had been sold but that he might be able to "oblige a few people" if they could pay accordingly. The result was a near riot.

"What a spectacle," Bohne wrote to Madame Clicquot. "How I

wish you were here to enjoy it. You have two-thirds of the best society of Königsberg at your feet over your nectar. I seek orders from no one, I just reveal the number of my hotel room and a line forms outside it."

It was no surprise. The champagne he was selling was Veuve Clicquot's famous 1811 vintage, the Cuvée de la Comète, an extraordinary champagne that vignerons said had been blessed "by the beneficial passage of Halley's Comet."

"It has no equal," Bohne exclaimed in a second letter to Madame Clicquot. "Delicious to taste, it is a real assassin, and whoever wishes to know it should tie themselves to the chair. Otherwise they may find themselves under the table with the crumbs!"

Veuve Clicquot was ecstatic. When the czar lifted his ban that August, she sent a second shipload of champagne to St. Petersburg. The result was the same.

The entire venture had been so successful that the House of Veuve Clicquot was able to withdraw from the Central European market and concentrate almost exclusively on selling champagne to Russia. Bohne, who was richly rewarded by his employer, bought himself a villa and settled into comfortable retirement in his native Germany.

Over the next few years, Russian demand for champagne swelled, making the country the second largest consumer after Great Britain. Nearly every major champagne house claimed a piece of the market.

By the 1850s, however, champagne's salesmen were growing restless. Europe had begun to feel old and stale. There were no more challenges, no new frontiers.

Until they looked west.

To the Champenois, America was the great untapped continent. Although small quantities of champagne had been sent there from the time of George Washington and even before the American Revolution, most producers regarded the United States as a hazardous place to do business. It was distant, unsophisticated and thought to be inhabited by "wild Indians."

Charles-Camille Heidsieck saw it differently. Bright, audacious, and the most flamboyant member of a very colorful family—it was his father who had ridden into Moscow on a white horse—Charles founded the Charles Heidsieck champagne house before he turned thirty. Now, he believed, he would make his mark in America.

Heidsieck arrived in Boston in 1852, the first head of a champagne house ever to visit the United States. Although he found Boston "very puritanical," he was impressed with the energy of the country, a feeling that grew stronger as he pushed inland toward Syracuse, Buffalo, and Niagara Falls. By the time he reached New York City, his enthusiasm knew no bounds. In a letter to his wife, Heidsieck exclaimed, "This truly is a land of opportunity!" He wasted no time in retaining an agent before returning to France, where he made arrangements to send a huge shipment of champagne to the United States.

Orders came pouring in. Americans, it seemed, couldn't get enough of his champagne. It was as if he'd struck gold. Five years later, Heidsieck was on his way back to New York, this time with twenty thousand *paniers,* or straw-lined baskets, each containing fifteen bottles of champagne.

He was welcomed like a returning hero. Receptions were

held in his honor, and his picture was carried by all the newspapers. He stood six feet three inches tall, sported a goatee and mustache, and had large, deep eyes that seemed to smile. "Our Charlie is back again," screamed one headline. Soon everyone was calling him "Champagne Charlie." [15]

On his next trip, Heidsieck came determined to combine business with pleasure. He arrived not only with more champagne but also with some of the latest pistols and hunting rifles, weapons that had been wrought by the best gunsmith in Paris. "More perfect specimens of the firearm we have never seen," raved one newspaper. "They are marvels of beauty and strength." The paper went on to say that Heidsieck knew as much about guns as he did champagne and was one of the best shots in France. [16]

The spectacle of a pistol-packing champagne magnate tickled the fancy of Americans, noted one writer, a fact Heidsieck himself acknowledged in a letter home. "I must tell you that for the moment I am the most important person in New York. I can't make a move without journalists on my heels." More than any other champagne salesman of the time, Heidsieck understood the value of publicity. "It's sometimes a nuisance but the more noise made about me, the easier it will be to sell my champagne," he said. When the *New York Illustrated News* announced the first ball of the season at the Metropolitan Hotel, it emphasized that Heidsieck would be one of the guests. *Harper's Weekly* in turn reported that "Monsieur Charles Heidsieck will soon be heading west to hunt buffalo." The article included a picture of the dapper Heidsieck posing with his rifle.

Over the next nine months, Heidsieck traveled everywhere, and by every means America had to offer: by stagecoach across New York; by paddle wheel steamers up the Mississippi; by horse and iron horse through Ohio, Texas, and Missouri. "One tries one's best to see everything that flies past the windows," he said. There were primeval forests, alligators sunning themselves on the banks of rivers, blue herons and wild turkeys in flight, and magnolias as big as the largest oaks in France. "Everything is so beautiful, the nature so varied, so smiling yet so wild, so sweet yet so daunting, that you can hardly think of anything else," he wrote.

Further west, he saw new settlements being carved out of the wilderness. He also took part in a cattle roundup, "a highly exciting affair," he recalled, especially the branding. "The burning iron was applied, the hide sizzled, and the animal bellowed with pain and rage."

At the end of the day, as the "sun set on a fiery horizon, we were bathed in an atmosphere of incredible purity." That night, "not a breath of air stirred, the heavens were warm and clear and there were millions of stars."

But there was also something ugly in the country, something Heidsieck failed to pick up on when he first visited the South. "The cotton fields are filled with Negroes of all ages and both sexes," he observed. "They seem happy, are easily moved to laughter and burst frequently into song. They lack for nothing and live more comfortably than many a white farmer. I think they are whipped more frequently in novels than in real life."

His attitude changed dramatically, however, when he visited a slave market. "A prospective buyer comes up. He wishes a plowhand, a coachman or valet at a low price. The colored man rises and the buyer has him open his mouth. He examines his teeth, feels his arms and legs, makes him walk and jump, all in silence, without a word being exchanged between him and the dealer." Heidsieck found it all dehumanizing and was appalled that human beings could be treated as merchandise. He watched as a cook was sold for $1,000 and a children's nurse for $750, all the while trying to conceal his emotions and remain impassive, "but what I witnessed was different from the language which was gripping my heart."

The issue of slavery had become increasingly divisive. As abolitionists called for an end to the institution, Southern states threatened to withdraw from the Union. On April 12, 1861, a Virginian named Edmund Ruffin aimed his rifle at Fort Sumter and pulled the trigger. It was the first shot of the Civil War.

When Heidsieck heard the news in Reims, he was alarmed. Half of his assets were now tied up in America, and there were several thousand bottles of champagne that he had not yet been paid for. Heidsieck scrambled for the first ship bound for the United States.

The scene in Boston was in stark contrast to what had greeted him on his earlier trips. The city was draped with Union flags, and soldiers were everywhere, drilling and filling the air with loud "hurrahs" as they marched back and forth. Heidsieck went straight to New York, where he immediately contacted his agent. He was stunned when the agent said he wasn't going to pay him, that he didn't *have* to pay him because of a new law that had been enacted absolving debtors of their obligations. The law was designed to deny the South revenue by allowing Northerners to withhold payments for cotton they had purchased. Unfortunately, nearly everyone tried to take advantage by refusing to pay any bills they owed. Heidsieck appealed to his agent's sense of honor but the agent shrugged him off.

Heidsieck was in serious trouble. Without the money, there

was no way he could pay his own bills. The solution, he decided, was to go south, to New Orleans, and try to collect directly for the champagne that had been shipped there.

It was a dangerous, exhausting journey. Because of the war, Heidsieck had to zigzag across several states, including Ohio, Illinois, Missouri, and Kansas, to reach his destination. He barely escaped death when his train derailed in Louisiana. Eventually he made it to New Orleans, only to find that no one there had any money. What they did have was cotton, bales and bales of it stacked in warehouses. It was worth a fortune in Europe, which had been cut off from its Southern suppliers because of the Union's naval blockade. Heidsieck decided to take a chance and accept cotton in payment for his champagne. The problem was getting it out of the country. When he learned that the port of Mobile, Alabama, had not yet been blockaded, he hauled the cotton there and hired two ships.

But time was running out. By early 1862 Union armies were closing in and the naval blockade was growing tighter with each day that passed. "The minute the ships are loaded, I want you to set off," Heidsieck told the captains. He also ordered them to take different routes in hopes that at least one of the ships would get through.

A few days later, Heidsieck's hopes were dashed. One of his ships had been fired on and sunk, its entire cargo lost. Although there was no word about the second ship, Heidsieck was consumed with worry and had only one thought: get home as soon as possible to try to salvage his business. But by now—April 1862— the way north was completely blocked. Heidsieck resolved to go back to New Orleans and try to catch a boat to Mexico or Cuba, where he could make connections to Europe.

Hearing that a paddle wheel steamer was about to attempt a trip to New Orleans, Heidsieck convinced the captain to take him on board as a barman. He also agreed to carry a diplomatic pouch from the French consul in Mobile to his counterpart in New Orleans.

On May 1, the steamer *Dick Keys* slipped into Mobile Bay and turned west, churning past Biloxi and hugging the coast of Mississippi in order to stay out of sight of the Union navy.

Four days later, New Orleans came into view, and everyone breathed a sigh of relief. What no one realized was that the city had fallen to the Union the day before they left Mobile. Before anyone could disembark, soldiers boarded the vessel and began searching it. The diplomatic pouch Heidsieck was carrying was seized and opened. To his shock, it contained not only government dispatches but also offers from French textile manufacturers to supply uniforms for the Confederate Army. Heidsieck tried to explain, but the commanding officer, General Benjamin F. Butler, cut him off and ordered troops to seize him.

Heidsieck was charged with spying and thrown into Fort Jackson, a prison perched on a swampy patch of the Mississippi Delta from where, it was said, no one ever escaped. As the glamorous man once feted as "Champagne Charlie" languished in a fly-infested, mud-filled cell, family and friends wrote letters to Napoleon III begging him to pressure the U.S. government into freeing Heidsieck. Butler, who had been nicknamed "the beast," was incensed. "I don't give a shit about France or its emperor," he said. "No one's going to push me around. Heidsieck is nothing but a French dog, and he deserves to be hanged."

Butler refused to allow Heidsieck visitors, but finally consented to a visit by the French consul. The diplomat told Heidsieck that everything possible was being done to secure his release but that he "should prepare for the worst." And that was not all; the consul had other depressing news. Heidsieck's second ship had been intercepted and its cargo of cotton burned.

As days passed, the heat, humidity, and squalid conditions took their toll. Yellow fever claimed the lives of many prisoners, including Heidsieck's cellmate. There were also alligators, natural wardens of the prison, which tried to crawl through the uncovered windows of the cells whenever the river rose. Inmates fought them off by throwing rocks into their gaping jaws.

In one of two letters he managed to smuggle out, Heidsieck told his wife, "In eight days, I will have been in prison for three months. Conditions are indescribable but I refuse to give up."

It would not be until November 16, 1862, that campaigning on Heidsieck's behalf finally paid off. On instructions from President Abraham Lincoln, who had been concerned about "the Heidsieck incident," the secretary of war ordered Heidsieck's release. Heidsieck was more dead than alive when the gates opened. He was so gaunt and frail that some of his closest friends didn't recognize him.

It took the entire winter for Heidsieck to recover. Not until the following spring did he finally make it home. He was depressed and thoroughly demoralized. His business had gone bankrupt, and his wife had begun selling their property to pay off bills.

And then a miracle occurred.

On a cold winter's evening, there was a knock on Heidsieck's door. When he opened it, a messenger handed him a note. It said that an elderly missionary, visiting his family in a nearby village, wanted to see him immediately. Although the hour was late, Heidsieck set off by horseback through the deep snow.

When he finally reached the house where the priest was staying, Heidsieck was given a packet of papers and a map. "These are yours," the old man said. Heidsieck unwrapped the packet and found a stack of deeds to land in Colorado, all made out in his name. The priest explained that the brother of Heidsieck's former agent in New York was ashamed of how his brother had rebuffed Heidsieck's request for payment. He had staked the claims in hopes of paying back at least some of the money his brother owed.

Heidsieck was speechless, but when the missionary opened the map and pointed out the location of the lots, he was absolutely dumbfounded. The land included one-third of the city of Denver. What had been a tiny village of barely three hundred residents when the claims were first staked was now one of the biggest and wealthiest cities in the West. The deeds were worth a fortune.

Heidsieck sold the land and, with money from the sale, paid off all of his debts. Within a few months, the House of Charles Heidsieck had been reborn.

It was about the same time that Robert Tomes was stamping his last invoice and preparing to leave for home. During his eighteen months in France, it had been his good fortune to taste some of the better champagnes. Unlike those he'd drunk with friends at New York City's Union Club, with their cloying sweetness, the wines he was served in Reims were elegant and much drier. He was immediately impressed. "It was the first time in my life that I had enjoyed a glass of champagne, as wine," he said. "I now found, instead of tossing off my glass and swallowing its contents with a gulp, as I had been wont to do in order to secure the evanescent sparkle and hasten the expected exhilaration, that the wine trickled slowly, drop by drop, over the gratified palate. My host caught the expression of my satisfaction, and said: 'You don't get such wine in America'; adding, with a roguish twinkle of his eye, 'we keep that for ourselves and friends.' "[17]

Tomes encouraged champagne producers to change their attitude and be more sensitive to the palates of foreign customers who, by then, were consuming 80 percent of the champagne being made. In what constituted a farewell note, he accused producers of catering to "the gulping crowd," of making champagnes that all taste as if they were "brewed from the same vat." He leveled some specific criticisms. Heidsieck's champagne, he said, "no longer pleases the taste of the fastidious." Though "wholesome and pure," it is "too sweet for a discriminating palate." Roederer's is "loaded with sugar" while Moët & Chandon is "manufactured for the masses" and not admired by European connoisseurs.

Tomes's most stinging indictment was reserved for Veuve Clicquot, which he said was "smothered in sweetness." Unlike other houses, "that of the Widow Clicquot never varies its wine to suit varying tastes. A bottle of Clicquot in America is the same as a bottle of Clicquot in Russia or elsewhere." Tomes warned that "Clicquot wine is fast losing prestige and will, before long, become obsolete if not adapted to the more discriminating taste of modern drinkers."[18]

His warning, however, had little impact on the house of Veuve Clicquot, which was still catering to the sweet tooth of Russia, its primary market. Years would pass before Clicquot would turn to a drier style of champagne.

Meanwhile, far greater concerns were creeping in. For all the bright accomplishments of the nineteenth century—the technological and industrial breakthroughs, the expanded transportation system, the transformation of Paris into a modern city—the glow of Louis-Napoleon's Second Empire had dimmed. The economy was slipping, corruption and nepotism were flourishing, and political unrest was growing. Many despised the 1852 constitution that gave the emperor almost absolute power. They deplored his reckless military adventures, his attempt to annex Belgium and Luxembourg, and his effort to set up a satellite empire in Central America by sending French troops to Mexico.

Like his uncle before him, Napoleon III had surrounded himself with ministers and other officials chosen more for their loyalty to the Bonapartes than to the welfare of the country. To ensure that loyalty, he gave them extravagant gifts (his favorite general received four thousand dollars' worth of chocolates) and paid them huge bribes. He skimmed millions from the national treasury, setting up secret accounts to funnel money to his family and mistress. Mindful that French regimes rarely lasted more than twenty years, the emperor also kept $75 million on deposit for himself in a London investment bank.

A certain wariness, even fear, had begun to permeate the country. It could even be felt at Robert Tomes's hotel in Reims,

where people were generally carefree and talked about everything. "But of politics you hear not a word," Tomes said. "Louis
Napoleon has put his firm finger on every lip. No one dares
whisper the words *liberté, fraternité, egalité,* or hum the faintest
stave of the Marseillaise." [19]

But in 1867, as Tomes set sail for New York and a country that
had only begun to recover from a devastating civil war, he could
not have guessed that in just three years, the country he was leaving behind would be plunged into a war of its own—and that his
beloved Champagne would bear the brunt of it.

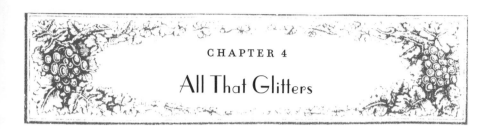

CHAPTER 4

All That Glitters

The first mail arrived at Pommery & Greno just before 9:00 A.M. The next delivery came about 11:00, followed by another after lunch. Before the day was over, there would be at least one more bag of mail. Under Napoleon III's Second Empire, la poste, as it was called, was everyone's chief means of communication. It was so swift and reliable that a letter mailed from Paris in the morning could be in Reims that afternoon. Businesses could count on several deliveries a day, and so could individuals.'

But even by those standards, the volume of mail at Louise Pommery's champagne house was staggering, which is why she was always up by 5:00 A.M. For the next four hours, she would sit at her desk, pen in hand, and respond personally to as much of it as possible.

There were orders from clients, letters from her agents around the world, notes from family and friends. "Many thanks for your warm letter," wrote a friend who was ill. "Hearing all your news brought me a great deal of pleasure." Not all of the correspondence was so cheery. A customer in London wrote that some of the champagne he'd received was undrinkable. Another complained that his bottles were corked badly. "I am returning them to you immediately," he said. "They should never have been sent in the first place. Such wretched work as this injures your name." But then, there was this note from her agent in London: "I have just made contact with the wine buyer for Cunard Lines whose magnificent floating palaces carry all those distinguished Americans to Europe. Could you please send me some of your 1868? I know for sure that a champagne any drier would not please the Americans."

Lately, however, much of Louise's mail concerned growing tensions between France and Prussia. "If hostilities erupt," asked a Belgian wine merchant, "would you consider setting up a warehouse with a considerable quantity of your champagne in Antwerp?"

By the spring of 1870, war did seem likely. It was almost as if the two countries' leaders were inviting it. Napoleon III, eager to divert attention away from his domestic difficulties, railed about about the dangers of Prussian militarism. Otto von Bismarck, who saw war with France as a way to unite Germany's quasi-independent states under Prussian domination, blamed France for most of his country's ills. He never missed an opportunity to remind his countrymen that France had invaded Germany thirty times over the past two centuries.

Another war was something champagne producers could ill afford. They had only just recovered from two other conflicts, the Austro-Prussian War of 1866 and the U.S. Civil War just before. Both had devastated the economies of those countries and resulted in numerous bankruptcies, all of which left champagne producers with stacks of unpaid bills. The possibility of another war was particularly distressing to Louise Pommery's financial manager. "It's truly aggravating to see our nation being drawn into unnecessary combats that can be so disastrous," he wrote. "Remember that stupid expedition to Mexico?" He was referring to Napoleon's attempt to set up an empire there. "When are we going to be done with all of this?"

As the sabre-rattling increased, friends urged Louise to take her two children and move to her country home in Chigny, a village on the Montagne de Reims which was surrounded by woods and vines. "It would be safer there, and you would also have the consolation of your roses," said one person who knew of Louise's passion for the flowers. But her agent in London, Adolphe Hubinet, counseled her to leave the country altogether. "If you come here, I would willingly put my house in London at your disposal," he said.

Louise, aware that Champagne would be the primary battle-ground if France and Prussia went to war, nonetheless replied that moving was out of the question. There was a business to run and workers who depended on her, she said. There were also numerous charities she supported for schools, orphanages, and the arts.

What claimed most of her attention, however, was a major building project aimed at turning the House of Pommery & Greno into what Louise said would be "the most beautiful business in the world."

Reaching that point had not been easy. The company was struggling when she inherited it from her husband ten years earlier. It was her husband's business partner, Narcisse Greno, who encouraged her to take an active role in the business. He was soon so impressed with her business acumen that he ceded the entire operation to her.

Although the firm made a bit of wine then, champagne was not Pommery & Greno's main business; it was wool-trading. One of Louise's first decisions was to sell off the wool business and concentrate on making champagne.

A few years later, she startled everyone when she purchased some land on the edge of Reims that had once been the site of a rubbish dump and began work on a new champagne facility. Offices and other buildings were to be modeled after some of the great English country houses whose architecture she admired. The cellars, however, with their hundreds of thousands of bottles, would be the main showpiece. Twelve miles of limestone were excavated for the caves. Louise also commissioned a sculptor to carve giant bas-reliefs celebrating champagne into the walls. These included scenes of Bacchus and an allegory of the five senses, along with tableaux evoking an appreciation of champagne in earlier times. Louise believed that art and champagne "ennobled" each other, and she was determined to show that.

Most Champenois, including Louise, had been supportive of Napoleon III when he was elected president in 1848. His modernization of France's industry and expansion of the railway system had done much to help Champagne. But Louise and others began having second thoughts after he declared himself emperor. There were too many scandals and charges of government corruption. The previous February, during the Carnival Ball in Paris, Napoleon had been seen stumbling around, his eyes glazed from opiates, his speech slurred. According to one who was present, the emperor was "surrounded by drunken officers and prostitutes dancing the cancan." The party "finally ended at dawn with everyone collapsing in a rack of champagne bottles."

On July 19 Louise heard the news that she and nearly everyone else feared but expected: Napoleon had declared war against Prussia.

It was a minor diplomatic flap that brought things to a head. Spain had deposed its Bourbon queen (a descendant of France's Louis XIV) and wanted to replace her with a nephew of King Wilhelm I of Prussia. When France protested, Wilhelm backed off but reserved the right for someone else in his family to inherit the throne. And there the matter might have ended had Bismarck not interfered. The chancellor, who had been looking for a "red rag to taunt the Gallic bull," intercepted Wilhelm's written response and reworded it to make it sound as if the king had insulted France.[2]

Napoleon responded as Bismarck hoped: he declared war and dispatched troops to the Franco-German border. In Paris, crowds at train stations chanted "Rout the German blockheads," and held out bottles of wine to the departing troops. In Champagne, however, the reaction was subdued. Louise Pommery ordered workmen to cease construction on her champagne house and to start walling up her champagne instead. Other producers, aware of an old saying, "The German hates the Frenchman but loves his wine," began hiding their champagne as well.

Two weeks after Napoleon's declaration of war, three hundred twenty thousand Prussian troops, followed by tens of thousands of reservists, poured across the border, overrunning Alsace-Lorraine and chalking up victories almost faster than they could be located on a map. Only one thing slowed them down: "wretched Champagne." That's what one Prussian officer labeled it after temperatures suddenly plunged and torrents of rain turned the chalky landscape into a morass of sticky gray muck. It caked onto soldiers' boots, seeped inside, and made each step sheer agony. Supply wagons sank up to their axles in the waterlogged terrain as horses strained futilely at their harnesses.

In the vineyards, the picture was just as grim. But there was something strange about it, even eerie. This should have been the hottest and driest time of year. Instead, growers dressed in heavy clothing slogged through the mud as their vines were battered by the relentless downpour. Lost on no one was the fact that the weather had changed almost the moment the invasion began. Once again, vignerons said an ancient legend was proving true: God sends a bad harvest to mark the beginning of war.

This one, the Franco-Prussian War, would be the bloodiest of the century. New weapons made killing faster and easier. The French had the mitrailleuse, the world's first machine gun, which they nicknamed "the coffee grinder" and their enemy called "the hell machine." Terrifying though it was, the mitrailleuse was no match for Prussia's long-range artillery. The damage inflicted by both, however, was enough to shake even the most battle-hardened soldier. "It was senseless butchery," recalled a Prussian sergeant after one battle. "There were heaped-up bodies everywhere, yet one looked in vain for a single intact undamaged corpse. I spotted a beautiful pair of cavalry boots lying on the ground and picked them up; there were legs and feet still inside." [3] The carnage was so terrible, said another witness, that even Prussian victories seemed more like bloody defeats.

As every attempt by French forces to advance and counterattack was thrown back, Napoleon, against all advice, announced he would go to Sedan, near the Belgian border, and take personal command. The Germans couldn't believe their luck. Because Sedan was surrounded by high bluffs, all they had to do was bring up their artillery. There would be no way for the French to maneuver, no way for them to retreat; Napoleon and his one hundred thousand men would be cut to pieces. "We've caught them in a mousetrap," said a Prussian officer with glee. One of Napoleon's generals put it more bluntly: "Here we are in a chamber pot, about to be shitted upon."[4]

On September 1, Bismarck's big guns opened up, spreading "a circle of fire the like of which no French troupier had ever seen," said one historian. "Twenty thousand Prussian shells exploded in this narrow space in the course of the day, harrowing up the soul of every French soldier."[5]

The next morning, a tearful Napoleon, surrounded by his men, surrendered his sword to King Wilhelm. Thirty-eight thousand French soldiers had been killed, wounded, or taken prisoner.

The war, however, was not over. Napoleon was deposed and a new Government of National Defense assumed power in Paris, rejecting Bismarck's demands that France cede Alsace-Lorraine and pay all war costs.

The Prussian chancellor now turned toward the French capital to bring the government there to heel. It was a route he and his troops happily realized would first take them through the heart of Champagne and straight into Reims. Although the distance from Sedan to Reims was only fifty miles, it was a march no one, including American General Philip Sheridan, would ever forget. Sheridan, a veteran of the U.S. Civil War, had been sent to

Europe as an observer by President Ulysses S. Grant. What he witnessed defied imagination. "Almost every foot of the way was strewn with fragments of glass from champagne bottles, emptied and then broken by the troops," he said. "The road was literally paved with glass, and the amount of wine consumed (none was wasted) must have been enormous."

Three days after their victory at Sedan, the Germans arrived in Reims, where Bismarck announced that a victory dinner would be held in honor of King Wilhelm. The site chosen, the Palace of Tau, was especially fitting, for it housed the talisman of Charlemagne, the Germanic leader who became emperor of France and most of western Europe in the ninth century. On the night of the dinner, two giant barrels were cut in half and filled with ice, into which hundreds of bottles of champagne were plunged. According to one of the guests, everyone "drank long and deeply."

The following day, the Prussians got down to business, declaring all of Champagne under military occupation. Homes, schools, and churches as well as other public buildings in Reims were requisitioned to house the thirty thousand troops stationed there.

Madame Pommery was still walling up her champagne when she was notified that her home had been requisitioned by the new military governor, Prince von Hohenlohe.[6] Unable to clear away the tools and debris before he arrived, Louise hoped the military governor would think it was simply part of the construction on her new facility.

But Hohenlohe was not fooled. Shortly after installing himself, he summoned Louise to his office. "I understand that champagne as prestigious as yours requires good ventilation when it is stored." Hohenlohe paused, letting his words sink in. Then, before Louise could reply, he added, "Don't worry, I promise that your champagne will not be touched." He gave similar assurances to other producers.

Hohenlohe also instructed troops to keep their distance from the vineyards and not interfere with the harvest. Like most Prussians, he hoped to ride out the occupation as quietly as possible, perhaps even enjoy a little time "living like God in France," as the Germans were fond of saying. With its architectural treasures and culture founded on wine and food, France, for most Germans, was a glittering contrast to "putrid Prussia."

For a while, everything went smoothly. Then someone took a shot at a soldier standing outside a café. The sniper could not be found, but the Prussians felt they had to make an example and fined the café owner 250 bottles of champagne.

The incident was followed by other attacks, and Hohenlohe, aware that most households had at least one hunting rifle, issued a decree ordering all civilians to surrender their firearms. As guns were turned in, Hohenlohe began to relax.

Shortly thereafter, the military governor received word that an important visitor was en route to Reims to assess the occupation. Count Alfred von Waldersee was Prussia's military attaché to France, and already a legend for his exploits as a spy. Four years earlier, during war with Austria, he posed as an artist and managed to sketch the entire defense network around Prague, then in Austrian hands. More recently, he charmed his way into the boudoir of the mistress of Napoleon III's chief aide-de-camp. He *said* it was to gather military secrets.

Hohenlohe was determined to make a good impression on

the colorful Waldersee and invited him to lunch at Madame Pommery's. As everyone sat down, the governor proudly described how he had put an end to the recent trouble by confiscating everyone's guns. "At last, there are no more armed civilians left," he said. "My proclamation has been obeyed."

Madame Pommery quickly interrupted: "I can assure you, sir, that some citizens still have arms." With that, she pulled a small revolver from her pocket. "It will never leave my side."

The two men were stunned.

"Madame, in the governor's house!" blurted Hohenlohe.

"Sir, I must remind you that this is *my* house. And I still have firearms belonging to my family hidden away. Perhaps you would like to search for them." (The guns had been hidden beneath the floorboards.)

A shocked silence followed before Waldersee spoke up: "Keep your weapons, Madame. It is not we Prussians who disarm the ladies, it is they who disarm us."

Madame Pommery's outburst revealed an uncomfortable fact: the occupation was not going well. Curfews, arbitrary taxes, and the constant presence of armed troops had created a festering resentment among the general population. Nor did it help that many champagne houses were owned or managed by Germans from the Rhineland, most of whom had become naturalized French citizens and who had never disguised their contempt for their Prussian "cousins," whom they considered barbarians.

Inevitably, attacks against the Prussians multiplied. Most were carried out by bands of civilians and army deserters known as franc-tireurs (snipers), who engaged in a kind of guerrilla war by ambushing convoys and military patrols, blowing up bridges, sabotaging railway lines, and doing all they could to make life miserable for the enemy.

The Prussians responded with force. Insurgents were summarily executed; villages supporting them were burned. When a young man was brought to Reims for execution by firing squad, Louise Pommery rushed to Hohenlohe's office and begged the military governor to spare the man's life. Hohenlohe, moved by her passion and eloquence, commuted the man's sentence to imprisonment.

A few weeks later, three doctors were arrested for recruiting franc-tireurs and spying for the French government. Hohenlohe, fearing a full-scale insurgency, sentenced the men to death. When Louise heard about it, she was horrified. They were close personal friends of hers, and she felt compelled to intercede. With a bitterly cold winter setting in, Louise stressed to Hohenlohe how vital the three physicians were to the community. Hohenlohe refused to lift the death sentence, saying leniency would only make the situation worse. But Louise was tenacious and would not back down. Finally, Hohenlohe yielded but said the men would remain in custody. This time, that was not good enough for Louise.

Those who knew Madame Pommery described her as someone who could be very persuasive, or, as one friend put it, "a woman men found hard to refuse." She was petite, dark-haired, and pretty. Every picture of her shows a woman whose eyes seem to bore through the camera, as if she is interested in what the viewer might say. In every photo and painting, Louise is elegantly dressed, seemingly reserved but on the verge of smiling. The men she surrounded herself with were unmarried and fiercely devoted to her.

Prince Hohenlohe was as susceptible to Louise's charms as anyone. Before she left his office that day, the military governor had issued orders for the doctors to be freed.

As 1870 drew to a close, all of France—but especially Champagne—seemed to be in a state of depression. Winter was colder than anyone could remember, and Prussian soldiers were everywhere. Despite Hohenlohe's orders not to touch anyone's champagne, troops helped themselves to whatever they could. To make matters worse, the economy was practically at a standstill. Champagne sales fell more than 50 percent because of damaged railway lines and Prussian restrictions, which made it difficult if not impossible for producers to get their champagne to market. "Can't you find some way of sending something to us?" pleaded Antoine Hubinet from London. "What about from your warehouses in Belgium or Holland or even Timbuktu? People here are willing to pay any price."

Although the occupation was only four months old, it felt much longer. Just before Christmas, Louise received another letter from Hubinet. "I know this is a painful time for our country," he said, "but I send you my best wishes for the holidays, and hopes for a better New Year. I urge you to remain confident and not lose hope."

It was the kind of sentiment being exchanged in Paris. Instead of "bonne année" (Happy New Year), it was "bon courage" (keep your chin up). Bismarck had surrounded the city and effectively sealed it off, warning that unless the government surrendered, he would start shelling. For Paris's two million residents the situation was desperate. Food was nearly gone, and people were burning their furniture to keep warm. Between three and four thousand people were dying from the cold and hunger each week.

Faced with such a bleak situation, Georges Braquessac, owner of Café Voisin, one of the city's finest restaurants, felt it was incumbent on him to do what he could to provide some holiday cheer. He decided to put together a Christmas Day menu that no one would ever forget.

On the menu, which was headed "99th Day of the Siege," there was elephant consommé, bear chops, stuffed donkey's head, and marinated kangaroo, all animals from the zoo which had been slaughtered on orders from the government to help feed the city's starving population. The pièce de résistance, however, came from elsewhere: it was "Le Chat flanqué de Rats," cat garnished with rats.

Fortunately, the cellar of Voisin, at 261 rue St-Honoré, was well stocked and the wines chosen for the occasion were, in their own way, as remarkable as the food. They included 1846 Château Mouton-Rothschild, 1858 Romanée-Conti, 1861 Grand Vin de Latour, and 1864 Château Palmer. There was also Port from 1827.[7]

Among such stars, however, there was one that sparkled the brightest: champagne from the house of Bollinger.

Three days after the New Year began, Bismarck's patience ran out. Artillery shells and incendiaries fell on the city like a blizzard, striking schools, churches, hospitals, apartment buildings, and train stations. It was from one of the latter, the Gare d'Orléans, that the government decided to launch a last-ditch appeal for help—by hot air balloon.

The idea had been inspired by a young novelist named Jules Verne, who only a few years earlier had published his first book, *Five Weeks in Balloon.* Verne's enthusiasm for air travel was shared by his friend, the photographer Félix Nadar, who actively promoted the plan to the government. The two reasoned that since trains were no longer running and Paris was cut off, the besieged city's train stations could be converted into balloon factories and launching pads. That would help solve one of the great problems that had plagued the French throughout the war: How to communicate with one another. Often, because telegraph lines had been cut, one part of the country was completely ignorant about what was happening in another. Carrier pigeons were employed but their use was limited by what they could carry. They could also be unreliable because male pigeons were often "distracted" by females and hence never reached their destination.

Thus, the government decided to give balloons a try. The first were launched in October, when Bismarck began encircling the city. Most were unmanned, but one carried the Minister of the Interior, Léon Gambetta, to Tours, 150 miles south, where he believed it would be easier to conduct the war.[8]

In the early morning hours of January 9, workers prepared balloon number 55, named the *Marquis de Duquesne,* for launching. Its destination was Bordeaux, where Gambetta's government delegation had fled after Tours became unsafe. The balloon carried coded military documents outlining Paris's plight and a plan aimed at breaking the Prussian siege. At 3:00 A.M., the *Marquis* lifted off into the darkness and drifted away . . . in the wrong direction. Instead of southwest, it floated northeast.

Twelve hours later, workers in one of Pommery & Greno's vineyards glanced up to see the *Marquis de Duquesne* floating overhead. Like several other balloons, it had been carried off course. (One launched toward Tours ended up in Norway.) As the *Marquis* gently descended into the vines, workers rushed toward it. It took them only moments to discover the balloon's cargo. Before a Prussian patrol could spot them, they stashed the important documents into grape-pickers' baskets and piled empty champagne bottles on top. The documents were then taken to Madame Pommery. With help from friends at la poste, Louise eventually managed to smuggle the documents to Bordeaux.

But it would have made little difference. The siege of Paris had become unbearable, and Bismarck was now warning that unless the government surrendered, he would occupy the entire country instead of the fourteen départements Prussia then controlled (there were eighty-nine in all). With French forces in tatters and plagued by mass desertions, officials finally gave in and signed an armistice that took effect on January 26. Although it would take four more months to hammer out a peace treaty that gave Bismarck and Prussia everything they wanted, the war was effectively over.

The peace, however, was not an easy one. Bismarck announced that troops would remain in France as a kind of insurance policy to make sure the government lived up to the terms of the treaty: ceding Alsace-Lorraine and paying a war indemnity of five billion francs, the equivalent of $15 billion today. Combined with its own staggering war costs of $36 billion, France found itself nearly bankrupt.

Champagne was in particularly dire straits. Not only had the region borne the brunt of the occupation, but business was in the doldrums. Transportation remained crippled, crops had rotted on the vines, and more than two and a half million bottles of champagne had been pillaged.

Despite the awful situation, Louise Pommery decided this was the moment to try something she had been contemplating almost from the day she inherited her champagne house: she would make dry champagne. Other champagne-makers had toyed with the idea but rejected it because of the cost and risks. Dry champagne, or brut, was more expensive and difficult to make. It wasn't simply a matter of cutting back on the amount of syrup and sugar. Better grapes had to be used, grapes that were more fully ripened, which was tricky given Champagne's cool, northerly climate. Dry champagne also required longer aging—three years instead of one—which meant tying up capital and valuable space in the cellar. But the biggest risk was that most people knew only sweet champagne and liked it that way. There were hints that customers might prefer something else if it were available. But they didn't come from France, they came from Britain, Pommery's main market.

As early as 1848, an English merchant named Burnes had tried to interest some of his clients in dry champagne. Britain had so many sweet wines like port, madeira, and sherry, which they drank with dessert, that Burnes believed they might be inclined to try something else, a wine that was not sweet but one they could drink throughout a meal.

Somewhat to his surprise, French champagne-makers were resistant to the idea, fearing their reputations would be ruined and they would lose the customers they had. When Burnes ap-

proached Louis Roederer for some samples of undosed champagne, Roederer flatly refused. "As long as I live, there shall be
no bowing to the dry Baal in my cellars," he said. Roederer had
made his name selling sweet champagne to Russia. What he
didn't say was that many champagne-makers relied on syrup and
sugar to mask faults in their wine, such as excess acidity that resulted from picking unripened grapes.

Eventually, Burnes persuaded a few smaller producers to give
him what he wanted, but only if their names were kept off the labels. When Burnes returned to London, he presented the champagne to a fashionable men's club. They turned up their noses at
it. Burnes tried again with another group. This time, he was
more successful. Those who tasted the drier samples loved it.
Soon, British merchants were asking champagne producers to
include a little dry champagne in their shipments.

Like Burnes, Madame Pommery was not successful when she
first began experimenting with dry champagne in the 1860s.
Some clients complained about the color and limpidity; it was
brownish and unclear. Others said it tasted raw. When Louise
sent some samples to her agent in London, Hubinet rejected
them, warning that she risked "negating the reputation you've
earned for the elegance and delicacy of your champagnes." Nevertheless, he encouraged Louise to keep trying, that tastes in
Britain were beginning to change and the demand for dry champagne would increase.

Everything was put on hold in 1870 but when the war ended,
Louise resumed her experiments—only to find that much of her
staff was skeptical. At an in-house tasting, one employee said
her champagne "went down like a razor blade." Another said it
made him grind his teeth. The biggest skeptic was Henri Vanier,

Pommery's financial manager, who reminded everyone that "Making dry champagne is not like making an omelette. It takes time, costs more money, and we risk losing customers who like our champagne the way it is. That's why the big houses aren't making dry champagne."

But Louise had already made her decision: they were going ahead. It was why she had built a new champagne house in the first place. Her goal was to make something different and special.

She began by contacting growers and saying she would buy all of their grapes on one condition: that they pick when she told them to. Growers, who always worried about sudden changes in the weather, often picked their grapes before they had ripened. Louise promised to absorb any losses if growers did what she asked.

The first three years after the war were disappointing. Weather remained poor and the grapes Louise had to work with were less than ideal, resulting in champagnes that were tart and green. "Hold back on trying to sell these bad years," she told her salesmen. "But when the good years come, knock loudly on doors, for then we shall command the market."

It was in 1874, a vintage heralded as the best of the century, that Louise Pommery blew doors off their hinges. The champagne she made was so good and commanded such a high price that a British poet composed an ode in its honor. Entitled "Ode to Pommery 1874" and written to be sung to *Auld Lang Syne*, it began, *Should auld acquaintance be forgot / 'Twixt human friends and wine?* The sixth and final verse went as follows:

Farewell, then, Pommery Seventy-Four!
With reverential sips
We part and grieve that nevermore
Such wine may pass our lips.[9]

Even Vanier, Louise's curmudgeonly old finance manager, who had warned that making dry champagne could be "hugely embarrassing," was blown away. "Our brut," he now told clients, "is meant only for people who appreciate fine sparkling drinks, who prefer finesse and bouquet to an excess of gas and sugar which some houses use to cover up the thinness of their wines. When the cork pops, our champagne will satisfy the palate, not just the ears."

Louise's Brut '74 was the first truly dry, or brut, champagne to be sold on a commercial basis. It not only turned Pommery & Greno, then a small company, into one of the largest and leading champagne houses, but it also transformed the entire industry.

To celebrate her good fortune, Louise Pommery declared a holiday. Every year on her birthday, March 18, she gave her entire staff the day off. In return, they always sent her roses, her favorite flower.

Late in the afternoon of March 16, 1890, word came down that the annual day off would be one day earlier.

Louise Pommery was dying, but her first concern was her workers. She did not want them to miss their holiday if she did not survive past her birthday. "Please do not send flowers this year," she said. "Save them to dress my coffin."

Two days later, on her seventy-first birthday, Louise died.

France had never given a state funeral for a woman, but this funeral came close. Twenty thousand people, including representatives from the national government, coursed through the narrow streets of Reims as Louise's casket, buried beneath an avalanche of floral tributes, was borne from her house to the city's great cathedral. The procession was led by hundreds of schoolchildren, all carrying flowers that had been sent by family, friends, clients, and those who had been touched by Louise's generosity. Following in the wake were Louise's own children and her four hundred workers, all wearing black armbands. Although the distance from Louise's house to the cathedral was only a few blocks, it took the cortege more than two hours to work its way through the jammed streets.

During the service, Louise was remembered not only for what she meant to the world of champagne but also for everything she had done for various charities. She was also praised for saving one of France's greatest paintings, Jean-François Millet's *Les Glaneuses (The Gleaners)*. When it was about to be sold to a foreign buyer, she purchased it herself and donated it to the Louvre.

The president of France also paid a personal tribute. Noting Louise's love of roses, he issued a decree changing the name of Chigny, her country home where she had her beloved rose garden, to Chigny-les-Roses.

The most touching eulogy of all, however, came from the mayor of Reims, Dr. Henri Henrot, whose grief nearly prevented him from finishing. "Were it not for this outstanding woman, I would not be here today," he said. Dr. Henrot was one of the three physicians whose life Louise saved during the Franco-Prussian War.

Three years later, another funeral was taking place, this one in Paris. Pedestrians stopped and watched as elegant horse-drawn carriages came from all directions, moving slowly along the cobblestone streets until finally coming to a stop near the Church of the Madeleine, where passengers descended. The women were gowned in black silk, men wore dark suits and black armbands. Footmen in livery guided mourners inside and settled them in velvet-covered chairs as a cherrywood coffin, borne by four pallbearers, was gently placed in the middle of the room. As the pallbearers stepped back, the deceased's closest friend moved toward the casket and opened it.

Revealing dozens of bottles of champagne on ice!

And why not? The funeral was at Maxim's, a name synonymous with glamour and good times. According to one of the mourners, the funeral was actually a party for "a friend who died too young but whose love of champagne was well-known." [10]

That was what the Belle Époque was all about, any excuse for a party, any excuse for champagne. It was a time when everything sparkled; the people, the conversation, the décor, but especially the wine. Life was lived in public; everyone went out to be seen, to be entertained, and to enjoy themselves. Champagne was their constant companion.

Maxim's was the great meeting place, the "temple of champagne" as some called it, but it wasn't the only watering hole. Champagne flowed everywhere, at parties, horse races, Turkish baths, and especially in cabinets particuliers, private rooms of restaurants where men entertained their mistresses and where, it is said, they may have eaten less but drank more. On the Côte d'Azur, a Russian whose job it was to supply food for the czar created a splash at one of his banquets by turning the center of each table into a lake of champagne, with ice sculptures of swans floating on the frothy surface.

Nor was champagne's popularity confined to France. Jazz musician Jelly Roll Morton described how he made a name for himself in the brothels of New Orleans by collecting all the unfinished bottles to "make up a new bottle from the mixture."[11] In Great Britain, the Prince of Wales always had a boy follow him on hunting parties with a basket filled with bottles of champagne.[12] Cases of champagne were even being carried by caravans of native porters to thirsty British officers in Africa.[13] "Is there anyone in the civilized world whose eyes do not light up and face does not smile when he hears the word champagne?" mused one champagne lover.[14]

Certainly, champagne producers had reason to smile. Prices were at an all-time high. Even peasants who tended the vineyards had money to spend. "It's like a rain of gold," said one grower.[15]

Three Universal Expositions, or World's Fairs, between 1878 and 1900 drew visitors to Paris from all over the world. These fairs, where champagne flowed like Niagara Falls, helped fuel a soaring optimism that was epitomized by the construction of the Eiffel Tower in 1889 and, after that, by the most exciting decade of all, the Gay Nineties.[16]

Every day seemed to present something new. Horseless carriages began cruising down the Champs-Elysées. Paris got its first telephone booth, and opened its first métro line. Marie

Curie discovered radium. Louis Pasteur developed a vaccine for rabies.

Given the downtrodden state of France in 1871, it's amazing that any of this even happened. At the end of the Franco-Prussian War many in France feared it would take thirty to fifty years for the country to recover. But France not only recovered, it came roaring back thanks in large part to the country's modern industrial system and the extensive railroad network that had been developed during the Second Empire.

It was a period as rich and varied as any France had ever known, and champagne was an integral part of it. Champagne became the password that confirmed the importance of a moment: the birth of a child, a marriage, the launching of a ship, old friends meeting again. Hardly a novel, poem, or play could be written without some mention of bubbly. Alexandre Dumas said he always kept a glass of champagne by his inkwell "to lend the pen inspiration." Pushkin described it as "a wine blessed by the Gods." Rudyard Kipling warned, "If the aunt of the vicar has never touched liquor, look out when she finds the champagne."

By the end of the nineteenth century, champagne was firmly fixed as part of the national character. "It resembles us, it's made in our image," said the writer Adolphe Brisson. "It bubbles like our spirit, it is piquant like our language, it sparkles and chatters and is constantly in motion."

In 1881 the National Assembly, in what may have seemed like an unremarkable piece of legislation, passed a "bill-sticking" law that allowed posters to be put up on walls. Combined with technological advances in printing, the impact of the law was revolutionary for it marked the advent of modern advertising. The first large lithographed wall poster was commissioned by

France-Champagne, a small champagne house that no longer exists. Designed by Pierre Bonnard, the poster featured a beautiful woman in a wispy, low-cut gown holding a glass of champagne, from which a river of froth was pouring out. It created such a sensation that Henri Toulouse-Lautrec was inspired to try his hand at poster-making, some of his work depicting champagne at the newly opened Moulin Rouge.

Although everyone in Champagne was eager to jump onto the advertising bandwagon, one man led the way. "I can stamp my name on any surface," declared Eugène Mercier, and he did, not only on posters but also on fans, corkscrews, ice buckets, lipstick tubes and, most notably, the side of a balloon.

Mercier, who founded his own champagne house when he was only twenty, was a man of boundless energy ("I sleep fast," he explained) and unlimited creativity. He caused a stir at the 1889 Exposition when he arrived with a team of twenty-four white oxen hauling the world's largest wine barrel, a cask that took sixteen years to build and contained the equivalent of two hundred thousand bottles of champagne. The barrel was so huge that roads had to be widened and houses had to be bought up and demolished in order to get it from Épernay to Paris.

Eleven years later, when the next Exposition came along, every champagne producer was acutely aware of the importance of advertising, of making sure their name was known. There was an extravagant Palace of Champagne designed by a major architect, but many houses also built pavilions of their own in an effort to entice as many of the fifty million visitors as possible to taste—and buy—their champagne. Competition was fierce. Everyone vied for the privilege of having his champagne poured at the grand dinners. One of those dinners was a banquet for twenty-two thousand mayors.

Once again, however, Mercier found a way to rise above the crowd, this time with a hot air balloon tethered near the Château de Vincennes on the eastern edge of Paris. The balloon could carry as many as a dozen passengers, giving them a bird's-eye view of the city while they sipped champagne and nibbled on snacks served from the bar in the basket. Mercier's goal was to illustrate how light and airy his champagne was. What he failed to anticipate, however, was the weather.

On November 14, as the 1900 Exposition drew to a close, violent winds ripped the balloon from its moorings and sent it and its startled passengers drifting toward the northeast. At first no one was too concerned. As the balloon passed over Épernay, ninety miles from Paris, people poured out of their houses and saluted it with glasses of champagne.

By nightfall, however, the winds had increased. Passengers in the balloon threw out the anchor in an effort to bring it down, but all they managed to do was rip up a few trees along with the rooftops of several houses. "Help, help," they cried, but people on the ground thought the cries were merely those of drunken revelers.

Finally, sixteen hours later, the balloon settled down in some trees in the Belgian part of the Ardennes forest and the shaken passengers climbed out. Within a short time, Belgian gendarmes were at the scene. When they discovered several bottles of champagne in the balloon, they fined Mercier for "illegally importing champagne" into the country.

Mercier could not have been more delighted. News of the incident was flashed around the world. "It's the cheapest publicity I ever got," he said.[17]

In the end, however, it wasn't balloons or posters that made the difference: it was the ingenuity of the people whose goal was to stamp the magic of champagne on the consciousness of the public. People like Champagne Charlie and Louis Bohne had, in different ways, set the stage for those who followed during the Belle Époque.

One of them was George Kessler, Moët & Chandon's agent in the United States. Moët was then, as it is now, the largest champagne house, but its market share in America lagged far behind Mumm's. In 1902 Kessler learned that a group of VIPs would be gathering in New York City to celebrate the launching of kaiser Wilhelm II's newly built yacht, *Meteor*. The kaiser sent a bottle of German sparkling wine, or sekt, for the christening along with several cases for the lavish luncheon which was to follow.

Unlike his grandfather King Wilhelm I, who had practically drunk his way through Champagne, the kaiser was a xenophobe when it came to wine. Only German ones passed his lips. He once accused Bismarck of being unpatriotic when the chancellor refused to accept a glass of sekt from him. Bismarck, who preferred French champagne, replied, "My patriotism stops at my stomach." On another occasion, Wilhelm admonished some of his officers at a reception for having the temerity to offer him French champagne. "Take it away and bring me my sekt," he growled. "It's just as good."

The officers, who appreciated the difference between sekt and champagne, hurried to the cellar. There they soaked the labels off several bottles of sekt and pasted them onto bottles of champagne.

"You see," said the kaiser when he was served a glass, "I told you sekt was every bit as good as champagne."

So one can appreciate the importance Wilhelm placed on having his favorite wine for the christening. Certainly George Kessler did, and he sensed an opportunity.

On the appointed day, as Germany's ambassador to the United States prepared to welcome President and Mrs. Theodore Roosevelt and other invited guests to the launch site in New York's harbor, Kessler made his move. With some sleight of hand, he managed to substitute a bottle of Moët for the kaiser's sekt.

The dismay the Germans must have felt when they saw the First Lady of the United States shatter a bottle of French champagne across the bow of their imperial yacht can only be imagined. And that was before lunch. As guests were being seated, they discovered magnums of Moët on every table.

Kessler's audacity provoked an international incident. An embarrassed and irate Kaiser Wilhelm immediately recalled his ambassador. Kessler and his employer, however, were delighted. The name of Moët & Chandon was emblazoned in newspapers across America. Moët sales there took off.[18]

Spoiling the kaiser's party wasn't Kessler's only triumph. Four years later, following the San Francisco earthquake, Kessler dispatched a railroad car filled with champagne to console the victims. Once again, the name of Moët & Chandon was in the headlines.

While Kessler and others were busy bringing champagne to the West, an American with just as much flair was bringing the West to Champagne. In 1905, the Buffalo Bill Wild West Show opened in Reims to great fanfare. Audiences were entranced by the riding, roping, and shooting by real cowboys and cowgirls, like Annie Oakley. They especially loved the Indians and the reenactment of Custer's Last Stand. But when the fashion-conscious French learned that Mrs. Custer herself had helped choose the costumes for the performance, they were practically charmed out of their seats—so charmed, in fact, that one champagne house began making Buffalo Bill Champagne, complete with the cowboy's picture on the label.[19]

In some ways, the champagne industry was not all that different from the Old West. It was a rough-and-tumble world where few laws existed. This was the era of snake oil salesmen where the catch phrase was "anything goes." Mass advertising was new, but the idea of truth in advertising was unheard of. Although champagne had become big business, rules and regulations to keep it in check had not kept pace. Protection for consumers and even producers was practically nonexistent. Into this vacuum gallopped a special kind of outlaw: the name rustler.[20]

One of the most daring was Léon Chandon, who realized that if his name were printed just right, people would confuse the champagne he made with that of Moët & Chandon, and buy more of his bubbly. Not only were Léon's bottle labels nearly identical to Moët & Chandon's, but his corks were branded with the same star. Léon's ploy was so successful that another Chandon, this one Eugène, formed a company of his own and began peddling champagne, too.

And it was all perfectly legal. At least, there was nothing in the books that said such things were illegal.

When the cellarmaster at Ruinart Père et Fils decided to set up a champagne house of his own, one of his first acts was to hire a retired cavalry officer named Paul Ruinart as a front man. Soon, bottles of Champagne Paul Ruinart were rolling off the assembly line.

There was also champagne made under the name of Victor Clicquot, whose real job was that of a bricklayer. There was almost another Clicquot, this one a bootmaker from Reims, but his misfortune was being a cousin of the famous and formidable Veuve Clicquot. When she heard what her cousin was up to, she put the fear of God in him and forced him to back off. "The world will never know what it lost in terms of a champagne-maker," said one producer, "but Reims would have lost a trusty bootmaker."[21]

For Gustave and Léon Bousigues, it was a little more complicated. The brothers realized from the very beginning that their name lacked that certain je ne sais quoi when it came to attracting customers. So they changed their name to Bley and began selling champagne under the name Bley Frères. Sales, however, continued to sputter.

It was in Strasbourg that the Bleys found the solution to their problem. While dining at a brasserie, they discovered that the name of their waiter was Roederer. No matter that his first name was Théophile, or that Théophile's knowledge of champagne was limited to the leftovers in customers' glasses. For a few francs, the Bleys persuaded Roederer to accompany them back to Reims and let them use his name to sell champagne.

Louis Roederer, the *real* Roederer, was irate and took the Bleys to court, one of the first times legal action had ever been taken. "What the Bleys are doing is like a thorn in my foot," he complained.

Roederer, however, was about the only one who was concerned. Even the court seemed indifferent, ruling that the Bleys had done nothing wrong. A man, the judges said, has the right to use his own name.

Such legal laxity meant that the public was often deceived. "Time and time again," observed Robert Tomes, "I saw would-be connoisseurs smacking their lips over an indifferent bottle of the false champagne and loudly declaring that they recognized the flavor of the genuine Roederer."

The house of Lanson also found its name being misused. A group in the Congo produced a sparkling beverage called Lanson Black Label. The label, however, was yellow. Instead of a coat of arms, it was adorned with two elephant heads. In California, a different company got the design and color correct but they called their "champagne" Château Lanson.

The biggest name heist, however, was pulled off by another group of Americans. As early as the 1850s, a few firms in the United States had been making sparkling wine on the side, but with the growing popularity of champagne, companies were soon specializing in it. One of the first was the Great Western Wine Company of Hammondsport, New York.

Although the winery had won numerous awards for its sparkling wine, owners decided they could make even more money if they had a more prestigious address. To arrange that, they met with officials from the U.S. Postal Service and explained how the soil and climatic conditions of their region were much like Champagne's. They pointed out that just down the road from their winery was the town of Bath, its name borrowed from a city in England. There was also New Amsterdam which became New York. Postal Service officials quickly got the idea.

Within a few days, a small branch post office was opened on the premises of the Great Western Wine Company. The official address: Rheims, New York, which was the common spelling for Reims in those days. But the folks from Great Western apparently didn't stop there.

In the 1880s a small delegation reportedly set off for France. After crisscrossing the country, they met an old woman who had once been a cook. She also happened to be a widow. What's more, her last name was Pommery. Money changed hands and Madame Pommery agreed to return to the United States with the Americans.

In no time at all, the House of Pommery was reborn, this time in Rheims, New York.

The Belle Époque was the Golden Age of Champagne, but as the twentieth century dawned, the glamour and excitement that characterized the era was being replaced by a growing anxiety.

Cheaper grapes had begun pouring in from the south, undercutting growers in Champagne whose livelihoods depended on selling *their* grapes to the big champagne houses. The railroad, which had been such a blessing for Champagne, had suddenly become a curse for its growers as champagne producers snatched up the cheaper grapes. With their "rain of gold" drying up, growers' incomes tumbled and relations with champagne producers soured. "They live in châteaux," grumbled one grower, "we live with holes in our roofs." [22] A series of bad harvests in the 1890s and early 1900s only added to their malaise.

On July 14, 1909, residents of Landreville, a small town in the

Aube part of Champagne, gathered to celebrate Bastille Day. It wasn't much of a celebration. "Hardly anyone took part in the parade, and no one paid very much attention to the few who marched by," wrote Louis Estienne in his journal. "It was all extremely sad."[23]

Several days later, French newspapers reported with pride that a Frenchman named Louis Blériot had just made the first solo flight across the English Channel.

"That's a fine thing for France," said Estienne, "but it does nothing for us here. Everyone is discouraged. Life may be changing but we have to find a way to live."

That was becoming increasingly difficult, for growers and many others as well. The frantic whirl of the Belle Époque seemed to be spinning out of control. Throughout the country, there was growing labor unrest, questions about the role of Jews in society as a result of the Dreyfus Affair, tensions over separation of Church and State, and challenges to the government by monarchists, anarchists, and communists.

The Belle Époque, as one historian noted, had become "a dance on top of a volcano," one that would erupt sooner than almost anyone could imagine.[24]

CHAPTER 5

When the Marne Drank Champagne

On a cold winter's afternoon in January of 1911, villages along the River Marne were bombarded with the sounds of bells, bugles, drums, and hail guns. It had just been learned that a truck carrying four thousand bottles of "foreign" wine—wine from outside Champagne—was on its way to Épernay to be turned into champagne.

Responding to the alarm, three thousand angry winegrowers armed with hoes, hatchets, and sharpened vineyard stakes were soon marching on Damery, a village not far from Épernay. There they intercepted the truck, pushed it and its cargo of wine into the river, and sent the driver running for his life.

The wine had come from the Loire Valley. It had been bought by a number of houses for turning into champagne because it was cheaper than the white wine produced in their area. Local vignerons, whose livelihoods depended on selling their wine and grapes to champagne-makers, complained they were being undercut and driven out of business. Not only that, they said, but using wine and grapes that did not come from Champagne was wrong, and the result was not *real* champagne.

Such complaints had been voiced many times before, and although authorities always promised they would investigate, nothing ever seemed to change. On the seventeenth of January, when growers were alerted about the foreign wine heading for Épernay, their patience finally ran out.

After scuttling the shipment, they turned toward the champagne house of Achille Perrier, chanting "A bas les fraudeurs!" (Down with cheaters). Alerted by his gardener that "all hell was about to break loose," Monsieur Perrier hid in the home of his concierge. Minutes later, growers and their families broke through the front gates and swept into the courtyard. There, they discovered a wagonload of more foreign wine, which they rolled out to the street, up onto a bridge, and heaved into the Marne. Others forced their way into the Perrier cellars, sabotaging grape presses and smashing fifty thousand bottles of champagne. By the time police arrived two hours later, everyone had disappeared.

The following day violence erupted again, with mobs sacking two other champagne houses, this time in Hautvilliers, home of Dom Pérignon. Once again, everyone had vanished by the time gendarmes appeared.

"Unmask the guilty ones!" blared the headline of one newspaper. But when authorities held a public inquiry to find out who was responsible, they were greeted by stony silence. "Well," said the presiding magistrate sarcastically, "it appears it was everyone, and it was no one."

The violence in Damery and Hautvilliers quickly spread to other towns and villages, but it was just the beginning. For the next six months, Champagne would be in a state of insurrection. *Les Émeutes*, as the riots of 1911 were known, would bring down two French governments and push the region to the brink of civil war.

Violence was in the air nearly everywhere as the twentieth century entered its second decade. In Britain, troops clashed with striking dockworkers, coal miners, and suffragettes. In Russia, the czar put down a violent uprising by Bolsheviks. Anarchists in New York battled with police while students from the Sorbonne rioted and fought with troops in Paris.

But even against that background, it came as a shock when the sleepy villages of Champagne exploded in mayhem.

Vignerons had always led solitary and docile lives. Educated largely by the Church, they had been taught to be obedient and to accept their lot in life. "It was a time when we believed in the policeman, the teacher, and the priest, and trusted them implicitly," one said.

Life was dictated by the vines and Mother Nature. Vignerons didn't just work the earth, they were riveted to it, their attachment almost religious in its intensity. Caring for the vines was a sacred trust, for each vine had its own story, evoking memories of ancestors who had labored there before.

Most vignerons, more than 80 percent, owned no more than one acre of land. That land consisted of tiny unconnected plots of vines that were no bigger than bedsheets, often separated from each other by several miles. Although it took time to trudge from one plot to another, that was all for the best as far as vignerons were concerned. It was their form of insurance. If frost or hail struck one parcel, it would probably miss the others, so there would almost always be something to harvest.

But in 1890, everything changed abruptly and their cherished way of life was ripped apart. That year saw the first sizable invasion of foreign wine and cheaper grapes, mainly from the Loire Valley and southern France, arriving in Champagne. In Épernay, the train station was so jammed with baskets of grapes and barrels of foreign wine that travelers could hardly move. Almost overnight, grape prices in Champagne plunged more than 50 percent.

Temperatures dropped, too. The winter of 1890 was one of the worst ever, and the paralyzing cold seemed to linger forever. For the first time in decades, bands of wolves were spotted roaming the vineyards, searching for something to eat. Spring arrived late, bringing with it heavy rains that added to the gloom of vignerons.

These were proud, hardworking people. The idea of begging, of having to ask for handouts, was humiliating and painful, but many had no choice.

"Please buy my grapes," pleaded one grower in a letter to a major champagne house. "I'll take anything you offer. My wife is sick in the hospital and I can't pay for her care. I have five children and nothing to feed them."

Another grower lamented, "I have grapes as beautiful as the jewels of Ali Baba sitting in my cellar but no one will buy them."

But champagne-makers were unrepentant, saying they had a right to make a living, too. "If we can buy our grapes for less, even if they don't come from here, why shouldn't we?" one asked.

And that was the point: it was all perfectly legal. There was only one law on the books that regulated the content of champagne, and it was virtually useless, stating only that 51 percent of a sparkling wine's grapes had to come from Champagne for the wine to use that name. Where the other 49 percent came from was up to the champagne-maker. More disturbing, if the champagne-maker wanted to use something other than grapes, well, that was okay, too, because the law didn't stipulate that champagne had to be made entirely with grapes. Some unscrupulous producers mixed in apple and pear juice. There were also rumors of champagne-makers being seen in England buying up large quantities of rhubarb.

The potential for fraud, and a quick profit, was enormous. "It's easy to make a lot of money in Champagne," one champagne-maker boasted. "All you have to do is use cheaper grapes. The quality will be different but most people won't notice."

Harder to ignore was the way many champagne houses obtained those grapes. They dispatched operatives, known as commissionaires, to the countryside. Their job was to buy grapes as cheaply as possible. Many of these men were little more than thugs who squeezed growers for everything they could, paying derisory prices and demanding bribes. Usually, bribes took the form of extra grapes which the commissionaires could sell for their own profit. If growers complained or refused to go along, they could end up with no one buying their grapes. "Keep your tongue between your teeth and say nothing," one vigneron cautioned his fuming neighbor. "That way, they'll at least pay you something."

Those who did manage to sell their grapes often found their

noses being rubbed in it. "Come along and let's have a glass of *your* wine," a commissionaire would say after concluding a deal. "It's not bad."

Inevitably, rumbles of discontent swept across the land as growers began wondering how they could escape the growing financial misery that threatened to overwhelm them. On a warm spring day in 1907, they found their answer.

Massive demonstrations by winegrowers erupted in the Midi. Eighty thousand people marched through the city of Narbonne while more than half a million took to the streets in Montpellier. As in Champagne, grape prices in that southern winegrowing region had fallen sharply. Mostly it was due to overproduction; the Midi was awash with cheap red wine. Protesters, however, blamed "fabricators of fake wine" for the problem. Winemakers, they said, were using cheaper wine from North Africa and Spain to stretch their wines and boost the alcohol content. Some added port and cognac to enhance the bouquet and even blended in beet juice.

Prime Minister Georges Clemenceau, known as "the Tiger" for his hard-line approach to demonstrations, was not about to take any chances. He declared a national emergency and ordered troops into the Midi. Their presence only inflamed the protesters, who began hurling stones and insults. Soldiers responded by opening fire, killing at least five demonstrators and wounding many others.

News of the incident spread quickly. People throughout the country were horrified, but it was the army that was most shaken. Many of the troops who were present that day were reservists from the Midi. Seeing family and friends bloodied and beaten came as a severe shock. Entire platoons sat down in the streets and refused to obey orders. In one case, an entire division mutinied.

As protests by growers gained force, Clemenceau backed down and ordered troops to withdraw, promising that their grievances would be addressed.

Within days, his government passed a series of laws aimed at protecting winegrowers from fraud and assuring them a fair price for their grapes. The laws also stipulated that wine would have to be made "exclusively from the alcoholic fermentation of fresh grapes or fresh grape juice." Not with beet juice, not with apple juice or any other ingredient. Only grape juice. It was the first time wine had been defined legally.

Unfortunately, the new measures applied only to the Midi. They did nothing for Champagne. But the Champenois had learned an important lesson: To change the law, they were going to have to break it.

Reaching that point had been a slow and painful process. With the exception of that wonderful year in 1889, nearly every harvest between 1889 and 1907 had been deplorable. Yet sales of champagne had more than doubled. How can that be? What's going on? growers asked each other. Someone's making money, but we're not seeing any of it.

Then, in 1890, when it was discovered that a number of houses were colluding to fix grape prices, the misgivings of growers increased. Their frustration and sense of helplessness was only made worse when honest champagne houses would condemn fraud but then stand back and do nothing while the fraud continued.

But it was the arrival of phylloxera, a disease that had already ravaged every other wine region of France, that drove the deepest wedge between vignerons and champagne-makers and set growers on a collision course with the government.

Growers had long believed that Champagne's chalky soil and colder climate would keep their vineyards safe from the vine-eating louse. When they heard, on August 5, 1890, that the insect had been detected in a small parcel of vines, most were convinced it was a hoax, a plot by the big champagne houses to scare them off so they could buy up their vineyards for next to nothing.

Even as the disease spread, first slowly and then by leaps and bounds—from four acres in 1892 to thirteen in 1897 to 237 in 1899 and to 1,581 by 1900—a newspaper that had just been launched for vignerons, *La Révolution Champenoise*, cautioned growers not to lose sight of the real enemy. "Phylloxera isn't the only parasite in our vineyards," it said.

When the regional government of the Marne formed a Grand Syndicat composed of growers, champagne-makers, and experts from the Ministry of Agriculture to tackle phylloxera, most vignerons refused to cooperate. By then, their distrust and lack of confidence had become so great that they rejected offers of financial assistance to treat their vines from the government and various champagne houses. When vineyard inspectors showed up on their property, growers drove them away with clubs and sharpened vineyard stakes. Many believed that the inspectors were planting the bug in their vineyards.

But the problems in Champagne went far beyond the distrust between growers and producers. There were also deep divides between growers themselves.

That was illustrated by a drawing that appeared in a national magazine. The drawing showed a kindly mother figure with an arm around each of her two daughters. One daughter was blond, the other brunette, and they were both beautiful. The mother, who was depicted as a bottle of champagne, symbolized the province of Champagne. The blond daughter represented the Marne, while the brunette was the Aube. Each carried a basket overflowing with grapes. Their mother was saying to them, "Embrace each other, my little darlings, there is enough here for all of us."

But that is not how many vignerons felt.

Champagne consisted of two primary winegrowing areas, and each was very different from the other. The Marne was the more important one, with thirty-seven thousand acres of vines. It had the best soil, grew the best grapes, and made the best champagne. Growers there looked down at their cousins in the Aube, contemptuously calling them les fousseux, after the hoe vignerons used to grub out rocks from vineyards. What's more, they said, the Aube was not really part of Champagne at all. It was closer to Burgundy, and its vineyards geographically nearer to Dijon than to Reims or Épernay.

But growers in the Aube argued that their soil was more like Champagne's than Burgundy's. They also pointed out that their rivers flowed north, not south as they do in Burgundy. More important, their main city of Troyes was the ancient capital of Champagne. "How dare those people in the Marne say they are more Champenois than we are," groused one grower. "We have always been part of Champagne, and always will be."

And that was the crux of the problem. Where exactly was Champagne? No one had ever defined its borders. No one had ever determined with any precision which vineyard areas were entitled to call their wines champagne.

For vignerons in the Aube, who possessed less than five thousand acres of vines, it was a life-and-death matter. In previous years, they had sold most of their wine to cafés and brasseries in Paris. Now, with cheaper wine coming into the French capital on trains from the Midi, they could no longer compete. The only market left to them was the champagne industry in Reims and Épernay. If they lost that, they would be dead.

Sorting out who belonged to Champagne was left to the national government. Officials had hoped the whole matter would just go away, but after the riots in the Midi and rising tensions in Champagne, they realized they could no longer duck the issue. On December 17, 1908, officials announced that only the Marne, and a few vineyards from the neighboring département of the Aisne, had the right to call themselves Champagne.

The Aubois were stunned. "They've slit out throats," one said. "If we're not part of Champagne, what are we, part of the moon?"

Growers in the Marne were not happy, either. They were insulted that their fine wines had been ranked with what they called the "bean soup" of the Aisne, a region better known for growing beans than grapes.

Fraud, meanwhile, had reached epidemic proportions. The adulteration of champagne with beet juice, apple juice, and rhubarb by unscrupulous producers, along with the continuing influx of foreign wine, threatened to destroy the reputation that legitimate champagne houses had worked so hard to achieve. It was estimated that as many as twelve million bottles of "champagne" were being sold each year in excess of the region's production of grapes. So endemic was the problem that one prominent English merchant cautioned his clients to be wary. "No wine is riskier than champagne," he said, "because no one can be sure what is in it."

But it was the vignerons who were paying the price, and nevermore so than in 1910. That year, everything that could go wrong, did. Harvests between 1902 and 1909 had been merely awful, but 1910 was catastrophic. Vineyards were attacked by insects, mold, and mildew. There was frost until mid-May, then hailstorms and heavy rains that washed away entire hillsides. Growers and their families waded through knee-deep mud trying to rescue the few vines that remained.

As early as June, everyone knew there would be next to nothing to harvest, and they were right. The amount of grapes picked was 96 percent less than the previous year. One vigneron managed to make only a single bottle of wine, and that to keep as a souvenir. Another picked so few grapes that all she could do was make a tart.

Winter arrived, and no one had any money. People walked barefoot through the snow looking for work. Many abandoned their vineyards and left Champagne to become vineyard workers in Algeria. Some simply gave up and committed suicide. One grower's wife who had just given birth to twins cried in anguish, "How will we ever feed them? If only we could throw them against the wall as we do with unwanted kittens."

A Paris newspaper sent one of its reporters to investigate the situation. He was shocked by what he saw. "It is hard to believe that such grinding poverty could exist in Europe in the twentieth century," he wrote.

With many growers facing bankruptcy and more than three-quarters of them being forced to mortgage their property, Champagne was fast becoming a powder keg, one that finally exploded on that cold January afternoon when vignerons went on the rampage in Damery.

Once again, the government puzzled over what to do. "The prime minister is no help," grumbled one legislator. "He says white to one side and black to the other." Mostly, the government was panicked, fearing it could face another 1789 if the situation were not defused.

In the end, the government, paralyzed by indecision, essentially did nothing. On the tenth of February, it passed a law that merely reaffirmed the status quo, namely, that the Marne and Aisne were part of Champagne, and the Aube was not.

The Marne exploded with joy. The Aube simply exploded. As people in the Marne declared a holiday and danced in the streets, vignerons in the Aube trudged through the icy winter fog to gather in tiny village cafés and mull over what to do. The picture seemed hopeless—until a man named Gaston Cheq stepped forward.

Cheq was an unlikely leader. He wasn't a vigneron; he was a potter who had to find other work when he got sick from the glazes. When the dispute between the Aube and Marne erupted, Cheq found his second calling.

Though barely five feet tall, his outsized personality inspired the Aubois and gave them confidence. "Be strong and united, and there will be a gold mine ahead for you," he said.

"Little Cheq," as followers called him, sported a droopy mustache and looked for all the world as if he would be more at home on the stage of a music hall. He was, in fact, a poet and musician. For him, every occasion was good for a song. He once wrote a song about repairing water pipes.

In no time at all, Cheq became the soul of the movement. One of his first actions was forging growers into Bataillons de Fer (Iron Battalions), a reference to the Aubois's iron determination to be reintegrated into Champagne. It also referred to the hoe growers used to root out rocks from their vineyards. This was no ordinary hoe but rather an iron hook curved like a question mark ending in a sharp point. It was a heavy-duty instrument, strong enough to scrape out the most stubborn of stones. Hammered flat, this basic vineyard tool was transformed into a lethal lance.

Cheq's battalions, armed with their fousseux, marched through the Aube, rallying communities to their cause. Each wore a pink medallion on his chest that said,

> *Champenois nous fûmes,*
> *Champenois nous sommes,*
> *Champenois nous resterons,*
> *ET CE SERA COMME ÇA!*
>
> *(Champenois we were,*
> *Champenois we are,*
> *Champenois we will stay,*
> *AND THAT'S THAT!)*

Towns and villages responded to the call. In Landreville, the mayor locked the door of the village hall and posted a sign that said, "This door will not open again until it's in Champagne." Throughout the region, tax papers were burned and government officials were hung in effigy. Town councils resigned en masse— more than 125 had quit by March—bringing the entire administrative life of the Aube to a standstill. In Paris, parliamentary representatives from the Aube put a stranglehold on the national government by refusing to approve the budget. The prime minister and his cabinet resigned.

But it was a beautiful Palm Sunday in April when everything came to a climax. More than ten thousand people, including growers and their families, local government representatives, and others from the Aube, boarded special trains for a giant demonstration in Troyes.

Massive crowds had already gathered in the ancient city by the time the trains arrived. Cheq's Iron Battalions, conspicuous with their sharpened fousseux, had been the first to arrive.

The mood was euphoric. Carrying banners and red flags, and singing revolutionary songs—some of which had been written by their leader—the demonstrators converged on the headquarters of the regional government. Along the way, one group came upon a shop that someone said was selling champagne from the Marne. It was promptly sacked.

By the time marchers reached the heart of the city, their numbers had increased to twenty thousand. Everywhere one looked, there were signs proclaiming, "Death to the Marne" and "Champagne or Death." Also in view were hundreds of armed troops, watching from the sidelines in case of any trouble.

Troyes's mayor welcomed the huge throng. "Given today's magnificent display of solidarity," he said, "the government must understand that it has no alternative but to reintegrate our region into Champagne without any restrictions." He was wildly cheered.

But it was Gaston Cheq everyone was waiting for. Having arrived late, the diminutive leader was lifted from his open car and passed over the heads of delirious supporters to the speaker's platform, which had been draped with bunting and flags. Addressing the sea of humanity, Cheq issued a plea for *all* Champenois to come together. "People of the Aube, people of the Marne, we are all brothers, and our wines are brothers, too. Our real enemies are those who make fake champagne and believe that money is the most important thing."

Cheq understood the feelings of inferiority that gripped most vignerons, and he encouraged them to stand up for their dignity. "Your hoes are every bit as valuable as guns," he said.

His words were greeted by thunderous applause. Journalists covering the event said they "had never seen such an imposing spectacle."

By then, the size of the crowd had mushroomed to forty thousand. When some of the demonstrators scaled the iron gates in front of the Préfecture de Police to hang red flags, troops tried to break up the rally. They were greeted with catcalls and chants of "Vive le dix-septième," a reference to the division that had mutinied during demonstrations in the Midi four years earlier.

But that was it. There was no real trouble as crowds, convinced they had made their point, began drifting back to their trains.

And they *had* made their point. Two days later, the Senate met in Paris to debate, yet again, who really belonged to Champagne. Officials agreed that the law of 1908 had been a disaster that turned Frenchman against Frenchman.

The debate was one the most closely followed ever. Throughout Champagne, in both the Aube and the Marne, people crowded into cafés and stood outside telegraph offices waiting for the Senate's decision.

At 5:00 P.M. the keys of telegraphs began to hammer out the news. The Senate recommended that the law of 1908—the law that had excluded the Aube from Champagne—be annulled.

This time it was the Aube that exploded with joy, and the Marne that simply exploded.

By 9:00 P.M. the blare of bugles and the beating of drums reverberated again through the Marne. Rockets from hail guns lit the night sky, calling growers and their families to arms.

Vignerons and their families, many of whom had already gone to bed, burst from their homes brandishing hatchets, hoes, and sharpened vineyard stakes. It wasn't just the Senate's decision. It was everything: being cheated by greedy producers, being bullied by commissionaires, being defeated by bad weather and terrible harvests, and, most of all, being crushed by the unrelenting misery of their lives. "Our empty stomachs have armed us," one vigneron said.

Little was safe from their wrath. In Dizy, homes were pillaged, pianos were hacked to pieces, and cars were burned. The cellars of De Castellane Champagne were ransacked. In another village, a bomb injured three people. At midnight, the Marne's regional governor boarded a train to assess the violence. Within a short time, he was telegraphing Paris. "We are in a state of civil war," he declared.

As violence escalated through the night, thirty-five thousand troops began pouring into the Marne. One of them was François

Beaujan, an infantryman whose regiment had arrived by train in Épernay in the wee hours of the morning. He and the others were greeted by a reddish glow on the horizon, but it wasn't the sun. "When we were told that it was the town of Aÿ burning," Beaujan said, "we were absolutely flabbergasted."

Most of the men in his regiment were from Paris and Normandy and had no idea of what had been going on, that they were facing what one officer said was a "veritable revolution."

"All I could think was, 'My God, what are we going to do?' " said Beaujan.

By daylight, as smoke drifted up from charred buildings, the rioters had coalesced into one enormous mob numbering more than ten thousand. Their target was Épernay, the ancient market town that was one of the most important for bottling and shipping champagne. Shouting "Death to cheaters!" and "Down with the Aube!" they blocked trains, overturned trucks, and attacked champagne houses they claimed had engaged in "oenological skulduggery."

On the outskirts of the city, however, the marchers found their way blocked by troops who had been ordered to protect Épernay at all costs. They then turned toward Aÿ, a winegrowing village three miles to the northeast, where they attacked everything in sight, even champagne houses known and respected for their honesty.

"These aren't vignerons," one witness said. "They're savages."

A reporter for a London newspaper wrote, "Warehouses and cellars of champagne merchants had been absolutely gutted. At one corner four roofless smoke-grimed walls marked all that remained of the warehouse of MM. Bissinger. Everything inside had been wrecked, and fire had done the rest. . . . The smoking ruins were melancholy proof of the vignerons' madness."

In the road were iron hoops, splintered barrels, and hundreds of account books "scattered in indescribable confusion, all sodden with wine which filled the air with its fumes."

By midday, the pilots of two army monoplanes that had been sent to survey the scene described the situation as complete chaos. It was the first time aircraft had been used in a quasi-warlike situation.

In the streets below, mounted cavalry tried to beat back the rioters with their sabers. Women, who were often more militant than the men, threw themselves in front of the horses. Their husbands pulled down telegraph wires and strung them across the roads, tripping reinforcements who were trying to get into the town.

Growers had another weapon in their arsenal as well: their bugles. Most vignerons were army veterans. Each time the cavalry blew the call to charge, vignerons sounded retreat, confusing both riders and the horses.

For the soldiers, it was too much. They had been issued two bullets each but told not to shoot. If they drew their sabers, they were ordered to use only the flat side. "Exercise patience but be energetic," they were told. Frustrated about what to do, many soldiers simply did nothing.

Even officers were befuddled. Mounted troops were ill-suited for Aÿ's narrow streets. Often, they found themselves trapped, unable to maneuver, and being pelted with bottles and bricks. When they tried to give chase, their assailants would disappear into the rabbit warren of cellars that ran under the town.

Le Déjeuner d'Huîtres *by Jean-François de Troy, the first painting of sparkling champagne, which hangs at the Musée Condé in Chantilly.* (RÉUNION DES MUSÉES NATIONAUX/© HARRY BRÉJAT)

*The father of champagne,
Dom Pérignon.* (COLLECTION
MOËT & CHANDON/© XAVIER
LAVICTOIRE

*Abbey of Hautvillers, where
Dom Pérignon lived and
worked.* (COLLECTION MOËT &
CHANDON/© MICHAEL KENNA)

*Cellar workers wore masks
to protect themselves from
exploding bottles.* (COLLECTION
CHRISTIAN SCHOPPHOVEN)

Portrait of the Sun King, Louis XIV, by Hyacinth Rigaud, Paris, Musée du Louvre. (RÉUNION DES MUSÉES NATIONAUX/© HERVÉ LEWANDOWSKI)

Nicole-Barbe Clicquot, the famous Veuve Clicquot who, with her cellarmaster, developed the technique of remuage. (COURTESY OF VEUVE CLICQUOT-PONSARDIN)

Napoleon visits his old friend Jean-Rémy Moët. (COLLECTION MOËT & CHANDON)

Cover sheet for the song "Champagne Charlie." (COURTESY OF CHARLES HEIDSIECK CHAMPAGNE)

Champagne Charlie's exploits in America were covered avidly by newspapers.

(COURTESY OF CHARLES HEIDSIECK CHAMPAGNE)

A champagne tasting at Pommery & Greno, 1860. (COURTESY OF POMMERY & GRENO)

Louise Pommery, whose vision and courage turned Pommery & Greno into a major champagne house, circa 1885. (COURTESY OF POMMERY & GRENO)

At the funeral of Louise Pommery crowds filled the streets of Reims to pay their last respects, March 21, 1890. (COURTESY OF POMMERY & GRENO)

The world's largest wine barrel, which Eugene Mercier built for the 1889 Universal Exposition in Paris. Houses had to be demolished to allow the barrel to pass through the streets. (COLLECTION MOËT & CHANDON)

The ill-fated Mercier balloon as it lifted off from Paris at the 1900 Universal Exposition. (COLLECTION MOËT & CHANDON)

Vignerons rally in Troyes to protest low grape prices, 1911. (COURTESY OF MÉDIATHÈQUE, ÉPERNAY)

Vignerons in Bar-sûr-Aube burn their tax papers during the champagne riots of 1911. (COURTESY OF MÉDIATHÈQUE, ÉPERNAY)

French dragoons clash with rioting vignerons in Aÿ, 1911. (COURTESY OF MÉDIATHÈQUE, ÉPERNAY)

French troops march through the vineyards on their way to the front, 1914. (COLLECTION CHRISTIAN SCHOPPHOVEN)

La gloire de la culture germanique.
(*Providence Journal*, États-Unis.)

Germany was determined to destroy Reims Cathedral, where France's kings and queens were crowned. (COURTESY OF MÉDIATHÈQUE, ÉPERNAY)

The cathedral in flames after German bombardment in September 1914. (COURTESY OF MÉDIATHÈQUE, ÉPERNAY)

LA GRANDE GUERRE

The first harvest under the bombs, 1914, in which many grape pickers were killed. (COURTESY OF MÉDIATHÈQUE, ÉPERNAY)

LES VENDANGES DE 1914
NOS VIGNERONS CHAMPENOIS ONT VENDANGÉ SOUS UNE PLUIE DE FER

Above left: *French troops with gas masks in the trenches.* (COLLECTION CHRISTIAN SCHOPPHOVEN)

Above right: *It was called the "war of the trenches," jagged lines that extended more than five hundred miles from the Swiss border to the North Sea.* (COLLECTION CHRISTIAN SCHOPPHOVEN)

Left: *Soup being delivered to French troops through the ruined landscape, 1915.* (COLLECTION CHRISTIAN SCHOPPHOVEN)

Most champagne houses suffered heavy damage, among them Pommery & Greno which was the firm closest to the front lines, circa 1916.
(COURTESY OF POMMERY & GRENO)

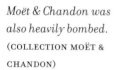

Moët & Chandon was also heavily bombed.
(COLLECTION MOËT & CHANDON)

Damage to Veuve Clicquot-Ponsardin.
(COURTESY OF VEUVE CLICQUOT-PONSARDIN)

To escape the bombs, thousands of people moved underground into the crayères, eating, sleeping and working there. (COURTESY OF POMMERY & GRENO)

There were also underground hospitals. Here, a mother has just given birth. (COURTESY OF MARY ROCHE WHITTINGTON)

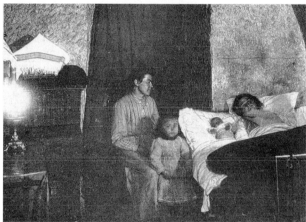

With most of the men in the army, the bulk of the cellar work for the champagne houses was done by women. (COURTESY OF POMMERY & GRENO)

Children went to school underground, 1916. (COURTESY OF POMMERY & GRENO)

A physical education class. (COURTESY OF POMMERY & GRENO)

Making wire muzzles to keep the corks in place. (COURTESY OF POMMERY & GRENO)

Shelling of Pommery & Greno was so heavy that parts of its crayères, one hundred feet underground, collapsed. (COURTESY OF POMMERY & GRENO)

French troops did their own share of pillaging, as the pile of empties at Pommery & Greno testifies. (COURTESY OF POMMERY & GRENO)

German soldiers surrendering to French colonial troops near Reims. (COLLECTION CHRISTIAN SCHOPPHOVEN)

Cartoonists had a field day. "Okay, buddy, you want to take Champagne? Fine, while waiting, here's a cork." (COLLECTION CHRISTIAN SCHOPPHOVEN)

— Alors vieux ! tu espérais prendre la Champagne !
Ben, en attendant, prends un bouchon !..

Germans were depicted as unsophisticated, drunken bumblers. "Their first taste of champagne," the caption says. (COLLECTION CHRISTIAN SCHOPPHOVEN)

Kultur Allemande, par HENRIOT.

Sa première mise en pratique en Champagne.

Rue Royale, Reims. Destruction was so great that Reims became known as "the martyred city," 1918. (COLLECTION CHRISTIAN SCHOPPHOVEN)

Reims's great cathedral was reduced to a burned-out shell. (COURTESY OF MÉDIATHÈQUE, ÉPERNAY)

Maurice Pol-Roger, Épernay's heroic mayor. (COURTESY OF POL ROGER & CIE)

At war's end, the Champenois were faced with a new enemy, phylloxera. Here, vignerons inject carbon disulfide into the soil in an attempt to save their vines, 1919. (COLLECTION CHRISTIAN SCHOPPHOVEN)

By 1931, champagne was so popular that it was being carried by porters to British troops in Africa. (COLLECTION MOËT & CHANDON)

"Just let the rioters be," one exasperated officer finally told his men. "They know what they want, they know what they need."

As hours passed, the violence became more and more senseless. Drunk on wine and slogans, the rioters made their way up the slopes overlooking Aÿ, where they set fire to straw that had been placed on vines to protect them from frost. It was an act that appalled many, reported one journalist. "Growers would as soon strike a baby as trample a young vine shoot underfoot," he said. When other vignerons realized what had happened, they began to cry. "It's too much, too much," they said. "We didn't believe it would go this far."

By the end of the day, thousands of vines had been burned and trampled. At least forty buildings, including six champagne houses in Aÿ along with their cellars and warehouses, lay in ruin. Nearly six million bottles of champagne had been destroyed. Rivers of wine flowed through the streets, and gutters choked. Vignerons said, "That was the day the Marne drank champagne."

It was over in less than twenty-four hours. Having rampaged all night and the following day under a hot sun, the riots died of exhaustion. Demonstrators had had little to eat and much to drink. By evening, most had returned home or collapsed in the streets.

Although no one had been killed, France was stunned by the viciousness of the riots. Two parts of Champagne had nearly gone to war with each other. Two governments—two prime ministers and their cabinets—had been forced to resign because of their inability to deal effectively with the situation.

Authorities moved swiftly to arrest those involved, but punishment did not always fit the crime. A fifteen-year-old girl was imprisoned for a month after offering a bottle of stolen champagne to a worker. Another person was given ten months in prison for stealing two champagne bottles, both empty.

The government had been able to identify these "criminals" by taking advantage of a new technology: local newsreels. Movie theater operators had hauled their cameras into the streets to film the riots, then ran the clips at night.

Because of the tense atmosphere, those accused of leading the riots were transferred to another part of France for trial. Acknowledging that many of the demonstrators' grievances were legitimate, some of the major champagne houses such as Moët & Chandon sent representatives to testify on their behalf.

Amazingly, no one was killed. The only casualties were two winegrowers who committed suicide, ashamed they had been arrested.

Champagne, meanwhile, was placed under military occupation, but with so many troops in the region—there were more soldiers than vignerons—it was a curious kind of occupation. Many were billeted in the homes of vignerons while others, like Private Beaujan, were quartered on the premises of champagne houses.

Beaujan and his unit were lodged at Ayala, whose elderly cellarmaster was understandably uneasy. After thanking the soldiers for their protection, he asked them in the gentlest way possible not to touch his champagne. "My children," he said, "my champagne has just been bottled and I must ask you to respect it. But in return, and for every day that you are here, each one of you will receive, morning and evening, a canteen of white wine that has not yet been made into champagne.

It is excellent wine but you will be able to judge that for yourselves."

Private Beaujan later confirmed that it was indeed excellent wine and that no one touched the cellarmaster's champagne.

That fall, most of the troops were withdrawn to make room for grape pickers arriving for the harvest. Many a young girl reportedly shed a tear as the troops departed.

But a few soldiers stayed behind. They married local girls, settled down in Champagne, and became vignerons themselves.

That fall witnessed a bountiful harvest. There were plenty of grapes, the quality was outstanding, and grape prices rose.

In Paris the government took advantage of the calm to patch together a bill that divided Champagne into two levels: Champagne and Champagne-Deuxième Zone, or second zone. The Marne was given the Champagne designation, enabling it to retain its first-class status. The Aube, though relegated to second-zone status, could at least now consider itself part of Champagne.

No one was completely satisfied. The Marne, which still regarded the Aube as a stepchild, resented having it admitted to the "club." The Aube, in turn, chafed over the fact that "second zone" in reality meant "second-class," and hence inferior wine.

More important, everyone realized that this was only a temporary compromise, that all of the issues dividing Champagne and which had nearly plunged the region into civil war were still unresolved. Most suspected the government was just buying time while it tried to figure out what to do next. And they were right. Much to everyone's dismay, lawmakers announced that further discussions would not be held until the summer of 1913. At the same time, there were good reasons for moving cautiously. Officials were acutely aware that whatever they ultimately came up with in terms of an appellation for Champagne, it would have ramifications for every other wine region in France.

What they didn't fully appreciate was that all the old antagonisms in Champagne were still smoldering and could easily burst into flames again.

More conscious of how precarious the situation was were the major champagne houses. They acted quickly to form a committee that would make sure growers received a fair price for their grapes. They also took a stand against fraud and took steps to eliminate the abuses of the commissionaire system.

It was not enough for growers in the Aube. As the weeks and months passed, they grew more and more restless. "We're being treated like bastards," said one vigneron, summing up the feelings of most.

By 1913 angry protests were flaring up nearly everywhere in the Aube. "We'll keep marching until we win," growers vowed. "Champagne or revolution!" went the cry. In one village, when a policeman tried to take down a sign protesters had erected, "they rolled him into the gutter," reported the local newspaper the next day.

Tax strikes were launched as well. "Taxes?" one vigneron sneered. "If they want us to pay taxes, we'll pay deuxième zone taxes."

More upsetting to the government in Paris, which had watched the protests with growing apprehension, were the German flags that many demonstrators were now carrying. There were also signs reading, "Vive l'Allemagne, Vive la Prusse" (Long live Germany, Long live Prussia).

With rumblings to the east of France and declarations by Kaiser Wilhelm II that Germany should be a world power, such sentiments sent a shudder through government circles. Author-ities now realized that it was imperative that they come through with the bill they had promised two years earlier.

By the summer of 1914, lawmakers finally introduced a mea-sure they hoped would be acceptable to all parties. But before both houses of the French National Assembly could vote on it, their work was interrupted by news that a Serbian nationalist in Sarajevo had just shot dead Archduke Franz Ferdinand and his wife.

World War I had begun.

CHAPTER 6

Up the Bloody Slopes

Pommery & Greno's cellarmaster was breathing hard. It was a steep climb up the circular staircase to the roof of the champagne house, but the view was worth it. Immediately to the north lay two of Pommery's prime vineyards, Clos du Moulin de la Housse and Clos de la Pompadour. To the east was the park Louise Pommery had planted with rare trees and shrubs forty years earlier. Far to the south, on a clear day, one could just make out the vine-covered slopes of the Montagne de Reims. A mile or so to the west was the heart of Reims, dominated by its magnificent cathedral.

The view, however, was not what had drawn Henri Outin to the roof of Pommery. It was a low, rumbling sound from the north, like the distant thunder of an approaching storm. Somewhere beyond the horizon were seven German armies, 1.5 million men, the largest military force ever assembled.

Three weeks had passed since France and Germany had declared war on each other. Now, as Outin scanned the horizon, he knew it wouldn't be long before the enemy was in sight.

Few in Champagne, however, seemed alarmed. When war was declared on August 3, people responded with enthusiasm. Train stations were packed with young men who had just been called up and were eager to go to war. Families and other loved ones cheered them on, waving flags and singing patriotic songs. Despite what had happened in 1870, nearly everyone believed that the élan and bravery of the French soldier would be enough to overcome the firepower of the Germans. "The boys will be home by Christmas," went the popular refrain. Perhaps even before the leaves fell, some said.

That was certainly the hope of champagne-makers, given that the harvest was only a few weeks away. It had been one of the most brilliant summers in memory with a "grilling sunshine" which vignerons said would assure a full ripening of the grapes.

By mid-August, however, the buoyant mood of the country had begun to change. French troops were floundering under the relentless onslaught of German artillery. By the end of the month, France's offensive had collapsed. More than one hundred sixty thousand French soldiers had been killed in a series of bloody engagements, their units ripped to shreds by the Germans' superior firepower.

From the moment the kaiser's armies had begun moving, nothing had been able to halt their advance. Luxembourg fell, and then Belgium. As the Germans swung south, sweeping across the Franco-Belgian border into Champagne, news of German atrocities began filtering in, casting a shadow across the country. In the Belgian town of Dinant, six hundred men, women, and children had been herded into the city's main square and shot. In Louvain, a small university town known as the Oxford of Belgium, German troops set fire to more than one thousand buildings, including its famed library, destroying priceless manuscripts and medieval paintings, along with two hundred thirty thousand books.

On Sunday, August 30, Henri Outin once again made his way to the top of Pommery. The "storm," he noted in his diary, was nearly upon them.

> For the first time, we can hear the cannons thunder all day long. The railway station is overrun. The best families of Reims camped all last night in front of the station. There are dogs, kids, and suitcases scattered all over the courtyard. Everyone is trying to leave.[1]

That same day, Outin was summoned in by the head of Pommery to assist in an unusual task.

> This afternoon, we buried fifty thousand gold francs in a vineyard next to the Moulin de la Housse. This treasure is meant to pay our workers and help families of those workers who have been called up to the army. Every Friday night from now on, we'll go out and dig up enough to take care of everyone's needs.

Fragments of Outin's diary were discovered many years later in the archives of Pommery. They provide a rare and poignant glimpse of one of the most defining moments in Champagne's history.

> Wednesday, September 2: A day of anguish! There is gunfire toward the east. All day, the French have been

blowing up bridges. We are cut off. No more newspapers,
no more mail, no telephone, no telegraph. Reims is a prey
abandoned to the enemy.

Thousands of French troops had been sent to Champagne to blunt the German offensive, with many being billeted in the enormous cellars of champagne houses. Now they were pulling out suddenly, taking up new defensive positions south of the city. To Outin's chagrin, the troops were not only leaving Reims wide open to the Germans, but the one thousand five hundred who had been camped in his cellars had made off with hundreds of bottles of his champagne.

Early the following morning, the mayor of Reims posted a public notice, pleading with citizens to remain calm. "With the German army on our doorstep, ready to march into our city, I beg you to avoid any provocation," he said. "It's not your responsibility to try to change events; it is your responsibility not to aggravate them. We beg of you silence, dignity, and prudence."

Just before noon, German forces marched into Reims. With them was a soldier they had taken prisoner in order to show them the way to city hall. The soldier, however, was unfamiliar with Reims. When the Germans mistakenly ended up at the tramway office, they were mocked by crowds. The troops then grabbed a civilian and forced him to guide them. This time, they ended up at the theater. The taunts of the crowds grew louder, and the embarrassed Germans became furious.

Eventually, they reached their destination and declared that Reims was now under occupation. It was a sobering moment, recalled Henri Outin, and yet, "We couldn't help laughing at their misadventure. One laughs even in sadness."

But the laughter didn't last long. It was interrupted by what Outin described as "an impressive musical gong." The "gong," it turned out, was the sound of breaking windows. German artillery had opened fire on the city. The Germans, upset at having been ridiculed, were letting the Remois know who was in charge.

The rain of shells sent citizens scrambling for shelter, many heading toward Pommery.

I see them coming with looks of utter dismay; And so many children! As they approach, three shells fall on our buildings. Soon, thousands of people are huddled in the darkness of our cellars. The candles give little light. A wounded woman arrives, a poignant sight. Many are praying aloud. They are convinced this is their last hour.

The shelling ceased after half an hour. Cautiously, Outin and others emerged to survey the damage. Several people had been killed and a number of buildings in the vicinity of the cathedral had been destroyed. The cathedral escaped unharmed, and for good reason. "It's because our gunners were given a formal order to respect it," the German commandant said.

Their goal was to restore calm and a sense of normalcy as quickly as possible. Stores and factories were ordered to reopen. Citizens, especially champagne producers, were told to go about their regular business. At the same time, soldiers were explicitly ordered not to do anything that might disrupt the business of champagne.

For the most part, the orders were obeyed. Although there were a few incidents—the most serious being soldiers who burned down the house of a young woman who spurned their attentions—troops generally behaved. They even paid for their champagne and apologized if they had to pay with German gold. More important, they stayed away from the vineyards, realizing that champagne was a precious resource. "The Germans were so sure of their victory," said one vigneron, "that they were already considering our vineyards as their own fiefdom."

Within a couple of days, most people, according to Henri Outin, "had grown used to the spiked helmets."

Our conquerors are not at all arrogant. One can sometimes see them surrounded by children who play with their weapons. The soldiers give them sweets, maybe plundered in Belgium? For the most part, the officers are approachable and often friendly with the population.

But in neighboring Épernay, which was occupied a day after Reims, the atmosphere was tense. Residents were fleeing as refugees poured in, driven from their homes by battles that were still raging. Adding to the chaos was the fact that nearly every civil servant—including the regional governor and the police and fire chiefs—had fled, taking with them all of the municipality's funds. The only official left was Maurice Pol-Roger, who not only headed a major champagne house, Pol Roger et Cie, but also served as the city's mayor.

Before the Germans arrived, he had vowed to remain on the job. "I will stay no matter what happens, to reassure and to comfort those who wish to leave but cannot. And I will do all that is humanly possible to defend them." [2]

His vow was soon put to the test. The Germans notified him that he was expected to keep order in the city and that he would be held personally responsible, on the pain of death, for any trouble that occurred. When a soldier was shot, the Germans renewed their threat, warning Maurice that he would be executed unless he promptly produced the person responsible. The mayor launched an appeal for information. It turned out that the "assailant" was the soldier himself, that he had accidentally shot himself in the foot.

The Germans, however, did not ease their pressure on the mayor. Three more times, they threatened to stand Maurice in front of a firing squad, once after accusing him of trying to disrupt their operations by cutting the city's gas supplies and electricity, and again when a delivery of salted meat the Germans had requisitioned failed to turn up. Another time, they held him hostage and threatened to burn the city to the ground unless he paid a huge fine.

Because other officials had absconded with all the money from the city's treasury, Pol-Roger paid the fine out of his own pocket, and with help from a few friends. With Épernay devoid of funds, he also had notes printed up to pay its workers and the city's bills. Maurice backed the temporary currency with his own money. It was the only way citizens could survive without the public monies, he said, and anyone who refused to honor the notes would be arrested. The people and shops of Épernay accepted the mayor's notes without question.[3]

The occupation of Champagne's two major cities was a moment for the Germans to pause, to catch their breath and replenish supplies before moving toward the big prize: Paris. "If we had soldiers like yours, we would already be there," an officer confided to Henri Outin. "Your soldiers are better than ours, but they are so badly armed."

The French, however, had managed to regroup, Outin noted, and were now proving more resilient than they had been when the war first began.

Maybe the tide is turning. The constant barrage, which has been our anguish, is now our hope.

Such hopes, however, depended largely on an old soldier who had been called out of retirement. With the French government having withdrawn to Bordeaux, just as it did in 1870 when Bismarck's armies threatened to destroy Paris, General Joseph Gallieni was ordered to defend the city "stone by stone."

Fearing that the kaiser's forces could be soon laying siege to the French capital, Gallieni moved like a whirlwind, shouting orders for a defensive cordon to be built around the city. With two-thirds of the population having fled, the general conscripted all remaining able-bodied men to do the work. He then ordered demolition charges to be laid under every bridge across the Seine.

In a move that alarmed many Parisiens, however, Gallieni also drew up plans for the destruction of the Eiffel Tower. Built twenty-five years earlier as a symbol of soaring optimism in celebration of the centennial of the French Revolution, the tower now housed an elaborate military communications system that Gallieni said could not be allowed to fall into enemy hands.

The Germans, however, had just crossed the Marne River and were only twenty-five miles from Paris. To push them back, the French army desperately needed reinforcements, so Gallieni did one more thing: he called a taxi. More precisely, he called more than a thousand of them. With trains already in full use by the military, the taxis were the only means of ferrying Paris's six thousand garrison troops to the front.

The "taxis of the Marne," as they became known, began assembling in front of the Invalides around midnight on September 6. They departed the following day, each taxi carrying four to five soldiers. "We traveled in style," said one soldier, "until we reached the front; then everything really went downhill."[4]

From the roof of Pommery, Henri Outin and several vignerons watched the Battle of the Marne unfold.

> September 12: *We had an unforgettable grand show; a big battle in open country, and we had a ringside seat! Flames belch forth. The artillery duel has started. German infantrymen withdraw, stopping at times to lie down and fire back. The French clearly have the upper hand. Our emotions are running high. We are so excited that we forget to have lunch.*

At four o'clock that afternoon, a German commander in Pommery's observation tower screamed orders to troops quartered in the cellars to evacuate immediately. It happened so suddenly and in such a harsh manner that Outin and the others were frightened. But as troops left the premises and long lines of soldiers filed out of the city, the cellarmaster realized the occupation was over.

> *We may have forgotten lunch, but we do not forget to celebrate this historic moment. One of us runs to the cellar and brings up a magnum of Pommery 1906.*

By next morning, just a little more than a week after Reims and Épernay had been occupied, the two cities were liberated. Celebrations quickly broke out.

Main streets are teeming with people. Many shed tears of joy and emotion. Early-rising civilians have come back from the previous day's battlefields carrying weapons, spiked helmets, and other souvenirs which they sell for a good price.

As French troops moved in, people threw candy, bread, and fruit at them, even money. They also handed out glasses of champagne. Other glasses of champagne, only half-drunk, were left behind on the table at city hall, which had been used as head-quarters by the German command, testifying to the haste with which the enemy had departed.

It was a miracle, people said, "the miracle of the Marne." A cartoon depicting the Germans' retreat appeared in the local newspaper. It showed a bottle of champagne mounted like a cannon, its cork exploding into the backsides of fleeing German soldiers.

The symbolism was right on target. A French soldier recalled that it hadn't really dawned on him that they had won "until we saw piles of abandoned guns and unused ammunition on the field of battle. But what struck us most of all were the incredible number of empty champagne bottles that covered the battle-field, bottles that had been pillaged from local cellars." Scores of abandoned German trucks also littered the landscape, their tires shredded by the broken glass of discarded bottles.

Then, as troops advanced, they came across something even

more startling: vast numbers of German bodies lying in ditches and along the road. They were not dead, however, just dead drunk. Thousands were taken prisoner. "We harvested them like grapes," an officer said. "Champagne can claim a legitimate role in our victory. It was our dearest ally." [5]

The euphoria, however, was short-lived. France's victory was not the smashing blow many perceived it to be. "We all said, 'The Boche have gone, the war is finished,' " remarked one Remois, "but the Boche had not gone. They had only left town to dig themselves into the hills outside the city. The war was not over. It had just begun."

But what a deadly beginning. Two hundred thousand French soldiers had just lost their lives. The month before, one hundred sixty thousand had been killed. Their British allies had casualties of more than eighty thousand, over half the troops they had sent. Germany, in turn, had lost nearly a quarter of a million men.

In a sense, World War I was the continuation of a war that had started forty-four years earlier. France still smarted over its loss of Alsace-Lorraine in 1870. "The piece of territory that was torn from France forty-four years ago is a scar that is not yet healed," said a newspaper. France also was haunted by Germany's growing military and industrial strength.

Germany, in turn, felt trapped by an encircling string of alliances France had created with Russia, Great Britain, Serbia, and Italy. It was also jealous of France's prestige and ability to rebuild itself after the Franco-Prussian War. German leaders were convinced that Paris still harbored Napoleonic ambitions of creating a United States of Europe dominated by France.

Germany's invasion of France also may have been motivated by another factor. Many Champenois were convinced that their neighbors across the Rhine coveted their vineyards, a belief that seemed to be borne out by the constant stream of German merchants into Champagne who bought juice from the second and third pressings of grapes to turn into sekt, their own sparkling wine.[6]

That conviction, and the deep-seated fear of German ambitions, was clear as early as the seventeenth century when the fabulist Jean de la Fontaine, who was born in Champagne, wrote, "I would rather see the Turks campaigning here than see the wines of our region be profaned by the Germans."

Another Champenois put it even more bluntly when World War I began. "Possessing our beautiful vineyards would crown all their achievements," said the writer Charles Moreau-Berillon. "Throughout the centuries, through big invasions and smaller incursions, it has always been our wine that attracted the Germanic hordes. They know, perhaps even better than we do, what riches are at stake and what a civilizing force champagne represents. Our celebrated wine goes to every point of the planet with the joy, gaiety, and elegance for which we French are known. The Germans wish to change all that, to crush our vision of happiness in a Teutonic fist."[7]

On September 14, only a day after the people of Reims had celebrated their liberation, that fist closed with brutal force. German artillery, perched on a crest only four miles away, opened fire, sending residents and those working in the vineyards running for cover.

In a Reims suburb, one champagne producer recalled how "the rain of bombs" forced hundreds to spend the night in his cellars.

Three days later, as shelling intensified, a messenger arrived at the champagne house of Veuve Binet asking for help. A nearby clinic had been hit and more than thirty wounded soldiers needed to be evacuated. The head of the firm, Charles Walfard, rushed to the site to find panic-stricken nuns directing him to the cellar, where another bomb had just exploded. "I stepped into what I thought was a pool of blood," he said, "only to realize that it was wine from a barrel that had been smashed. Then I stumbled over an obstacle. A man accompanying me lit a match, and we saw that it was the corpse of a nun who had been hit by shrapnel. A little further on, we found the body of another nun, and later under the rubble, a third." [8]

But a far greater tragedy was about to unfold. Twenty-four hours later, the cathedral of Reims came under fire. The first shell landed about 8:30 A.M., killing a beggar who had been sitting on the cathedral steps. The second decapitated the *Ange au sourire* (Smiling Angel of Reims), the most famous of all the statues decorating the cathedral's façade.

As shells continued to fall, priests and others inside raced to rescue religious treasures. The Germans claimed the French were using one of the cathedral's towers as an observation post, a charge that was vociferously denied. The archbishop of Reims penned an urgent letter to the pope, pleading with him to denounce the bombing. The pope was noncommittal.

In an effort to stop the shelling, priests cobbled together a Red Cross flag out of the cathedral's vestments, and one of them, Father Robert Thinot, climbed to the top and hung it from one of the towers. It did no good; the Germans continued their bombardment.

Part of the cathedral had been converted into an infirmary for wounded soldiers, both French and German. "It was a horrible scene," said Father Louis Andrieux, one of the priests who had been caring for them. "The wounded began to cry out. Those who could walk fought for shelter near the pillars. Those who could not dragged themselves along on their hands, or begged to be carried, for shells were falling thick and fast."

Fathers Andrieux and Thinot had been part of the cathedral staff for many years. Their deep attachment to the cathedral was reflected in diaries they kept as the Germans laid waste to one of France's greatest monuments.

"As blocks of stone began falling from the pinnacles," said Andrieux, "the screams of the wounded increased, but these sounds were drowned out by the explosions which echoed in the immense building. Smoke and dust covered everything."

The cathedral was an important symbol. It was where France's kings and queens had been crowned, where "emperors had been created," as one historian wrote later. Destroying it, the Germans knew, would deal a devastating blow to French morale.

At five the next morning, as Mass was being said, the Germans opened up again, this time with even greater ferocity. "The great homogenous mass of stones shuddered and trembled with rage," Father Thinot remembered. "As each shell hit, the cathedral seemed to groan under the blows."

Incendiary shells began falling in midafternoon, igniting straw that had been spread on the floor as bedding for the soldiers. Scaffolding from restoration work caught fire as well. "Soon, the bells, loosened from their posts, fell with a terrible noise," Father Andrieux said. "We just had time to jump aside as the great Rose Window, freed from the melted lead of its frame, parted and fell with a crash."

As flames swept toward the roof, Andrieux and others rushed to gather up the remaining sacred objects, ripping open cupboards and flinging artifacts that had been used for the consecration of kings onto stretchers normally used for burials.

By then the heat had become so tremendous that the three and a half tons of lead that made up the cathedral's roof began to melt, turning every statue and gargoyle into macabre stalactites. "Suddenly, the tremendous construction burst asunder," Andrieux said, "emitting heat of terrible intensity and discharging into the nave a torrent of molten lead and a cascade of crackling beams."

The Germans begged to be let out, but guards refused to open the doors, fearful that angry crowds which had gathered outside would turn on them. Only after frantic pleas from Fathers Andrieux and Thinot did the guards finally relent. But then, the wind picked up, fanning the flames and sending showers of sparks along with burning debris onto neighboring buildings, setting them aflame.

The cathedral itself burned through the night, the flames creating an eerie glow that could be seen for miles.

By morning, hardly anything was left. The area around the cathedral was a charred ruin. Four hundred homes and other buildings had burned to the ground. As for the cathedral, it was no more than a smoldering skeleton, its roof, elegant statuary, and beautiful stained-glass windows gone. All that remained were the walls and the two towers—along with flocks of birds who had made their homes there.

That is what Father Thinot could not forget: the birds. "So many crows and pigeons thrown into the air by the explosion of shells, making noise throughout the night and all through the day following the fire. Now they circle endlessly around the carcass of the church, not understanding what has happened."

Nobody did.

The shelling of the cathedral provoked worldwide outrage, but the Germans had barely begun. For the next three and a half years, Reims would endure 1,051 consecutive days of unrelenting bombardment. Ninety-eight percent of the city would be destroyed; only forty houses out of forty thousand would be left standing. Reims would no longer be Reims.

For people the world over, Reims would become known as "the martyred city." [9]

In the midst of the carnage that September, there was still one thing that gave hope. The bright, sunny weather was holding and grapes were ripening to perfection.

Much was riding on the harvest of 1914. Since the turn of the century, there had really been only one good harvest, and that had been three years earlier. Champagne stocks were depleted and many cellars were now empty. While demand for champagne remained high, there was no way to meet it because there was almost nothing to sell. Everyone prayed that the coming harvest would be the one that would save them.

But everyone knew as well that it would not be easy. Most of the young men were in the army, leaving only women, children, and old men to bring in the grapes. Horses had been requisitioned, so getting grapes to the presses would be especially difficult. In addition, casks were in short supply and no one, particularly vignerons, had any money. Communications were a nightmare, too. Phones and telegraphs had been reserved for the military, so there was no way for vignerons and producers to contact each other.

No one appreciated the problems more than Maurice Pol-Roger. He was thirty when his father died, forcing him and his younger brother, Georges, to take over the responsibilities of running the famous champagne house. Less than two months later, on February 23, 1900, their cellars suddenly caved in. One and a half million bottles of champagne were destroyed, along with five hundred casks of wine which was to be turned into champagne. It was a tremendous loss that threatened to put the firm out of business. A newspaper in New York reported, "There will be a million and a half less headaches in the world because of an accident in Épernay." The paper went on to describe how the "immense cave-in" caused buildings elsewhere to collapse and nearby roads to crack apart. The disaster was attributed to the instability of the area's chalky soil.

Other champagne houses pitched in to help, offering the Pol-Rogers storage space, use of their pressing facilities, and even money to help keep their business going. Even with that assistance, however, the Pol-Rogers had barely recovered when World War I broke out. Georges was called up to the army, leaving Maurice to manage the firm alone.

The main problem was getting grapes from the vineyards to

the champagne houses. Normally, this was done by the vignerons, but because of the war, that was now impossible. Maurice decided that if the grapes couldn't go to the winemakers, winemakers would go to the grapes.

Under his direction barrels, presses, and other winemaking equipment were hauled from one vineyard to another. The new wine would be kept by the vignerons through the first fermentation. Whenever there was a lull in the bombing, it would be quickly moved to the cellars of champagne producers, where the rest of the work would take place.

The logistics proved as demanding as any military campaign. To facilitate the process, Pol-Roger organized a network of runners and cyclists, who went from one village to another, alerting vignerons as to when the barrels and equipment would be arriving. The runners also inquired if there was anyone who needed extra help. If anyone was short of money—and most were—Maurice dug into his own pocket.

Although vignerons and producers around Épernay were out of range of most of the German artillery, they had to endure a new kind of warfare. German airplanes could come out of the sky at any time—and did with frightening irregularity—swooping in and dropping their bombs on workers below.

There was another worry as well. Many feared it was just a matter of time before the Germans came back and regained control of the area. That was why Maurice decided to start picking on September 21, more than two weeks earlier than usual. Some thought he had made a terrible mistake, saying the grapes were still too green and acidic for making decent champagne. Maurice was convinced otherwise. "The 1914 will be the wine to drink with victory," he predicted.[10]

The picture on the northern side of the Montagne de Reims was dramatically different. There, with most vineyards in easy range of Germany's big guns, picking began under the bombs. "The women are panic-stricken by the whistling and bursting of shells," reported one vigneron. "They say they will not carry on with the work unless we stay with them in the vineyard."

It was the same at every other vineyard on the front line. The closest of all were those of Pommery, which were just a few hundred yards from the guns. Harvesting there had begun on October 8, but it was frequently interrupted by shelling.

Pommery had already come under fire a few days earlier, when several shells hit its offices. Cellarmaster Henri Outen summoned a priest to help him document the damage. The clergyman was Father Robert Thinot, who had written so movingly about the destruction of Reims's cathedral and the distress of the birds who had lived there.

Father Thinot was with Outin in the cellar when the walls and floor were rocked by a sharp explosion. Racing outside, the two men discovered that nineteen French soldiers had just been killed by a shell as they were digging a trench through the vineyard. More than twenty others were badly wounded. "Be ready to take cover," the French commander warned. "It's not over."

Most of the soldiers were in shock. They were reservists who had just been called up and mistakenly sent to the front. When Father Thinot tried to comfort them and explain that "the dead must now be taken care of," they stared at the ground, unable to move. Finally, he got them to begin digging a mass grave among the vines.

Digging was slow. When other shells landed near them, everyone threw themselves on the ground. It took most of the afternoon to finish preparing the grave. Paralyzed by grief, however, the soldiers could not bring themselves to bury the mutilated bodies of their comrades. "You're in charge, Father," said the commander. "It's up to you."

Thinot, with help from Outin, recovered a handcart from a nearby shed and began hauling the victims to the gravesite. It took them a couple of hours to complete the grisly task.

As the soldiers gathered to pay their last respects, Father Thinot began to speak. "Sadness strangles our hearts," he said, "but their souls are now in heaven." Thinot then dropped to his knees and blessed each of the victims. He then took branches from the surrounding vines and handed them out to the soldiers. "You may now make your farewells," the priest said.

One by one, the men approached the grave. With tears in their eyes, each soldier knelt and placed his branch in the grave.

The last words belonged to the commanding officer. "We have suffered so many losses, such grievous losses, and now what we must hope for, what we must pray for, is the end."

Thinot then pounded a wooden cross into the earth with the names of the victims scratched onto it.

It was one of the last services he performed in Reims. A few weeks later, Father Thinot enlisted in the army as a chaplain. He was ministering to the dying on the field of battle when he was killed on March 16 the following year.

The harvest of 1914 was a deadly one. Many women and at least twenty children lost their lives. A number of soldiers who were helping also were killed.

Yet even as shells rained down and they saw their friends die, the picking went ahead. There had been so many horrible harvests, and so much hope invested in this one, that people were willing to risk their lives to bring in the grapes. Every day for more than a month, women, children, and old men who had come out of retirement—even wine merchants from Paris—trudged up and down the bloody slopes.

In early August, it had been predicted that the harvest would yield four hundred thousand hectoliters of high-quality wine. Less than half of that was achieved.

By then everyone knew that another prediction was wrong, too. The boys would not be home for Christmas. The war, which had begun with such lightning speed, had bogged down. Millions of men were now digging themselves into an earthen line nearly five hundred miles long. That line, running from the Swiss border to the North Sea, would change the definition of war. It had always been thought of in terms of winners and losers, with a beginning and end.

But this war was different. It had become a murderous stalemate in which just holding on became a victory. No one advanced, no one retreated. They called it the "war of the trenches."

Those trenches cut through Champagne like a jagged knife, zigzagging across the region and slicing through vineyards. As winter fell and the year drew to a close, the chalky soil of Champagne turned those trenches into a hell of gray, clinging mud.

One French officer described it as the personal enemy of every soldier. "It throws its poisonous slobber out at him, closes around him, buries him. For men die of mud, as they die of bullets, but more horribly. Mud is where men sink and—what is worse—where their souls sink." [11]

Those first five months of the war saw more than half a million casualties, making 1914 the bloodiest year of the Great War. By December, however, the two armies, crouched in confrontation across a bleak and narrow strip of no-man's-land, were exhausted. Numbed by the senseless slaughter and staggering loss of human life, few seemed to know why they were fighting anymore. Reasons for the war had disappeared, just like much of the landscape, now shrouded in a blanket of perpetual winter fog.

On the night of December 24, Allied soldiers were surprised when they saw lights glowing from the trenches they faced. And then they heard music: Christmas carols being sung in German.

The soldiers didn't know what to make of it. But when the German singing ended, the Allies, timidly at first, sang back in their own language. As their voices gained in strength, an apparition appeared out of the fog and moved slowly toward them. It was a German soldier. He was brandishing not a rifle but a small decorated Christmas tree.

Within moments, the soldiers dropped their guns and poured out of their trenches to meet him. German troops did the same. Soon, on that barren stretch of ground where so much blood had been spilled, everyone was shaking hands, embracing each other, exchanging candy and cigarettes—and toasting each other with champagne.

By Christmas morning, they were laughing and playing soccer. "It was a perfect day," one soldier recalled. It was hailed as "the little miracle of Christmas." [12]

But not at the headquarters of the two sides. Before long, the generals had ordered their men back to the trenches.

The following day, the killing began again.

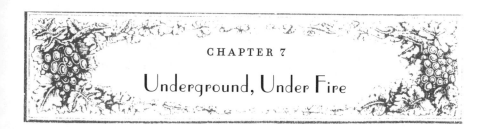

CHAPTER 7

Underground, Under Fire

As the orchestra finished tuning, the audience hurried to take its seats. Moments later, the much-loved sounds of Bizet's "Carmen" filled the air. What made this performance of the opera extraordinary was that it was being done one hundred feet underground, in the cellars of one of Reims's major champagne houses.[1]

Continuing bombardment by the Germans had forced most of the city's population to seek refuge in the vast limestone caves, or crayères, that housed the reserves of the champagne industry. Six hundred residents of Reims had been killed during the first five months of the war, and four thousand homes were destroyed. The cathedral, the city's most enduring monument and symbol of its glorious past, now stood burnt and blackened, a grim testament to all that had befallen Reims.

But it was just the beginning. On February 22, 1915, German guns opened up again, this time with even greater ferocity, pouring what one witness called "an avalanche of iron and fire" on the city. More than one thousand five hundred shells rained down that day, prompting a wholesale exodus, downward, into the crayères.

Once a hiding place for early Christians fleeing Roman persecution, these caves became home for more than twenty thousand people, a place of protection for human as well as bottled life.

Originally, the crayères were little more than giant chalk pits, underground quarries that had been excavated by Roman slaves who hauled out huge blocks of stone for building roads and constructing Durocortorum, the Roman name for Reims.

By the Middle Ages, monks had discovered that the cool and constant temperature of these caves made them ideal storing places for wine. As the business of champagne-making expanded, so did the crayères until they had become a warren of multilevel tunnels and galleries that snaked their way under Champagne for nearly three hundred miles.

Now, because of the shelling, it was as if Reims had been flipped upside down; everything on the surface was suddenly underneath: schools, churches, clinics, and cafés. City Hall was moved underground, as were the police and fire departments. Tailors, dressmakers, watchmakers, and cobblers set up shop there, too, alongside butchers, bakers, and even candlestick-makers.[2]

It was a shadowy, almost surreal, world in which everything from cooking, washing, and going to work was done in the glimmer of candles and oil lamps. "There was a constant search for light," said one woman who brought her pets with her, "and yet the birds sang without ever seeing the sun."

That wasn't the only music, however. There were also concerts, cabarets, cinemas, and live theater productions. Singers, actors, and actresses clamored for the distinction of performing for underground audiences. In the cellars of Veuve Clicquot, an extravagant dinner complete with cases of champagne was staged for several hundred mutilés, soldiers who had been badly wounded. One of them described it this way: "Those who still had legs danced, and even those without noses warmed themselves to life again, laughed and were happy." [3]

Life in the crayères was so unusual that journalists, politicians, and foreign VIPs badgered French military authorities for permission to visit. The president of France made several appearances, as did the king of Italy, the queen of Portugal, and the United States ambassador. Sometimes, when conditions on the front were calm, visitors were escorted through the crayères and out to a pillbox built in one of the vineyards. There, as if they were in a shooting gallery, they were handed rifles and told, "Try your luck. See if you can hit a Boche." [4]

Among the visitors was Paul Poiret, but his reasons for being there were more serious. Poiret, who was France's most famous clothing designer, had been summoned to Reims to design a new uniform for the military. The French had long believed their soldiers should always be well-dressed and look like heroes when going off to war. Hence the blue jackets and red trousers troops had worn since the mid–nineteenth century. By World War I, however, that had become impractical. Not only did red trousers present an inviting target, but the madder red dye for making them was no longer available because it had come from Germany. Poiret's idea was to create a more modern uniform that was horizon bleu (sky blue), one that blended more naturally with the landscape and was less conspicuous to the enemy. It was a design that would be quickly adopted by the French government.

Any discussion about uniforms, however, had to be postponed, for no sooner did Poiret arrive than Germany's artillery erupted. "I jumped into a hole, which led me to a narrow gallery," he said. "That, in turn, led me to a corridor which opened into a large vaulted cave."

These caves and corridors were those the military had opened up between the cellars of all the champagne houses to enable troops to march from an entrance beneath the railroad station directly to the front line—a distance of several miles— without ever going aboveground.

But Poiret may have felt more like Alice in Wonderland tumbling into a rabbit hole, for what he came upon next seemed like the Mad Hatter's Tea Party. "I was stunned to discover forty good Frenchmen sitting at an elegant table with candelabra, hams, and bottles of champagne. Monsieur Werlé, head of Veuve Clicquot, invited me to join them, which I did with pleasure.

"At five o'clock, someone came and informed us that the bombardment was finished, and I returned to the surface, only to realize that I could hardly stand up. Then I discovered sixteen champagne corks in my pockets. Could I possibly have drunk that much?"[5]

Life underground, however, was hardly a party. With each barrage, the crayères trembled, anxiety grew, and uncertainty deepened. Is my house still standing? people wondered. Has someone I know been killed? All too often, news filtering down from the surface was bad. At Heidsieck Monopole, two cellar workers and one of their wives were killed when the building they were working in was hit. At Krug, workers were loading cases of champagne onto a wagon when a shell landed in the courtyard, killing three of them instantly. Pol Roger's cellarmaster suffered serious head injuries when he was struck by shrapnel during another bombardment.

Although the crayères provided a measure of safety, they weren't completely bombproof. Sometimes, in the upper galleries, fissures and cracks would develop from the constant bombardment, resulting in cave-ins.

Most of the time, the shelling was erratic, following no regular pattern. But at other times, there seemed to be a definite point. As one champagne worker said, "Every time our soldiers scored a small success, the Germans took it out on Reims and bombed even harder." [6]

People remained underground for weeks or months at a time; some stayed for as long as two years. Children were born there, and old men breathed their last.

With hundreds sharing common facilities such as laundry and bathing, privacy was a problem. Families created living spaces for themselves by using pupitres, racks for remuage, as makeshift walls. Sometimes they added cardboard liners from champagne cases. "We lived and slept among the bottles," one said. [7]

For the children, the retreat underground seemed like the beginning of a never-ending vacation at first. The long, winding tunnels were perfect for playing cache-cache, or hide-and-seek, and other games. But then came the bad news: School was back in session. There were classes for every grade level, kindergarten through high school. Each school was decorated with patriotic symbols and bore the name of a military hero, such as École Joffre, named after the general who orchestrated the Battle of the Marne, and École Foch, named for the general who succeeded Joffre as commander-in-chief. There was also École

Gallieni, named in honor of the military governor of Paris who launched the taxis of the Marne.

Aside from the setting, schools operated in normal fashion, with space set aside for libraries and exercise. Classrooms in the crayères looked pretty much like any classroom with desks and blackboards.

But there were a couple of important differences. Six cows were stabled nearby to provide younger children with fresh milk. Also, every student carried a gas mask.

Although gas warfare had been outlawed by the Hague Conventions in 1899 and 1907, the Germans began using gas as a weapon in early 1915. At first, it was tear gas. On April 22, they switched to chlorine, setting open bottles along the frontlines and allowing the wind to carry the gas to their opponent's trenches. This was soon followed by deadlier gases, such as the feared mustard gas, which were contained in artillery shells. It was a new way to die in war, but hardly the only way.

Modern bullets had come into play—high-velocity, conical, and twisting—which lacerated the flesh and caused bones to burst. Never before had human bodies been so torn apart. The Germans were also bringing in guns with much greater firepower, the most terrifying being a cannon named "Big Bertha." Its seventy-five-mile range now made every town and village, as well as every champagne house, a potential target.

Virtually all of the firms suffered serious damage, forcing the entire champagne industry to move its operations into the crayères. Maison Henri Abelé was burned to the ground, Pommery and Lanson were reduced to rubble, and Roederer was shelled repeatedly, while nearly every building belonging to Moët & Chandon, including those where Jean-Rémy Moët had entertained Napoleon, was almost completely destroyed.

One of the first to be caught in the firestorm was Champagne's oldest house, Ruinart Père & Fils, which was founded in 1729. Like Pommery, it was situated near the front line in easy range of German guns. During the Battle of the Marne, most of the buildings, including the offices, were destroyed. Salvaging what he could, André Ruinart moved his office into the cellars. No sooner had he done so, however, than another barrage erupted, with one of the shells rupturing a water main and flooding Ruinart's underground office. Undeterred, André built a raft, mounted his desk onto it, and went back to work—afloat. Unfortunately, the cold and dampness were such that André became ill and died several months later.

Hermann von Mumm faced a different problem: he was German. His family had settled in Champagne in 1827 but had never taken out French citizenship.

In July 1914 Mumm called workers at his champagne house together to say that military authorities had advised him that war was imminent. "I want to encourage those of you who have been called up to do your duty as Frenchmen," he said. "While the war continues, you will still get your full salary; your wives may come to the cellars each month to pick it up. I plan to stay in Reims and do my duty as director of this company."

But it was not to be. Although Mumm had applied for citizenship, formalities had not been completed before the war started. Mumm was arrested and interned as an enemy alien in Brittany. His champagne house was confiscated by the French government and turned over to French managers for the duration of the war.[8]

For the rest of the champagne industry, the picture was becoming increasingly grim. Production had fallen to half its prewar level. Bottles, packing cases, and sugar had become nearly impossible to obtain. The shortage of bottles was particularly acute because so many glassblowers had been killed. While orders from neutral countries such as the United States were still pouring in, they were impossible to fill. Ports were blocked, German U-boats lurked off the coast, insurance companies refused to cover champagne shipments, and banks would not honor foreign checks.

Sales in France had dried up as well. In Paris, the agent for Pol Roger wrote, "The city is dead and no one is drinking champagne. The only restaurants that continue to work are Larue and Maxim's, and they shut at 8:00 P.M. The rest are all closed."[9]

Not only was Paris dead—a third of its population had fled—but resorts on the Côte d'Azur had closed down as well. "There is nothing we can do except wait," the agent said.

That was something Maurice Pol-Roger felt he could not afford to do. With northern ports like Le Havre and Calais shut down, he tried shipping out of Bordeaux. His first efforts were unsuccessful. One ship went down in a storm; another carrying a huge consignment was sunk by German U-boats.

By the end of 1915 the economic picture had slightly improved. Cafés and restaurants in Paris were reopening, albeit slowly. In addition, one of Maurice's agents had just signed a new customer: the British Expeditionary Force in France. "With this," the agent said, "we will now be able to tell our customers how Pol Roger is helping defeat the Germans."

There was, however, some unfinished business that Maurice was determined to take care of. He had not forgotten how the regional governor had deserted his post a year earlier, absconding with the city's funds on the eve of the German occupation. Now, a year later, Hervé Chapron had returned, and he was furious. Charging that his reputation had been impugned, Chapron sent his seconds to Maurice, demanding satisfaction and challenging him to a duel. Maurice accepted.

The two met on March 17 on the grounds of Château de Saran just outside Épernay. Each was accompanied by a personal physician and their seconds, and each was armed with an épée de combat, or small sword. The two foes wore gloves and were dressed in loose white shirts, dark pants, and boots. (Suspenders were prohibited, but the men were allowed belts.) On a signal from the referee, the duel began.

Maurice lunged first, inflicting a wound in Chapron's left shoulder. The duel was halted while a doctor quickly checked it; the wound was minor. With a nod from the physician, the duel resumed. Even though Maurice had drawn first blood, it was clear to all that Chapron was a much better swordsman. The préfet struck next, inflicting a dangerous wound in Maurice's right wrist, forcing him to drop his sword. Again, the duel was halted while the doctor examined Maurice. The injury was serious, said the doctor, who then announced he was calling an end to the duel. It had lasted only a few minutes.[10]

This was not intended to be a fight to the death. It was more of a ritual, a point of honor, and both were convinced that they had made their point. Although Chapron resumed his duties as préfet, Maurice resigned as mayor of Épernay, saying he had no wish to be associated with Chapron.

Honor and patriotism were sentiments increasingly seized upon by champagne-makers as the war progressed, and for good reason. Many champagne houses had been founded by German families in the nineteenth century, and the growing anti-German feeling in the years leading up to the war had cost them business. Deutz & Geldermann was particularly affected by the loss of sales. René Lallier, who had taken over the firm, decided to change its name to Champagne Lallier, but noted on the label of each bottle that it was the "successor to Deutz & Geldermann." When sales failed to improve, however, Lallier returned to the original name, adding an extra label saying that the owners of the champagne house were all officers serving in the French army. Finally, sales *did* improve.

Other producers gave their cuvées names such as Gloire Française and Champagne n'oublions jamais (we'll never forget). For soldiers in the trenches, there was Champagne des Poilus. There was also Champagne America and one for British soldiers in France called Alliance Creaming Tommy's Special Dry Reserve. And there was even one called Champagne anti-Boche.[11]

Although commerce between France and "the Boche" had been cut off, the German high command had not lost its taste for champagne, which was hardly a surprise. Even before 1870, the Germans admitted they loved good champagne and preferred it to their own sparkling wine, sekt. Now, they let it be known that they were ready to pay any price for the most prestigious marques, "no matter how exorbitant." Champagne-makers soon noticed an increase in orders from certain clients in Switzerland

and Holland. Only later did they learn that these "clients" were actually secret agents working for Germany, ordering shipments of champagne and then forwarding them on to Berlin.

Champagne-makers were less surprised to find that the fifty thousand French troops camped in the crayères were taking advantage of their bivouac. At Krug, a chapel had been set up in the cellars for troops, with cases of champagne serving as pews. The cases, destined for the United States, had been sitting there for some months because shipping lanes were blocked. When lanes finally reopened, workers began hauling the cases out, which is when they noticed that they seemed awfully light—and they were, because they were empty.

In the cellars of Mumm, soldiers obtained permission to hold a funeral Mass for a buddy who had been killed. Workers watched respectfully as the coffin was carried in. Then it was carried out. A few minutes later, the coffin returned, then went back out. When this happened again, one of the cellar workers intercepted the coffin and opened the lid. It was what everyone suspected.[12]

"We took the opportunity to liberate quite a few bottles," admitted one young soldier. His name was Maurice Chevalier.

As the second year of the war came to an end, champagne was being sent regularly to troops as a morale-booster; those in the trenches near Reims received two bottles a day. Champagne was also donated to military hospitals, the bottles marked "For the sick and wounded." Pilots kept track of the number of enemy planes they shot down by pinning champagne corks on the walls of mess halls. Newspapers told readers that the best way to honor returning soldiers was with champagne.[13]

In Paris, French prime minister Aristide Briand always

drank a bit of champagne with lunch, saying it helped him re-main optimistic "in these sad times."

Champagne had become a symbol of France's determination to survive. When it appeared that the Germans were about to break through French lines, the commander of French forces in Reims was ordered to abandon his position and withdraw from the city. He ignored the order.

"As long as there is champagne here," he said, "we will de-fend it."

It was a sentiment that a young man from New York would have shared. Alan Seeger was born into a family of wealth and privi-lege. It was also a very musical family. His brother, Charles, was a noted musicologist; his nephew Pete would become one of the most famous folksingers of his generation. Alan, however, was drawn to the music of words.[14]

In 1912 he moved to Paris to write poetry and pursue a literary career. It was not what his parents wanted—they hoped he would follow his father into business—but Alan was happy. He rented a room in the Latin Quarter where he reveled in the Bohemian life.

But there were rumblings of war, and when it finally broke out, Alan found he could not ignore it. At the age of twenty-six, he joined the French Foreign Legion. "It was unthinkable to leave the danger to others," he said, "to go on enjoying the sweet things of life while others were shedding their blood."

Danger and bloodshed, however, didn't seem to faze him, at least not in the beginning. In one of his first letters home after being sent to Champagne, Seeger wrote, "Wonderful days are ahead. You have no idea how beautiful it is to see the troops undulating along the road with the captains and lieutenants on horseback at the head of their companies."

It was October, and Alan was mesmerized by the beauty of the countryside, the vine-covered slopes full of dazzling autumn colors as an afternoon sun beamed down. Everything he saw moved him, imprinted itself on his memory, and made him feel more alive.

"How beautiful the view is over the sunny vineyards," he said, "and what a curious anomaly. On this slope, the grape-pickers are singing merrily at their work, on the other the batteries are roaring. Boom! Boom!"

Seeger would immortalize that scene in "Champagne, 1914–15," a poem he wrote about the land and each soldier who gave his life defending it.

> There the grape-pickers at their harvesting
> Shall lightly tread and load their wicker trays,
> Blessing his memory as they toil and sing
> In the slant sunshine of October days. . . .

It was a poem he worked on over a period of months, often by candlelight while hunkered down in the trenches. Sometimes, when there was a lull in the fighting, he would wander away to some quiet spot to write.

> In the glad revels, in the happy fêtes,
> When cheeks are flushed, and glasses gilt and pearled
> With the sweet wine of France that concentrates
> The sunshine and the beauty of the world,

Drink sometimes, you whose footsteps yet may tread
The undisturbed, delightful paths of Earth,
To those whose blood in pious duty shed,
Hallows the soil where that same wine had birth.

As time passed, the war became a hemorrhage of human life. Three hundred and thirty thousand French soldiers had been killed in the first four months; another six hundred thousand had been wounded. In 1915 four hundred thirty thousand troops were killed. The staggering losses and grim realities shook Seeger. In some ways, he found it easier to describe them as a reporter than as a poet. With an eye for personal detail, Alan was able to write articles in a style that freed him from poetic conventions.

On February 15, 1915, he filed this dispatch for the *New York Sun*: "Poor ruined villages of Northern France! They lie like so many silent graveyards, each little house the tomb of some scattered family's happiness."

Alan wrote those words from the wine cellar of a château where he and his regiment were camped. Unfortunately, the Germans had already been there and left little behind. "Most precious were the remains of a beautiful library," Seeger said, "the last thing to be violated by the rude hands that have ransacked everything else and left not a bottle of wine in the whole town."

What especially tugged at his heart, however, was a little girl's postcard collection "with their little messages of love or greeting." A few days later, Seeger came across some other postcards. These were on the bodies of German soldiers who had been killed months earlier. "I wish I had taken them down textually so you could share some of the emotion that was mine," he wrote to the *New York Sun*. "They were simple little family messages, reflecting a father's pride, a sister's love, a mother's fears. Far away in some German village, they have long since found his name in the lists of missing. But soon we will go out in the night and bury these bodies, and the manner of his death and the place of his nameless grave they will never know."

Not long afterward, Seeger and his fellow legionnaires were summoned to a review before France's commander-in-chief, General Joffre. Seeger's division, along with several others, gathered in a nearby town perched on a sunny plateau, one that seemed all the sunnier because it had been cleaned up by German prisoners of war.

As a monoplane circled overhead for protection, the soldiers were called to present arms. At that moment, the band broke into "La Marseillaise." "At the first bars of the familiar strains," Seeger said, "even the horses felt the wave of emotion that rippled over the field and whinnied in accompaniment. There was something sublime about it."

Alan and his buddies were in high spirits as they marched back to their camp. "That night, in our candle-lit loft, we uncorked bottles of bubbling champagne," he said. "Clinking our tin army cups, with the spell of the afternoon still strong upon us, we raised them there together, and we drank to the day."

The next day, it was back to the trenches, a world apart with its own rules and strategies for survival. Seeger and the others referred to themselves with pride as poilus (hairy ones). Their unruly hair, beards, and mustaches gave them strength like

Samson, they said, a strength they badly needed to deal with what they faced. Trenches frequently collapsed, burying whole units alive.

The dead and wounded lay next to the living because there was no way to evacuate them. Rats nibbled on corpses, and sometimes on men who were merely sleeping.

Seeger likened the trenches to the tiny, cramped cages Louis XI had created in the fifteenth century to torture prisoners. "We are not, in fact, leading the life of men at all, but that of animals, living in holes and only showing our heads outside to fight and to feed. It is a miserable life to be condemned to, shivering in these wretched holes, in the cold and the dirt and the semi-darkness."

It was from such darkness and misery that Seeger drew much of his inspiration, as in this verse from his poem called "The Aisne," one of Champagne's rivers:

> *Winter came down on us. The low clouds, torn*
> *In the stark branches of the riven pines,*
> *Blurred the white rockets that from dusk till morn*
> *Traced the wide curve of the close-grappling lines.*

Such gloom only added to the gnawing irritation Seeger felt about America's isolationism and continuing refusal to join the war. In "A Message to America," he wrote,

> *You have the grit and the guts, I know;*
> *You are ready to answer blow for blow.*
> *You are virile, combative, stubborn, hard,*
> *But your honor ends with your own back-yard . . .*

By spring of 1916 Seeger had become increasingly fatalistic. Each day he could feel the ground beneath his feet shake as bombs and shells came crashing down, the sky filled with so much metal that it seemed solid. At times it was hard to breathe, and harder yet to comprehend the horrendous carnage unfolding before him as long lines of young men would charge out of their trenches into a murderous artillery barrage, only to be "hurled up like waves breaking backwards into the sea."

In a letter to his mother, he wrote, "You must not be anxious about my not coming back. Death is nothing terrible after all. It may mean something even more wonderful than life."

That fatalism had become a personal premonition which Seeger expressed in "I Have a Rendezvous with Death," the poem for which he would become best known.

> I have a rendezvous with Death
> At some disputed barricade,
> When Spring comes round with rustling shade
> And apple blossoms fill the air.
> I have a rendezvous with Death
> When Spring brings back blue days and fair.

The days of June were incredibly blue and fair and seemed to lift Seeger's spirits as he headed into one of the biggest battles of the war. A million men would die on the Somme, but Alan was brimming with joy and excitement; he was impatient to get to the action.

On June 22 he celebrated his twenty-eighth birthday. A few days later, he and his fellow legionnaires got their orders: they would attack the next day. "My dream is coming true," Alan said to one of the other men.

The following afternoon, Seeger's unit made a charge up a hill northwest of Reims near the village of Belloy-en-Santerre. It was the Fourth of July. Halfway to the top, Seeger was hit, and fell mortally wounded, but fellow soldiers recalled how he cheered them on even as he lay dying.

His body was found in a shell hole the following day. Most of the men in his company had been killed as well. They were buried together in a mass grave.

"Of all the poets who have died young," a writer said, "none has died so happily." A French newspaper announced Seeger's death and saluted him by publishing part of his poem "Champagne, 1914–15," saying that "Cyrano de Bergerac would have been proud to claim it."

I love to think that if my blood should be
　So privileged to sink where his has sunk,
I shall not pass from Earth entirely,
　But when the banquet rings, when healths are drunk,

And faces that the joys of living fill
　Glow radiant with laughter and good cheer,
In beaming cups some spark of me shall still
　Brim toward the lips that once I held so dear.

By the time of Seeger's death, France had undergone a profound change. Gone were the bravado and conspicuous displays of patriotism. No longer did crowds flock to train stations to cheer soldiers headings to the front. Now, the conscription of young men was known as the impôt du sang, or blood tax. Never before had war cost so many deaths, particularly in so short a time. Fifty percent of those who would die in the war had been killed in the first year and a half. As one newspaper reported, "France is bleeding to death."

Nowhere was the pain more keenly felt than in Champagne, where some of the fiercest fighting was taking place. And for what, people wondered.

A wave of deep depression had swept over the region, a feeling that the country could neither win the war nor stop fighting it. The war in the trenches, with half of those trenches in Champagne, had bogged down into what was called "grignotage" and "tenir," nibbling and holding on.

As summer turned to fall, the management of Pommery & Greno decided it could no longer hold on. Pommery was not just a champagne house now; it was also a place of mourning.

Seventeen of its staff, including one of its directors, had been killed while working there. Telegrams arrived almost daily at Pommery with news that someone's husband, brother, or son had been killed or wounded at the front.

Situated on a high bluff only a few hundred yards from enemy lines, Pommery & Greno was extremely vulnerable to German gunners. No champagne house was closer to enemy lines; no champagne house took a more savage pounding. Every day, the shells came in; every day another part of Pommery disappeared in a cloud of fire and smoke.

Deciding the dangers were too great, Henri Outin, the firm's acting director and onetime cellarmaster, called an urgent meeting to announce he was suspending operations. "Here at Pommery, we have had the perilous honor of playing a major role in the defense of Reims," he said.

Its crenellated Victorian towers—those that were still standing—were being used as observation posts by the army. Machine guns, howitzers, and heavy artillery had been mounted in the vineyards. Pommery's cellars, which housed one thousand troops, extended nearly a mile into no-man's-land and opened directly into the trenches, making them invaluable for getting reinforcements to the front or evacuating the dead and wounded. Unfortunately, this also made Pommery a legitimate military target.

Outin, who had become acting director after the previous director had been killed during a bombardment of the champagne house, continued. "We have experienced some terrible days. Many of our friends and loved ones, women and even children, are no longer with us. Some of you have been wounded as well. For these reasons, we have decided that it would be better if we closed down."

Before any of the three hundred workers who had gathered in one of the underground galleries could respond, Outin explained that the munitions industry, located in the center of the country and far from any battle lines, was desperate for help. "It's safer there, and the salaries are much higher than what we can afford to pay you," he said. "We'll get you there, and at the end of the war, your jobs here will be waiting for you if still you want them."

The reaction of workers was swift and unanimous: We're not leaving. "Do what you must," one said, "but we're going to stay and continue making champagne for as long as we can."

No one felt more strongly about that than Albert Corpart, Pommery's long-serving vineyard manager. Corpart had worked in the vines all his life. He had joined Pommery as a young teenager and, over the years, worked his way up to become chief vigneron, a position of great responsibility and one he held dear, almost as dear as his family. Nearly every one of Pommery's vines had been planted by Corpart himself. He had raised them from small cuttings, then nurtured them in glass-roofed sheds until they were ready for planting. After more than thirty years in the vines, Corpart was not about to abandon them.

But continuing would not be easy. Everyone he had trained, all of the experienced workers, were gone, leaving Corpart with an inexperienced team of old men, women, and children. Equally upsetting was the state of his cherished vineyards, which were furrowed by trenches and strung with coils of barbed wire. Vines had been shredded by shrapnel while the ground, pock-marked by so much shelling, looked like the surface of the moon. Simply getting to the vines was an ordeal. The landscape was littered with unexploded shells, many of them leaking poisons into the soil that would contaminate the vineyards for years to come.

There was also a matter of getting permission. With the French military having requisitioned the property, Corpart now needed a military pass to enter the vineyards. Often authorities, citing the dangers, refused to grant it. When Corpart complained, they shrugged and said there was nothing they could do. Finally, one of the officers took him aside and said, "Look, people who don't hesitate to bomb our cathedral would have no qualms about sending a few shells onto tillers of the earth." Corpart was unswayed.

Military authorities weren't the only ones trying to stop him from venturing into the vineyards. His superiors at Pommery urged him to pull back as well, saying the risks weren't worth it. Friends pleaded with him to be more cautious. His wife begged him to stay home. Corpart refused to listen. The only ones who never tried to rein him in were members of his team, or, as Corpart described them, "old men unafraid of death and young people heedless of danger."

Finally, one day after Corpart led his team so close to a French battery that it was forced to stop firing, the military issued a direct order for him to stay out of the vineyards.

Corpart ignored it and was back in the vineyards the next day, staking up vines and repairing the damage. If someone asked what was happening, he would say, "Oh, not much," and his team would nod in agreement. What no one realized was that Corpart had sworn them all to secrecy. "If anyone including our bosses, but especially my wife, ever asks if there's been any shelling, deny it," he said.

According to Henri Outin, who had recorded in his diary what life was like during the first weeks of the war, Corpart was a master of the "pious lie."

> There was "never any bombing in the vines" or if you pressed the point, he might concede, "just a little, but nothing serious." He figured that no one would ever check.

But in case someone did check, Corpart always tried to cover up the damage. Like a golfer replacing his divots, he would fill in the dozens of shell holes and replant or replace those vines that had been ripped up or damaged. And his team was always there, loyal and completely devoted, according to Outin.

They followed his orders explicitly. If the direction of shelling changed, he would tell his people to move to a different part of the vineyard. If shells whistled too closely, he would order everyone to flatten themselves on the ground. He maneuvered his little team like soldiers in combat.

As soldiers watched him in action, they developed a grudging respect for "this tenacious man with the ruddy complexion and brilliant blue eyes." They even came to accept what one officer called his "entêtement," or pigheadedness. Most of all, they realized there was no way of keeping him out of the vineyards.

Corpart's pigheadedness, his single-mindedness, was something his family knew well. When his son was called up to the army and came to say good-bye, Corpart said, "As long as you're here, take the horse and go plow Clos Pompadour." The son did as he was told.

A short time later, however, German guns opened up. Worried for his son's safety, Corpart ran after him, but when he got to the vineyard, there was only the horse, still harnessed to the plow, rearing up every time an explosion occurred. The son was nowhere to be seen.

He was eventually found in a barn, hiding underneath some straw. Corpart was indignant. Dragging his son back to the horse, Corpart ordered him to unhitch the animal. "You have no right to take shelter until you've taken care of your animals," he said. All the while, the shelling continued, "close by and thick," as Corpart would later admit.

The next day, Corpart's son marched off to war. He would distinguish himself for bravery, but "Working in the vineyard that day was my baptism of fire," he said.

By 1916 nearly two hundred thousand shells had already fallen on Pommery & Greno, turning what had been one of the most beautiful properties into a wasteland. Hardly a building was left standing. The entire workforce was living in the crayères, among them Corpart himself, whose house had stood in the center of the vineyards until it was destroyed during a barrage.

In many ways, it had been much more than a house; it was also an historic landmark, a medieval mill that had been rebuilt with stones from an ancient monastery torn down during the Revolution. Corpart had watched the destruction, counting the shells as they reduced his home to rubble, and himself to tears.

But the chief vigneron had little time to grieve. There were two harvests to worry about, this year's, the 1916, and the one from the year before. Because of military regulations prohibiting nonessential civilian shipping, the 1915 harvest was still stuck in the vineyards. Late that summer, however, authorities finally gave champagne producers permission to start bringing their grapes into Reims.

The question facing Corpart was how to get those grapes, which had been pressed, siphoned into barrels but marooned for nearly a year, back to Pommery. Before the war, it had been done with a small suburban train that ran through all of the vineyard villages. Giant wooden barrels would be transported out to the vignerons, who would fill them and then send them back on the train. That was no longer possible because the Germans, when they occupied Reims in 1914, seized the train's locomotive engine, which had been made in Germany, and sent it back home. When Reims was liberated after the Battle of the Marne, the French army took control of le petit train, refitted it, and brought in another engine, but announced that the train would only be used for hauling military supplies and evacuating the dead and wounded. There was no room for grapes. Corpart had to find another means of transportation.

Corpart eventually found some old wagons, drawn by even older horses. The best horses had been requisitioned by the army. For the next two months, fourteen horse-drawn wagons, each loaded with a barrel, arrived every night at Pommery. Unloading had to be done quickly but quietly so that the Germans, who were only a few hundred yards away, would not hear them and open fire. The wind was also a factor. Even the slightest breeze, if it was blowing in the wrong direction, could easily carry the sound and give them away. This happened on several occasions. One night, a driver and several horses were killed.

By mid-September, the last barrel of "new wine" from the 1915 vintage had been unloaded. Corpart now turned to the 1916. For this, he would need every ounce of ingenuity and courage he possessed.

Unlike 1915, the weather had been poor. It had rained throughout the summer and grapes had failed to ripen. Vineyards were so mushy and waterlogged that working in them was often impossible. Rot and mildew had set in, but no one had the necessary equipment or chemicals, like copper sulfite, for treating the vines. There wasn't even any fertilizer because the army had seized most of the horses.

Few were under any illusions that 1916 would result in anything more than mediocre champagne, least of all Albert Corpart. Even if there was no changing that, Pommery's chief vigneron was determined to do whatever he could. Each day, he would lead his little team to the Clos Pompadour and Clos du Moulin de la Housse vineyards to check on the vines. Because of shelling, the route they took was usually underground, through Pommery's crayères and the dimly lit tunnels that extended all the way to the trenches and no-man's-land where the two vineyards were located.

Much of their work had to be done at night, crawling on stomachs through the mist, fog, or hazy moonlight lest the Germans spot them. At times, they were so close to enemy trenches that they could hear the soldiers talking. Corpart would whisper to keep quiet, keep moving, and, most of all, to be careful of unexploded shells that littered the vineyard.

Even in the darkness, he could see what the war had done to his beloved vines. It was a pitiful sight that almost broke his heart. Most of the vines were those he had planted twenty years earlier. Now they looked lifeless, broken. Many had been uprooted by the bombing. Others had yellowed and were turning brown because of the poisons that had seeped into the soil from chemical warfare. Ugly coils of barbed wire draped around the vines and along the trenches only added to Corpart's gloom, as did the graves of fifty French soldiers who had been killed in the vineyard and were buried where they fell. So much death, he thought. And then he remembered the women and children who had been killed picking grapes the year before.

Corpart's greatest fear was for the safety of those who worked with him. In addition to the normal precautions, he now insisted that each member of his team carry a gas mask. Poison gas had become a common item in the enemy's arsenal of weapons. As the harvest approached, clouds of poisonous gases frequently hovered over the vineyards. Corpart never forgot a soldier's description of one attack: "With each wave of gas, death enveloped us. It impregnated our clothes and blankets, it killed everything around us that lived, that breathed."

Breathing while wearing a mask, however, was extremely difficult, especially while doing the kind of work Corpart and his workers were doing. Nevertheless, the harvest went ahead and the grapes got picked. Although the quality was as bad as everyone predicted, the good news was that no one on Corpart's team was wounded or killed.

His "quiet courage, admirable serenity, and the magnificent example he set"—prompted the government to award Corpart one of its highest civilian honors: the Order of the Nation.[15]

CHAPTER 8

No Drums, No Trumpets

To most French, 1917 was known as "the impossible year."[1] Casualties rose, frustration within army ranks grew, and the United States continued to cling to its policy of strict neutrality. "America is too proud to fight," declared President Woodrow Wilson, arguing that the United States should not involve itself in Europe's power struggles.[2]

On April 2, following the sinking of five American ships by German U-boats, the president reversed himself and asked Congress to declare war. His about-face was spurred by the discovery that Germany was also trying to entice Mexico to join the war by promising to return Texas, Arizona, and New Mexico, territories Mexico lost to America in 1848. "The day has come," Wilson said, "when America is privileged to spend her blood and her might for the principles that gave her birth."

Suddenly, "the impossible year" began to seem a little less impossible. Even Germany realized the picture had changed as the first of three million doughboys, chanting "Lafayette, we are here," began pouring into France that summer.

But as France gained a powerful ally, it was losing another. After months of turmoil, the Russian czar abdicated and, by fall, a communist government had taken power.

For Champagne, the Russian Revolution was a devastating blow. Ten percent of its market vanished practically overnight. Bills for millions of bottles of champagne went unpaid as the new communist leadership branded champagne a "degenerate capitalist habit" and declared that vodka was the patriotic drink.

Champagne's connection to Russia stretched back to the early eighteenth century, when Peter the Great visited the province and first tasted champagne. Actually, he did much more than taste: he guzzled. So much so that he passed out in a drunken stupor in the crayères that today belong to Taittinger Champagne. Because Peter was so enormous, there was no alternative but to leave him where he'd collapsed until he came to. When he awoke, a priest was there to lecture him on the dangers of overindulging. This apparently had little effect because from then on, the Russian monarch made it a nightly habit to always go to bed with at least four bottles of champagne tucked in with him.

No champagne house profited more than Louis Roederer, which became the personal favorite of Czar Alexander II. On assuming the throne in 1855, he announced that he preferred Roederer's intensely sweet style to all others, including Veuve Clicquot's and Moët's. By 1868 two million bottles, or 80 percent of Roederer's annual worldwide sales, were going to Russia.[3]

Such was Alexander's passion for Roederer that he began sending his cellarmaster to Reims every year to select the best cuvées for his table. Fearful of being poisoned, Alexander insisted that his cellarmaster monitor every step of the champagne-making process, from the time wines were blended to when the champagne was bottled and corked.

There was something else the czar demanded as well: a special bottle that would distinguish *his* champagne from everyone else's. Normally, champagne came in thick, dark green bottles, much like those used today. Eager to please its best customer, Roederer designed an elegant, clear crystal bottle for Alexander's champagne. It was called, appropriately, Cristal. By World War I, six hundred sixty thousand bottles of Cristal were being shipped to St. Petersburg each year—exclusively for the czar.

The end of 1917, however, saw the house of Louis Roederer in desperate straits. The shattering impact of the October Revolution not only left Roederer, like other houses, with a stack of unpaid bills, but also with a huge stock of champagne so sweet that nobody else wanted it. "The only reason our firm survived, that we still exist today," observed a Roederer spokesperson, "was that no one else in Champagne had any money to buy us out."

In December, Russia signed an armistice with Germany, enabling the Kaiser to reinforce his armies on the Western Front with troops from the East.

It was depressing news for France, whose army was already plagued by a rash of mutinies by soldiers protesting "the senseless slaughter" and the hellish conditions that existed in the trenches. Three years of warfare, in which the front hardly moved, had turned the trenches into cesspools of filth, where rats, fleas, lice, and other vermin flourished among the corpses. Said one soldier, "You ate beside the dead. You drank beside the dead. You relieved yourself beside the dead. You slept beside the dead."[4]

In an effort to boost morale, the French National Assembly voted to give every one of its soldiers, all seven million, a bottle of champagne for New Year's.[5]

For Germany, the picture was also grim. Troop strength had shrunk 20 percent. Nearly one million of its soldiers had been killed, wounded, or captured over the previous ten months, and there was no replacing them, because Germany was out of reserves.

Many in France were convinced this was the time to take the offensive, but General Philippe Pétain, who had succeeded Joffre as commander-in-chief, was convinced otherwise. "We must wait for the tanks and the Americans," he said, noting that it would take several months before American forces were at full strength. Prime Minister Clemenceau, upset with what he felt was a defeatist attitude, replaced Pétain with Ferdinand Foch, one of the army's most intuitive and outspoken generals. "Pétain said we were beaten," Clemenceau explained, "while Foch behaved like a madman and wanted to fight on. I said to myself, 'Let's try Foch. At least we'll die with a rifle in our hand.' "[6]

German hopes were pinned on taking Paris. Military leaders believed that if it fell, the rest of France would follow. Achieving their goal, however, meant pushing through Champagne and crossing the Marne River, something they had failed to do in 1914. This time, they vowed, the outcome would be different.

That spring, as a second Battle of the Marne loomed, French military authorities ordered the total evacuation of Reims along with a whole string of vineyard villages on the Montagne de Reims.

Still huddled in the crayères, the people of Reims had endured more than a thousand days of consecutive bombing. "Death hangs over our city night and day," said Cardinal Louis Luçon, who believed it was his duty to remain despite pleas from church leaders and others for him to leave. "Death flies over us, it strikes down, it cuts down the army, it cuts down men, women, children, old people. We are all open to its surprises, and we don't know how to avoid its blows."[7]

Most citizens, like Luçon, did not want to leave. Now, however, they had no choice. With French troops standing guard, residents, many of whom had not been out of the crayères for months, emerged warily from their underground refuge and climbed onto buses that were to take them to Épernay. There, they were to be transferred to trains bound for Paris.

As the vehicles rolled out, passengers recoiled at the devastation surrounding them. Halfway up the Montagne de Reims, the buses paused to allow passengers a last look back. Much of their city was now in flames. No one harbored any illusions that there would be anything left when they returned.[8]

On July 14, France's national holiday, German forces began softening up their targets. In Épernay, which was evacuated a few weeks after Reims, the bombing opened up cracks in caves and underground galleries where millions of bottles of champagne were stored. It was so intense that people in Paris could hear it, eighty miles away.

The following morning, the second Battle of the Marne began in earnest. The kaiser himself had come to watch what he called "a drive for final victory." So confident were he and his generals that they had five trains standing by in eastern France, loaded with straw and packing cases. Once Reims and Épernay fell, the trains were to be sent there and filled with hundreds of thousands of bottles of the best champagne, "les marques les plus reputée." The champagne would then be transported back to Germany and put up for sale, with proceeds used to help pay war costs.[9]

As German forces converged on Reims, however, they were met by furious resistance. French troops had been reinforced by several divisions of colonial troops from Africa; the latter had been promised two bottles of champagne a day for as long as they held the city.[10] The Africans never wavered, said one French historian. "They held it to the end."

Unable to penetrate Reims, the Germans swept around it, heading south toward the Montagne de Reims and the Marne River. There, three days later, they were stopped again. According to an American witness,

Miles of close-laid batteries opened with stupendous thunder. The air above the treetops spoke with unearthly noises, the shriek and rumble of light and heavy shells. Forward through the woods, very near, rose up a continued crashing war of explosions, and a murk of smoke, and a hell of bright fires continually renewed. It lasted only five minutes, that barrage. But they were terrible minutes for the unsuspecting Boche.[11]

The stunned Germans tried to regroup, fighting back with even greater ferocity. Much of their wrath was directed at Épernay, where cracks in the underground galleries had now become so wide that work had to be abandoned out of fear they would collapse.

Instead, it was Germany's dream of taking Paris that crumbled. Although battles would continue for another four months, Berlin now realized that if it hadn't already lost the war, it could no longer win it. "How many hopes, cherished during the last few months, have collapsed at one blow," said Field Marshal Paul von Hindenburg. "How many calculations have been scattered to the winds!" [12]

By contrast, the mood of the French was buoyant; victory was finally within reach. A Paris newspaper printed a cartoon showing the kaiser's son struggling in vain to open a bottle of champagne and crying, "I'm thirsty, thirsty for glory, and I can't uncork it."

Almost forgotten by everyone outside Champagne was that another harvest was taking place under the bombs, the fifth of the war. That prompted yet another cartoon, this one showing a retreating German soldier fleeing with an armload of champagne. Chasing him was a French soldier, yelling, "You call that harvesting?"

In truth, it was French troops who did most of the "harvesting." Left alone for six months in the capital of Champagne, a city they were protecting, few could resist the temptations that lurked in the cellars of Reims's major champagne houses. At Pommery alone, three hundred thousand bottles were emptied by soldiers quartered in its crayères.

Most producers, however, were in a forgiving mood and accepted their losses with good grace. "What would have become of Reims and all its 'buried treasures,'" said Pommery's director of VIP visitors, "if our brave defenders hadn't taken advantage of the situation to comfort themselves physically and morally with our incomparable champagnes? The enemy was defeated and our stocks were saved, so it's better to pull a veil over these sad events and accept that what we have lost sustained the courage of the defenders of champagne."

On November 11, Germany signed an armistice with France and its allies. "At 11:00 A.M., the firing stopped," said historian Correlli Barnett. "Soldiers stood upright in unaccustomed safety listening to the birdsong, marveling that they had survived, mourning the dead." [13] Although a formal peace treaty would not come for another seven months, the Great War was finally over.

France exploded with joy, corks popping everywhere as people poured into the streets to celebrate. Maurice Pol-Roger, trying to satisfy orders that were now flooding his office, stuffed his car with straw and bottles of champagne and set off for Paris. The city was jammed; the Champs-Elysées was a crush of humanity. At the Place de l'Opéra, fifty thousand people gathered to sing "La Marseillaise," the national anthem. "Even the parents of the dead got caught up in it," reported one newspaper. "For one brief moment, they forgot their pain." [14]

In Reims, Charlotte broke into song as well. Charlotte was the name given to the largest bell in the city's cathedral. Forged in 1570, she had "sung" for every coronation but had come crashing down when the cathedral was bombed, laying half-buried in the debris. It took twenty men to raise the twenty-two-thousand-pound bell high enough for her to be rung again. "When she began to sing that day," the mayor said, "it was as if the sun had broken through the fog, as if the sky was blue again." [15]

But only for a moment. Escaping the darkness that had enveloped Europe for four long years was impossible. Thirteen million lives had been lost in the Great War, with France having suffered the most proportionately. More than one and a half million of its soldiers had been killed. Another three million were disabled, one million of them permanently. A whole generation had been practically wiped out.

Champagne alone lost over half of its population. One of its departments, the Aisne, lost two-thirds.

In Reims, which had endured 1,051 consecutive days of bombing, a newspaper headline summed up what was left in two words: "C'est Pompeii." Gone were homes, schools, hospitals, and factories. Virtually everything had been destroyed, including all of the lovely medieval wooden buildings with their intricately carved façades. The city's Renaissance city hall had been flattened. The famous Hôtel Lion d'Or, where U.S. consular officer Robert Tomes once stayed, lay in rubble, too.

But it was Tomes's "imposing neighbor," the one that had greeted him when he awoke each morning, that symbolized Reims's devastation most dramatically. The great thirteenth-century cathedral, where kings had been crowned for six hundred years, was no more than a burned-out shell. Its lead roof had melted away while the massive wooden beams that once supported it had collapsed into the interior. All that remained were parts of walls and a shattered façade. When the U.S. ambassador, Myron Herrick, saw what was left, he wept.

Sadness hung like a cloud over Champagne. People separated from loved ones posted public notices seeking news of their fate: "Monsieur and Madame Léon Simon of Loivre would like news of their mother, Madame Simon-Huraux, who disappeared during the bombardment of Marquigny." Another asked if anyone had seen his nephew and niece, Monsieur and Madame Noël-Bosserelle, "who were taken away by the Germans" when the village of Ligny was bombed.

Half of those killed would never be found or identified. In Dormans, the army began digging a mass grave for fifty thousand soldiers, the bodies so badly mangled and scattered that it was impossible to tell if they were French, British, American, or German.

As unexploded bombs were removed and gas, electricity, and running water were restored, people began returning. The local newspaper, which had to be published in Paris, ran a regular column, "Les Ruines de nos Villages," in an effort to help returnees prepare for what they would face. The notices read like obituaries for a whole way of life:

JANVRY: *Our village is little more than a pile of stones. Everything is gone. Shells and grenades are strewn across the ground. Vines have been burned by poison gas.*

BERMERICOURT: *There is nothing left, absolutely nothing. It is difficult even for those who lived here to tell where the village once stood.*

GERMIGNY: *The chaos is indescribable. The Germans cut the water supply and poisoned all the wells. They took all the metal, even the moving parts from clocks and sewing machines, and sent them back to Germany.*

MERY-PREMECY: *All the farm animals have been killed and been left unburied. Burying them will be difficult because fields are full of unexploded shells.*

BOUVANCOURT: *We should use German prisoners of war to clean up the fields and the most dangerous areas.*

CHAUMUZY: *It's a sad situation for our vines. They have been completely devastated by trenches, barbed wire, gas, and incendiary bombs. The land has so many craters that it's almost impossible to walk.*

Scores of winegrowing communities, much like the "poor ruined villages" Alan Seeger had once described, were damaged beyond recognition. Some were so badly mauled that they would never be rebuilt, among them Tahure, Mesnil-les-Hurlus, Perthes-les-Hurlus, Hurlus, Ripont, Beauséjour, Le Four de Paris, Le Rond Champ, Moronvilliers, Nauroy, Sapigneul. "They have left us with nothing but our land and our tears to water it with," said one vigneron, surveying his vanished village.

Even the land seemed dead, disemboweled by so much shelling that nothing grew any longer. Entire woods and forests had disappeared. Forty percent of Champagne's vineyards were out of production. In the village of Verzenay, barely 175 out of the 1,200 acres of vines were still standing. Where vines had been burned by poison gas, vineyards resembled cemeteries of blackened and contorted crosses, "a vision out of Dante's Inferno," as one local described it. So much land had been chewed up, contaminated by poison gas, and irrigated by the ooze of decaying corpses that fifty thousand acres were declared "zone rouge," or "red zone," meaning that they were considered forever sterile.

The cost of revitalizing vineyards and rebuilding towns and villages was astronomical, but money was something France did not have. The franc, which the government had propped up during the war, went into free fall, losing 80 percent of its value. Making everything even more difficult was a decision by the French government that no financial claims could be made against Germany and its allies for at least two years. An official explained that it was essential that passions be allowed to cool.

It was a severe setback for the Champenois who had shipped millions of bottles of champagne to Germany before the war but had not been paid for them. Exports, which had been Champagne's mainstay, shriveled to barely a third of prewar levels. As one producer explained, "There were no more Grand Dukes in Russia nor Magyars in Hungary; no more gay social life in Vienna and Warsaw."

Now, Germany, which found itself bankrupt, was lost as a market, too.

On January 27, 1919, a man wearing a top hat and heavy overcoat arrived in Reims aboard a special train. He apologized for being late, explaining that he had been delayed by "business" in Versailles. He was referring to the peace conference that had begun two weeks earlier.

The visitor was U.S. President Woodrow Wilson. He was welcomed by Mayor Jean-Baptiste Langlet who said, "You have seen cities celebrating, people pressing about you, waving flags and saluting you with excited enthusiasm. You will not see that here. This is a city in mourning. Here, you will find nothing but solitude and silence."

Given the city's shattered state, only a smattering of Reims's one hundred thousand residents had been able to return. The president's visit, which lasted several hours, was a somber one with few words spoken. At the cathedral, Wilson was presented with a small souvenir, a piece of stained glass from the cathedral's once-magnificent rose window. Already workers were clearing away the rubble of what the American president called "the symbol of German barbarity." [16]

A few months later, Reims had taken on a new look, one that startled visitors and was completely different from what it had been before. Tiny wooden buildings, little more than storefronts, had been thrown up practically overnight. Some said Reims looked like a town out of the American Wild West and California Gold Rush. Others said it looked like a mishmash of Swiss chalets that had lost their way. No one felt it was what Reims *should* look like, so Mayor Langlet met with his city council in an effort to come up with something more appropriate.

What they adopted was le plan américain, a program that brought in American financing to rebuild Reims's most important structures. John D. Rockefeller donated money to rebuild the cathedral's roof. Andrew Carnegie provided money for a new library. A group called the American Fund for French Wounded gave funds for construction of a children's hospital. The goal of le plan américain was to preserve as many of Reim's old charms as possible while transforming it into a modern city of the twentieth century.

But there was one important condition: all of the work had to be carried out by local engineers and architects. The council was determined to keep the spirit of their city intact, as well as to provide jobs for residents who returned.

To symbolize Reims's resurrection, officials chose a rose, the most common flower in Champagne's cemeteries. The Damascus rose, as it was called, was also a link to the city's past. It had been brought to Champagne in the thirteenth century by Count Thibault IV on his return from the Crusades and had flourished there ever since. The rose was to be incorporated as a motif into the façades of new buildings, but with one major change. There would be no thorns. "We've had enough of thorns," one resident said. "There have been too many in our history."

As if to underscore Reims's rebirth, a quiet little event occurred almost a year to the day after the city had been evacuated. A baby was born, the first in the new Reims. It was a boy. His godmother was a young American who was a nurse with the Red Cross.

Something else happened as well that illustrated how life in Champagne was returning to normal. Herds of wild boar were spotted in the vineyards and forests of the Montagne de Reims. "Nobody ever saw them go, and not one was seen during five years," said writer André Simon. "Then they all returned, but never told where they had spent the war years!"

On June 28, the Treaty of Versailles was signed, bringing the First World War to a formal end. France took advantage of its July 14 national holiday to stage a magnificent parade down the

Champs-Elysées. Thousands of soldiers from all the Allied powers took part in the July 14 celebration. They called it the Défilé de la Victoire (the March of Victory).

Although one enemy had been vanquished, another now had to be faced.

As the Champenois began clearing weeds and debris from their neglected vineyards, they could see that phylloxera had marched on even as the war raged. Trenches, barbed wire, poison gas—nothing had stopped its advance.

For forty years, the Champenois had sat in their northern citadel, secure in the belief that their region's colder climate and chalky soil would protect them from the deadly bug that had destroyed the rest of France's vineyards. They were wrong. The tiny aphid was now doing the same to Champagne's, and nearly every vineyard was under attack.

Phylloxera vastatrix, as scientists call it, arrived in France in 1862, a stowaway on a shipment of vines from America. It was first detected in the Rhône Valley. From there, it began its relentless march northward—through Burgundy, across the Midi, into Bordeaux—ravaging vineyards wherever it went. Within a few years, phylloxera had killed nearly all the vineyards in the southern half of the country.[17]

Because of its unusual life cycle the microscopic bug goes through about twenty stages, partly aboveground in a winged form, and partly underground as a wingless creature—no one could figure out how the bug reproduced or even spread. It defeated all attempts to kill it or cure the vines it attacked.

In desperation, the French government offered a prize of thirty thousand gold francs to find a remedy, then increased the amount to three hundred thousand gold francs. Thousands of ideas poured in. Drown it, some said, and if necessary, interjected Ferdinand de Lesseps, the engineer who had built the Suez Canal, channels could be designed to run through the vineyards for bringing water in. Better yet, others suggested, flood vineyards with white wine.

Other ideas were even more bizarre: burying live toads in the vineyards to draw away the poisons, planting Venus flytraps between the vines to eat the bug, sprinkling vines with holy water from the shrine at Lourdes, circling vineyards with strong-smelling plants that would repel the aphid. Some believed irrigating vineyards with shrimp bouillon or goat urine would do the trick. The best urine was said to come from human males. As a result, long lines of schoolboys were marched to the vineyards twice a day to do their bit to save France's rich heritage of vines. Railway stations got into the act as well, doing a lively business selling the desiccated remains of their urinals. The army joined the fight, too, by providing "insecticide" from the urinals of military barracks.

One proposed remedy tugged the patriotic heartstrings. It called for armies of vignerons to stand on the west side of their vines and pound the ground with heavy iron bars. This, it was said, would drive the insect out of France and into Germany. Alas, the vine louse had no sense of patriotism or geography.

The government's prize remained uncollected, sealed in the vault of the Banque de France. Meanwhile, vineyard production fell each year. No one could agree on what the best approach might be. The most effective appeared to be a form of chemical warfare, injecting carbon disulfide into the soil. The process, however, was clumsy, expensive, and time-consuming, involving giant syringes and a highly flammable chemical that often resulted in toxic side effects among those using it.

In despair, authorities decided to hold a meeting in Lyon where all the different "solutions" could be debated. So many people showed up that officials persuaded a visiting circus to postpone its afternoon performance and rent them its large tent.

As the day grew warmer, so did the arguments of scientists and propagandists inside the tent. When someone proposed replacing French vines with American ones which had been shown to be resistant to phylloxera, he was shouted down. American vines were responsible for bringing the louse here in the first place, opponents said. Others blanched at the thought of trying to make decent wine from American grapes such as Concord, Clinton, and Herbemont.

Finally Prosper de Lafitte, head of an anti-phylloxera committee, rose to speak. "Nothing I have heard today is going to work," he said. "Not toads, not urine, not carbon disulfide, and certainly not American vines, which we all know produce terrible wine."[18]

Lafitte went on and on, and his audience grew increasingly impatient, as did the line of people now gathering outside the tent for the next performance of the circus. Even the animals waiting to perform became restless. Suddenly, the monkeys broke loose and descended on the hapless Monsieur de Lafitte. The audience scattered as the beasts overran the podium. The only one who stood fast was Lafitte himself. As one of those who attended the meeting described it, "Monsieur de Lafitte continued to speak, firm and noble to the last."[19]

A solution did finally emerge, and it had an American connection: by grafting French vines onto American rootstocks,
scientists were able to grow vines that were resistant to phylloxera. Not only that, but the new plants also produced fine wine.
Over the next few years, during the 1870s and 1880s, vignerons
throughout the country began uprooting and replanting their
vineyards.

But not in Champagne, not even after 1890, when phylloxera
was first detected in a tiny plot of vines in the village of Tréloup.
Vignerons assumed it was a quirk, promptly burned the vines,
and figured the problem had been eradicated.

Four years later, however, twelve acres of vines had been infected. By 1898, the number had jumped to one hundred. With
each new attack, church bells in affected villages sounded the
alarm. Vignerons remained unmoved, as if by denying its exis-
tence, the pest would go away.

The great champagne houses, however, were convinced it
was a calamity in the making. That year, the Association Viticole
Champenoise, or AVC, presented a plan for fighting phylloxera.
They bought American rootstocks in bulk and handed them out
to vignerons, saying they would not have to pay for them until the
grafted vines were earning money.

Unbelievably, most vignerons refused to consider the offer.
"The phylloxera crisis had revealed a deplorable lack of confidence between the vine-growers and the champagne-makers,"
said historian Patrick Forbes. "Men who work on the soil may be
stubborn, conservative, unreceptive to new ideas; they may be
unduly suspicious of the motives of their fellow beings, too fiery
in temperament to take easily to discipline; but a situation like
the one that arose during the phylloxera invasion with vine-

growers refusing to make a concerted stand against a deadly enemy threatening their livelihoods was almost incredible."

Another factor was involved, too. These were people who put their vines ahead of everything else. The vines had been inherited from their fathers and grandfathers and were as dear to vignerons as members of their family. The thought of ripping them out was like amputating a part of themselves.

Even in 1899 when the number of ravaged acres more than doubled to 240, and the next year soared to nearly 1,600, most vignerons still refused to budge. When vineyard inspectors attempted to gauge the extent of the damage, they were chased away by vignerons wielding axes and sharpened vineyard stakes.

But there was no chasing away the real problem, which by 1904 had finally been detected in the most important vineyards of all, those on the Montagne de Reims. By 1910, on the eve of the Champagne riots, sixteen thousand acres, or nearly half of the Marne's vineyards, were dying from phylloxera. In the last official study, the year before World War I, the number of infected acres had climbed to twenty thousand.

Six years later, when the war had ended, only a handful of Champagne's vines remained untouched. Even the most skeptical and stubborn vigneron now realized that phylloxera was a fact of life and could no longer be ignored. Vineyards were uprooted and replanted with vines grafted onto disease-resistant American rootstocks. Grafting houses, funded by the government and major champagne houses, sprouted. Vignerons went to school to learn the art of grafting, their tuition footed by producers.

The Great War had taught everyone an important lesson: survival in the face of a common enemy depended on working together. That meant resolving differences peacefully, especially those that led to the riots of 1911. In 1919, the government passed a series of laws aimed at eliminating fraud, among them, no more mixing in rhubarb and apple juice to stretch their wine, or hauling in cheaper grapes from outside Champagne to make champagne. From now on, champagne had to be made exclusively with grapes from the region. In the process, a new term was born: "appellation d'origine," which meant that only the Champenois had the legal right to call their wine champagne.

Disputes between Champagne's départements were also addressed. The Aube, for instance, which had been relegated to second-class status when it was designated "Champagne Deuxième Zone," could now apply to have that label removed. Within a short time, the term was scrapped altogether.

For the first time in years, the picture seemed bright. Newly planted vineyards were healthy, cellars were full, and the opportunity for making money was looking better and better. There was also a major new customer: France. The country had long lagged behind the rest of the world in per capita consumption of champagne, because most French tended to gravitate toward their own local wines. The Bordelais drank Bordeaux, Burgundians preferred Burgundy, while people in the Rhône and Loire stuck with their own village vines. With champagne having carved out a unique identity for itself, this began to change. People everywhere were clamoring for bubbly, the result being that France was now rapidly overtaking every other country as a customer for champagne.

At last, the Champenois felt they could take time to celebrate. The war was over, phylloxera had been dealt with, and good times seemed to be ahead. Maurice Pol-Roger decided this was the perfect moment to uncork a bottle of his 1914 champagne, the one he had predicted would be "the wine to drink with victory." Brother Georges had returned home safe from the army and bomb damage to their champagne firm was nearly repaired. As Maurice pulled the cork, he recalled what others had said about that first vintage of the war: that the grapes were too green, that they would never make good champagne.

With one sip, Maurice knew immediately they were wrong and that his faith in the vintage had been proved right. The 1914 was bright, sparkling, and intensely alive. It was everything he hoped it would be.[20]

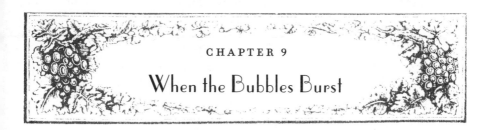

CHAPTER 9

When the Bubbles Burst

After all their struggles and traumas, the Champenois could be forgiven for hoping that they had now arrived at a point in their story when it could finally be written, ". . . and they lived happily ever after."

With the end of the war, it seemed as if their hopes were about to be realized. Everyone was eager to blot out the nightmare of the previous four years, and champagne was the perfect tool. As one writer described it, "War profiteers had money to burn while demobilized soldiers had girlfriends to woo or wives to woo back."[1] Many in the military had become used to drinking champagne during the war and they were determined to continue the habit.

It was an exhilarating time, an era known as the Roaring 20s. In France, it was called "Les Années Folles" (the Crazy Years). Skirts got shorter, women cropped their hair, and Chanel No. 5 was invented. At Le Mans, thousands gathered to witness the first twenty-four-hour road race. In Paris, eleven people were handed small wicker baskets, each with a ham sandwich and bottle of champagne, as they boarded a plane for the first commercial flight to London. On the Champs-Elysées, Josephine Baker and Sidney Bechet, performing in *La Revue Nègre,* mesmerized audiences with a new kind of music: jazz. It had been introduced to France during the war by American doughboys.

In the artist colony of Montparnasse, where writers like Ernest Hemingway and F. Scott Fitzgerald congregated, an enormous, elegant brothel called the Sphinx opened with fifteen girls. Five years later, there were sixty, all of them earning a percentage from the drinks customers bought. Many nights, more than one thousand bottles of champagne were sold. Some girls made so much money on their percentages that they never had to "go upstairs" with their clients.

Everything in those Crazy Years seemed to be light, gay, and sparkling, just like champagne. But the craziest thing of all lay ahead.

For all the euphoria, there was a feeling in Champagne that the good times might be fleeting. Cables and telegrams had been filtering in from the United States saying that crusades against alcohol by the Anti-Saloon League and Women's Christian Temperance Union were gaining strength. When President Wilson announced alcoholic beverages would no longer be served at the White House, the Champenois knew for certain something was up.[2]

Then, on January 20, 1920, an urgent cable from Pol Roger's agent in New York arrived: "Prohibition Bill signed by the president stops importation of wine. Hurry all orders!"[3] The cable was not completely accurate. President Wilson had actually vetoed the bill but Congress overrode it. Nevertheless, the result was the same: the United States was officially "dry."

In Épernay, a moment of panic set in. Maurice and his brother, Georges, had just shipped a large quantity of champagne to New York, and it was already halfway across the Atlantic. In a response to their agent, they expressed "deep regret that prohibition of export of our champagne to the United States is a fait accompli, but we hope this Prohibition Law will not be long-lasting."

Much to their relief, their ship was allowed to land because it had set sail before the bill became law, but it would be the last shipment of Pol Roger champagne to the United States for fourteen years.

Through legal means, that is.

Champagne producers quickly discovered that while Prohibition presented a legal obstacle, it was not an insurmountable one. Soon, more champagne was making its way into the United States than ever before. The best guess is that at least seventy-one million bottles reached America's shores in those "dry" years. Compared to annual sales just before World War I, that represented a three-fold increase. As one champagne-maker described it, "We did a fabulous business. We never had it so good."

For one thing, producers no longer had to pay customs duties to the U.S. government. For another, the risks of trying to sneak bubbly into the States fell mainly on smugglers.

Slipping champagne past authorities, however, required fancy footwork. With U.S. ports closed, champagne first had to be sent to places like the Bahamas, Bermuda, Mexico, and Canada, where booze was still legal. From there, smugglers took over.

St. Pierre and Miquelon, two poor fishing islands near

Canada, developed a whole new economy based on smuggling. With hundreds of thousands of cases of champagne and spirits off-loaded there, the French islands soon earned the reputation as "the alcohol warehouse of North America." Villages became boomtowns; hotels and restaurants sprouted. A cottage industry sprang up as residents recuperated champagne cases and shipping crates discarded by smugglers to repair their homes and build new ones. One of the most conspicuous was the "Cutty Sark Villa," a house built entirely out of whiskey cases.

Smugglers, meanwhile, repackaged their "merchandise" in unmarked cases, wrapping them in tar-soaked canvas to make sure they were waterproof before setting off for the U.S. mainland. Their ships would then anchor outside the three-mile limit where American authorities couldn't touch them. There the booze would be transferred to smaller, much faster vessels. If the Coast Guard appeared, smugglers would drop their contraband on a sandbar and try to retrieve it later. Other times, they left their cargo at a prearranged spot such as a sandbank closer to shore where bootleggers could pick it up at low tide in cars, trucks, and even horse-drawn wagons.[4]

The repressive atmosphere of Prohibition and the ease with which it was circumvented was evident when the Prince of Wales, a noted lover of champagne, paid an official visit to the United States in 1922. Banquets and toasts galore were part of the tour, according to H. Warner Allen, one of the reporters accompanying the prince. "To look at the decorated tables with their array of wineglasses, one might have supposed that for the moment the iron fetters of Prohibition would be relaxed," he wrote, "but it was not to be. There were plenty of glasses on the table, though never a bottle." He went on to describe the dinner:

Toasts were drunk in unfermented grape juice masquerading in a champagne glass. As the meal proceeded and the soul- and stomach-chilling beverage iced water got to work, conversation grew more and more frigid and forced. The stillness of a polar winter descended on the tables where the gaps of empty seats steadily widened. Who could drink with feeling or sincerity a toast given in unfermented grape juice?[5]

As far as Warner Allen was concerned, no one could, and no one did. Most of the guests had come prepared, arriving with bottles of champagne wrapped in newspapers under their arms. "Behind the screens and curtains, there was a certain activity," he wrote, notably the muffled sound of corks popping.

Many of those corks were from bottles of Charles Heidsieck. Of all the producers who did business during Prohibition, no one did it better than Jean-Charles Heidsieck, grandson of the famous Champagne Charlie. His adventures could have come out of a Hollywood movie script.

In 1922, the year the Prince of Wales made his official visit, Jean-Charles was sent to North America by his father to "find out what is going on." What he discovered was that there was a killing to be made. All that was required were guts and imagination.

One of his first ports of call was Nassau in the Bahamas where it was rumored a well-known bootlegger was spending the winter. Heidsieck spotted him swimming offshore. Looking around and seeing no one else on the beach, he stripped off his clothes, swam out, and introduced himself to the bootlegger. Within minutes, Heidsieck had an order for hundreds of cases of champagne. "It's the only order I ever received this way," he said.

And that was just the beginning. Heidsieck roamed the Caribbean, hatching deals in Bermuda, Cuba, and Jamaica. His biggest one took place in Mexico where bootleggers placed an order for 20,000 cases of champagne, the largest single order the champagne house had ever received.

Not all the orders fell into Heidsieck's hands as easily. "Go to St. Pierre and Miquelon," his father cabled him from Reims. "We sent some champagne there that has not been paid for."

It was a long way from the sunny climes of the Caribbean, but Jean-Charles finally found a small freighter in Canada that agreed to take him on board. It was loaded with sheep and cows and two other passengers, bootleggers named Reinfeld and Reitman. When they discovered who their shipmate was, they were thrilled. We would be happy to take the champagne off your hands, they told Jean-Charles. First, however, they had to get to the islands. Even though it was June, a terrible blizzard had come up, tossing the tiny ship around the Atlantic, and terrifying all the passengers, human and otherwise. "The mooing and bleating kept us up all night," Heidsieck remembered. That and the smell of the anchovies the bootleggers were wolfing down with their whiskey to fight off seasickness.

When they finally landed, Jean-Charles discovered his champagne was in a fish-drying warehouse and the manager was not about to release it without some compensation. "How would you like to be my agent for the islands?" Heidsieck asked. "You'll get a commission on all sales."

The new agent promptly sold the entire consignment to Reinfeld and Reitman.

Not all transactions went smoothly, however. In 1925, Heidsieck was contacted by three brothers in Canada named Bronfman, who said they were getting lots of booze into the United States. "We're already selling Pommery champagne and we'd like to do business with you, too," they said. "If you want to check us out, go to Windsor, Ontario." Windsor was just across the border from Detroit, separated by the Detroit River.

"I was told to cross a little field, follow a path along the water until I arrived at a little cabin mounted on stilts in a lake and hidden from shore by trees," Heidsieck said.

When he knocked at the door of the cabin, "it was thrown open and I found myself face to face with three individuals who looked like hangmen. One was a giant, one was a dwarf, and the other was normal-sized." All had their hands in their pockets. "It was clear they were holding pistols."

Heidsieck explained that the Bronfmans had sent him, that he was the one whose champagne the Bronfmans wanted to sell. The three eyed him suspiciously and said not a word. Finally they gestured Heidsieck inside and pointed him toward a chair. Heidsieck continued talking, trying to explain. When nothing he said seemed to make a difference, he reached into his pocket for some souvenir Charles Heidsieck pocketknives to give them. "The moment I put my hand in my pocket," he said, "the three goons drew their revolvers and pointed them at my head."

It took a few moments before the three gunmen understood what he was trying to do. Suddenly, a signal light flashed from across the water. "Let's go, the coast is clear," one said. A trapdoor was flung open and all four men scurried down a ladder into a boat loaded with whiskey and champagne. Much to Heidsieck's surprise, the rickety-looking craft shot out of the dock at fifty miles an hour. Within two minutes, its cargo was being unloaded in Detroit. A few minutes after that, they were back in Windsor where Heidsieck was told to go back to his hotel and wait until someone else contacted him.

This time it was several men wearing suits and slouch hats who came calling. Two had cigars stuck in their mouths and all were carrying mitrailleuses au camembert (machine guns). They blindfolded Heidsieck, hustled him to a car, and drove to another location. When Heidsieck got out, all he could see from beneath his blindfold were the bootleggers' black and white shoes. Heidsieck remained blindfolded while his deal with the Bronfmans (who, once Prohibition ended, founded Seagram's, the world's largest spirits and wine group) was negotiated.

"I was really proud of my experience," Heidsieck later said, "but from that time on, I never again put my hands in my pockets when I was around bootleggers. I was always cautious and tried to be discreet, especially when such dealings were being conducted in the United States."

That is something Heidsieck's colleague, Count Maxence de Polignac, learned the hard way. Polignac was the commercial director for Pommery & Greno. He had been receiving large orders for champagne from his agent, who was still in Chicago. "These are for a very important client," the agent said, refraining from divulging the name. There was never any haggling over price and bills were promptly paid. Polignac decided orders like this deserved his personal attention, so he made up his mind to go to Chicago and try to meet the mysterious client.

When he arrived, a welcoming committee was there to greet him. It was the FBI. Polignac's customer turned out to be the gangster Al Capone. The next day, newspaper headlines trumpeted the news: "French Count in the Clink." Polignac was released a few days later after paying a heavy fine.[6]

But Prohibition left behind some unexpected souvenirs. In 1959, a young couple digging for clams off Cape Cod saw a bottle bobbing in the water. Then they saw several more. Using their clam rakes, the two retrieved what clearly were champagne bottles. Although the labels had long since floated away, the bottles were still full. When they were taken to a nearby restaurant and opened, the brand on the corks read: "Charles Heidsieck, Extra Dry, 1920." Upon being told about the discovery, Jean-Charles said he was not surprised. "The bottles were obviously jettisoned by bootleggers who were being pursued by the Coast Guard."

What was a surprise was that the champagne, even after all those years, was still good.

Although no one knew how long Prohibition would last, champagne-makers realized it could not go on indefinitely, and they were determined to be prepared for its end. They began crossing the Atlantic in droves to assess the situation and determine, as André Simon pointed out, "what the chances were of creating or reviving a worthwhile demand for their brands in the United States. What was badly wanted was not commercial travelers hawking their wares but missionaries who might persuade the young people of America that champagne was the fairway, as opposed to the out-of-bounds of hard liquor and soft drinks."

Part of their gospel was that champagne was good for everyone's health. Journalists and foreign personalities were brought to Champagne for conferences where medical experts described how champagne helped prevent depression, appendicitis, and infectious diseases such as typhoid. A professor from the School of Medicine in Bordeaux reminded everyone of champagne's role in the war, "how this wine allowed the fighting men to endure the ordeals of the trenches. That's what kept their morale and hopes alive."

France's leading wine distributor, Nicolas, even put out a coffee-table book complete with illustrations by the artist Raoul Dufy. It was called *Mon Docteur, le Vin (Wine, My Doctor)*. The preface was written by Marshal Philippe Pétain, the former commander-in-chief of the French army. In his "Tribute to Wine," Pétain said: "Of all the supplies sent to our army during the war, wine was surely the mostly highly anticipated and appreciated by soldiers. In order to get their ration of wine, our poilus would risk danger, face down shells, and defy the military police. To them, supplies of wine were almost as vital as supplies of ammunition. Wine was a stimulant that improved morale and physical well-being. It contributed significantly—in its own way—to our victory."

The French government took part in the health blitz, too, issuing statistics showing that the oldest and healthiest people in France came from winemaking regions. "Drink better, drink less, drink longer," was the official slogan. It was a sentiment embraced by Dr. Gaston Guéniot of the French Academy of Medicine. Guéniot had written a book entitled *Living to Be 100*, in which he described how wine contributed to long life. He was 102 at the time.

When the French boxer Georges Carpentier knocked out the American Battling Lavinsky in the fourth round to take the World Light Heavyweight Championship, other doctors pointed out how the United States had lost its edge in sports. "Since Prohibition, the Americans have retrogressed in athletics," one said. "They have lost their superiority in world boxing championships, skiing, sailing, and tennis, and are now only able to maintain their superiority in foot races over short distances." [7]

Although such claims may sound far-fetched today, they were taken seriously at the time by nearly everyone. Few failed to notice that after Carpentier's victory, another Frenchman, Emile Pladner, scored a first-round knockout against the American Frankie Genaro to become the World Flyweight Champion.

Slowly but surely, Prohibition began losing its punch. There were increasing fears of being poisoned by bathtub gin, wood alcohol, or some other concoction of uncertain provenance. During his visit to the United States, H. Warner Allen was taken to a speakeasy in Greenwich Village, where he paid an "enormous sum" for what he said was the worst bottle of wine he ever tasted. "We swallowed down its nastiness in an atmosphere of dramatic secrecy that was as ridiculous as it was revolting." [8]

What finally brought Prohibition to its knees, however, was growing dismay over how otherwise respectable, law-abiding citizens were being turned into criminals—with one sip of wine. A presidential commission declared that Prohibition was unenforceable and created a climate of rampant gangsterism. Al Capone, it pointed out, who had been smuggling in massive quantities of champagne, employed an army of between seven hundred and one thousand gunmen while running an underworld empire that grossed $60 million a year. With gang wars on Capone's home turf leaving hundreds dead, the government and most Americans were now convinced Prohibition was not worth its price in lawlessness, and should be repealed.

By the end of 1933, it was gone, scrapped by a constitutional amendment which was ratified by the states in record time. But there was another reason why Prohibition disappeared so fast. A new and far more serious crisis had arisen.

Throughout the 1920s, Western economies had been behaving erratically. In France, the franc would rise, then fall, the victim of what one economist called "volatile extremist politics." To stabilize it, the government devalued the franc to a fifth of what it was before the war. Products sat on the shelves because few could afford to buy them. Domestic sales of champagne, which had been the mainstay of the industry, fell nearly 50 percent. Exports tumbled, too, as other countries erected tariff barriers. In one country where champagne had been selling for 32 francs a bottle, the price was now 230 francs.[9]

On October 21, 1929, the New York Stock Exchange took a sudden dive. Two days later, it was tumbling out of control. On October 29, it crashed. The Great Depression had begun.

To the people of Champagne, it seemed like yet another chapter in the same old dreary story. Good times never lasted; even in the best of times something was always lurking around the corner. Old-timers reminded others how Champagne had been "standing on top of golden hours" when the Franco-Prussian War erupted in 1870. A few years later, they added, during the Belle Époque, the 1911 Champagne riots broke out. Three years after that, just when peace between growers and producers had been restored, World War I exploded. It had been this way for centuries, they said. Now it was happening again.

The crash on Wall Street coincided with what everyone had predicted would be a terrific harvest in Champagne. "It was extraordinarily bad luck," wrote historian Patrick Forbes, "that at this crucial moment in the Champagne district's history, when the ravages of war and of phylloxera were on the point of being fully repaired and the winefield seemed destined to go forward from strength to strength, there should have occurred a world-wide economic crisis of unprecedented proportions."[10]

Cellars were full of outstanding wine, but there were no buyers. In 1934 Mother Nature rubbed salt in the wound by giving Champagne exactly what it didn't need: another bumper harvest of top quality. Now cellars were not merely full, they were bursting. Champagne-makers had almost 150 million bottles stuffed in their cellars but were able to export only four and a half million. "These were evil days indeed for winegrower and champagne-maker alike, as bad as any in the winefield's history," Forbes said.[11]

Champagne houses stopped buying grapes and laid off workers. Some resorted to making what was called Forty Day Champagne, an allusion to how hastily and sloppily it was put together. It sold for cut-rate prices and under phony labels to hide the maker's name and protect his reputation.

Still other houses reverted to making still wines, something that hadn't been done for one hundred years. "Champagne has lost its bubbles and its party dress," bemoaned one newspaper.[12] Another warned that "champagne is killing itself" by producing inferior wine. Some firms went bankrupt and vanished forever. Others were sold at rock-bottom prices.[13]

For those who worked the land, the situation was even more acute. Prices for grapes and other agricultural products had fallen so much that they were actually below what they had been in the sixteenth century. In desperation, vignerons banded together, pooled what little money they had, and tried to make their own champagne. Most were unsuccessful and soon gave up.

Some abandoned their vineyards, left the countryside, and sought work in the cities. Others were reduced to begging on street corners.

To many in Champagne it seemed like their only hope was finding a savior or a fairy godmother. What they found was someone more like a godfather, a man they rescued from the pages of history.

In turn, Dom Pérignon rescued them.

If ever there were an unlikely savior, it was the humble monk from Hautvillers. During the two hundred years since his death, no one had paid much attention to him. Even in Champagne, very few people had heard of him. Unlike his contemporary Louis XIV, Dom Pérignon had left no lasting monument like the palace of Versailles, had organized no glittering fêtes, had led no armies into battle. Rather, he'd worked quietly and unobtrusively, establishing respect for his religious devotion and the quality of his wines. In addition, many details of his life and work had been lost when the monastery at Hautvillers was sacked during the French Revolution.

All of which made it easy for a group of enterprising Champenois to rewrite history and organize a celebration marking the two hundred fiftieth anniversary of Dom Pérignon's "invention" of sparkling champagne. Their goal was to revive sales, and they were not about to let facts get in the way. Never mind that Dom Pérignon did *not* invent champagne, or that the date chosen for the anniversary was completely arbitrary. Everyone also ignored the fact that just eighteen years earlier, with World War I on the horizon, they tried to do the same thing. That one was hailed as the two hundredth anniversary. A major newspaper at the time carried a picture showing the cellarmaster holding a frothing bottle of champagne and exclaiming, "I have tasted the stars!" That event, however, was lost in the onrush of the war.

The *new* anniversary, the two hundred fiftieth, was a three-day party held at the restored abbey of Hautvillers. There were papers by leading scholars and speeches by government officials, all rendering homage to Dom Pérignon's genius. There was also a lot of champagne poured, so much, in fact, that no one noticed that not a single paper or speech ever specified exactly what it was Dom Pérignon really had done. But none of that mattered. The celebration achieved its purpose. Sales of champagne soared and Dom Pérignon became the man of the hour. He was heralded as the man who invented bubbly, the "father of champagne," and his name was suddenly everywhere, attached to celebrations, streets, and even cigars.[14]

(Not until the 1950s when serious historians began deconstructing the legend and sifting through the few existing records were Dom Pérignon's achievements finally put into perspective. But the aura remains. Today, the monk's name "belongs" to Moët & Chandon and is attached to its flagship cuvée, Dom Pérignon.)

By 1935 the worst of the Depression was over for Champagne, but the crisis had underscored the urgency of streamlining the industry and restoring its integrity. The Champenois now understood they could not afford to wait for the government to rescue them, that they had to depend on themselves. They also had come to realize that the success of champagne was fragile and that they must never cease protecting and trying to develop it. "Prosperity does not fall from the sky," one said. There was another lesson they'd learned, too: It was not enough to come together only during times of crisis; they had to remain united in good times as well.

The following year, five men representing different segments of the champagne community sat down in the garden of a major champagne house to formulate a plan. These were men who, in the past, had frequently found themselves at odds with each other but now realized they had to put aside their differences.

Like many gatherings in Champagne, this one began with a toast. "Here's to success," said the host, raising his glass, "but the only way to assure it is if we remember that we are all in the same basket of grapes."

Serious questions spilled out immediately. How can we prevent fraud and guarantee quality? How can we protect our rights as growers and producers? "And let's not forget the consumer," one representative injected. "They're the ones who keep us in business."

The most perplexing question concerned Champagne. "Where is it, exactly?" one person asked, noting that the precise boundaries of the growing area had never been set. Until then, it had been defined by custom and tradition. Growers planted vines where their fathers and grandfathers had planted them with little regard to soil conditions or other factors that determine the quality of grapes used for champagne.

After fourteen hours, it was clear the men weren't going to come up with all the answers, not immediately anyway. What they did do was establish a regulatory body called the Commission de Châlons, named after the town in which it met, to "protect the customs and traditions of champagne," their hope being that it would resolve once and for all the myriad of questions that had swirled around Champagne for generations. Champagne thus became the first wine in the world to subject itself to such stringent regulations.

As the five participants got up to leave, they were feeling rather proud of themselves. They were convinced they had achieved something significant. One of them stopped to count the empty champagne bottles on the table. He was astounded to discover there were twenty-five. "But it was with perfectly clear heads that we took the road home," he said.[15]

What the five men did not anticipate was that the "customs and traditions of champagne" they hoped to protect would be threatened by an old enemy. Germany had been humiliated by the Treaty of Versailles, which ended World War I. It was forced to return all occupied territory as well as Alsace-Lorraine, which it had annexed after the Franco-Prussian War. It also was made to pay war reparations, a staggering sum that practically bankrupted the country. German pride was bruised further when President Wilson exclaimed at the peace conference, "What abominable manners! The Germans are really a stupid people. They always do the wrong thing."[16]

The indignities of Versailles helped sweep Adolf Hitler into power in 1933. He vowed to overturn the treaty and make Germany the greatest power in Europe. "No one since Napoleon had thought in such audacious terms," historian Paul Johnson said.[17]

Hitler moved quickly. He pulled Germany out of the League of Nations, instituted compulsory military service, then occupied and rearmed the Rhineland. In 1938 his armies marched into Austria and Czechoslovakia. At a conference in Munich, Britain and France tried unsuccessfully to appease Hitler by ratifying the Austrian Anschluss and endorsing his claim to the Sudetenland. The following year, Hitler took over Poland. Britain declared war on September 3, and a few hours later, France reluctantly did the same.

For the French, this would be the third war against Germany in less than seventy-five years, and it was extremely unpopular. How will we survive? wondered writer Louis-Ferdinand Céline, who agonized that there could be as many as twenty-five million casualties. "We'll disappear body and soul from this place like the Gauls. They left us hardly twenty words of their own language. We'll be lucky if anything more than the word *merde* survives us." [18]

For most, the horrors of World War I were still vivid. "Any Frenchman over thirty remembered the blind wastage of young men in 1914–18, which had made France a nation of old people and cripples," wrote historian Robert Paxton. "That stark fact was brought home daily by the sight of mutilated veterans in the street. It took on particular urgency in the middle 1930s with the advent of the 'hollow years,' the moment when as demographers had predicted, the annual draft contingent dropped in half because so few boys had been born in 1915–19. One more bloodbath, and would there be a France at all?" [19]

It was a question the people of Champagne asked themselves every day. The region had lost so many people in the Great War that its population in the mid-1920s was actually less than what it had been in 1800. Now, with another world war on the horizon, the sense of dread, of déjà vu, was overwhelming. Once again, war had been declared just as the harvest was about to begin.

Once more, work in the vineyards would fall on the shoulders of women, children, and old people. In addition, the United States—again—would hold back initially and remain neutral.

This time, however, the Champenois were better prepared. During the eight months that passed before German armies, massing across the border, finally invaded, hundreds of thousands of bottles of champagne were hidden away. Some were moved to the furthest recesses of the cellars where they were unlikely to be detected; others were sealed up behind fake walls. One champagne house, Laurent-Perrier, went so far as to erect a shrine with a statue of the Virgin Mary to conceal its champagne.[20] Everyone was mindful of what former Prime Minister Edouard Daladier said, that wine was "France's most precious jewel," and that no jewel sparkled more than champagne. Everyone knew that seizing that jewel and taking control of the lucrative champagne industry was one of the Third Reich's goals.

On May 10, 1940, the long-anticipated invasion began. Within a month, France had surrendered, almost without a struggle, and more than a million and a half Frenchmen had been made prisoners of war. The country was carved in two, with the northern two-thirds, including Champagne, placed under military occupation.

The first two months of the occupation were chaotic ones for Champagne. Triumphant troops went from house to house, cellar to cellar, grabbing and drinking whatever they could lay their hands on. At Mumm, a man brandishing a key suddenly arrived at the front door and announced, "Ich bin Graff von Mumm! ("I am Count von Mumm!") He was the son of George Hermann von Mumm, who had been forced out twenty-five years earlier when the firm was confiscated by the French government as enemy property in World War I. Now, the younger Mumm had returned to claim what he said was rightfully his.[21]

Germany's victory had happened so fast that even its high command was startled. Not until September were German authorities able to regain control and restore order. By then, however, an estimated two million bottles of champagne had disappeared. If there was any consolation for the Champenois, it was that their towns and villages had been spared the massive destruction suffered in the previous war, and that there had been no battles in the vineyards.

In Berlin, however, Field Marshal Hermann Göring was hurriedly mapping out plans that would inflict a different kind of pain on Champagne. Göring had been charged with setting economic policy for occupied territories. "France is fattened with such good food that it is shameful," he said. "In the old days, the rule was plunder. Now outward forms have become more humane, but I intend to plunder, and plunder copiously."

Göring told his troops to "transform yourselves into a pack of hunting dogs and always be on the lookout for what will be useful to the people of Germany." However, for wine, and especially champagne, he didn't want a pack, he wanted pointers, people who could sniff out the finest France had to offer. With that in mind, the field marshal turned to the German wine trade, creating a corps of what some called "wine merchants in uniform." The French had another name for them: the weinführers. Their job was to buy as much good French wine as possible and send it back to Germany. The man put in charge of Champagne was Otto Klaebisch.[22]

Champagne-makers heaved a sigh of relief when they heard who had been assigned. Klaebisch had been born and raised in

France, where his parents were cognac merchants. In Germany, Klaebisch headed a wine import company that was the distributor for Lanson Champagne. "We were so happy to get somebody from the wine trade, and not a beer man," said Bernard de Nonancourt of Laurent-Perrier. Another added, "If we're going to be shoved around, it's better to be shoved around by a wine-maker than by some beer-drinking Nazi lout."

Their enthusiasm, however, was short-lived, for the shoving began almost immediately. Klaebisch appeared before the Commission de Châlons to lay down the terms. "Here's what the Third Reich expects," he said. "You will provide us with three hundred fifty thousand bottles of champagne a week, each of which must be stamped, 'Reserved for the Wehrmacht.' You will also be required to supply all German-controlled restaurants, hotels, and nightclubs in France." The weinführer stressed that Germany had first claim on champagne and that if there was any left, some of it might be used by producers to supply their French clients.

The commissioners were nearly speechless. The 1940 harvest had been minuscule, down 80 percent. Klaebisch's assurances that he would pay for the champagne did nothing to mollify them. Everyone knew that while prices supposedly would be "negotiated," the weinführer would pay what he wanted. What's more, Germany had already established a new exchange rate making the mark worth five times what it was before the war, thus enabling Klaebisch to buy as much champagne as he wanted for next to nothing. "It was nothing but legalized plunder," grumbled one producer.

Champagne-makers retaliated any way they could, using bad corks and dirty bottles, misdirecting shipments to Germany, and adulterating their cuvées. What they sometimes forgot was that the weinführer knew champagne and was a connoisseur. He had a keen palate, good nose, and often conducted spot-checks to make sure no one was trying to trick him.

This was forcefully brought home to François Taittinger, who had recently been brought in to help run the family firm. Like other producers, he was required to send regular samples to Klaebisch. One day, François was summoned to the weinführer's office. Klaebisch was at his desk, a frown on his face. Beside him was an open bottle of Taittinger's champagne. Before François could speak, the weinführer snapped, "How dare you send us fizzy ditch water!" François, who was only twenty and something of a hothead, replied, "Who cares? It's not as though it's going to be drunk by people who know anything about champagne."

Taittinger was arrested and thrown into Reims's Robespierre Prison, where he was held for several days. He had lots of company, for the prison had become a kind of "home away from home" for other champagne-makers guilty of similar offenses.

As months passed, Klaebisch grew more demanding, sometimes insisting on five hundred thousand bottles a week. Because he had grown wary of what champagne-makers were doing, he also ordered that a German officer be present whenever any workers entered the cellars.

Meanwhile, because of shortages caused by the war, champagne-makers were running out of bottles, corks, and sugar. Growers, in turn, were unable to obtain fertilizers or copper sulfate to treat their vines against diseases. Nor did they have enough hay to feed their horses, those, that is, which hadn't been requisitioned by the military.

No one had imagined having to face problems like this—or to

deal with someone like the weinführer—when the Commission de Châlons was set up. Everyone now realized they needed something, or someone, with more clout to represent them.

Only one figure seemed to have the personality and strength of will to stand up to Klaebisch. That person was Count Robert-Jean de Vogüé, head of the largest champagne house, Moët & Chandon. De Vogüé was related to many of the royal families of Europe, and his family owned some of the finest wine estates in France. His brother headed Veuve Clicquot, while a cousin ran one of the most prestigious domains in Burgundy. It was said that if you had a cellar stocked only with de Vogüé wines, you would still have one of the best cellars in the world.

De Vogüé agreed to take on the job of representing the Champenois. His first step, on April 16, 1941, was to form the Comité Interprofessionnel du Vin de Champagne, or CIVC, an umbrella organization enabling growers and producers to present a united front and speak with one voice. The most important voice, however, was his, and it was a voice Klaebisch was prepared to listen to.

The two men met regularly to work out quotas, negotiate prices, alleviate shortages, and settle any other problems that arose. While their meetings were always businesslike, it was apparent that the weinführer admired his counterpart and was impressed by his lineage. De Vogüé was a skilled negotiator and, at one point, was so persuasive that Klaebisch agreed to intervene with his superiors in order to free seven hundred French POWs whose skills, de Vogüé said, were essential for maintaining the production of champagne.

Nevertheless, the weinführer never hesitated to exert his authority if he felt he was being pushed or taken advantage of.

When Maurice and Georges Pol-Roger, for instance, complained that they could not meet one of Klaebisch's quotas, the weinführer retorted, "Work Sundays!"

By then, Klaebisch had begun to sense that other things were going on. Champagne had become a major stronghold for the French Resistance, the most secretive and best-organized in France. The crayères and underground galleries of champagne houses made ideal storage places for weapons and ammunition parachuted into France by the Allies. One of the biggest caches was at Piper-Heidsieck. The crayères also served as hiding places for those seeking refuge from the Gestapo. At the house of Krug, Joseph and Jeanne Krug hid allied airmen who had been shot down, concealing them in their caves until they could be smuggled out of the country. At Ruinart, one of the more unusual forms of resistance took place.

Workers there had noticed a distinct pattern to some of their champagne shipments. Wherever a surprisingly large consignment was sent, a military offensive usually followed. It first happened in 1940 when the Germans ordered tens of thousands of bottles to be sent to Romania where, officially, there was only a small German mission. Within a few days, German troops invaded the country. The following year, another huge order came in for bottles to be specially corked and packed so they could be sent to "a very hot country." That country turned out to be Egypt where Field Marshal Rommel was about to begin his North Africa campaign. The information was relayed to British intelligence.

The most vital center of resistance, however, was Moët & Chandon. It had been badly pillaged in the early days of the occupation, and many of its buildings had been burned. "Under the circumstances, we had no choice but to resist," Claude Fourmon, Moët's commercial director, explained. The entire management team was involved, none moreso than Robert-Jean de Vogüé, who headed the political wing of the French Resistance in eastern France.

By 1943 the Gestapo had grown suspicious and begun monitoring de Vogüé and his colleagues. On November 24, he and Fourmon were called to Klaebisch's office to discuss the harvest. A half hour into the meeting, the telephone rang and the weinführer answered it. A look of surprise crossed his face. Moments later, two men with revolvers drawn burst into the office and handcuffed de Vogüé and Fourmon. Both were accused of aiding the Resistance. Fourmon was sent to the concentration camp at Buchenwald. De Vogüé was hauled before a military tribunal and sentenced to death.

Shock waves rippled through Champagne. On November 29, for the first time in history, the entire Champagne community went on strike. Klaebisch called it "an act of terrorism" and warned of severe repercussions if the strike wasn't ended immediately. The protest escalated. The weinführer realized he held the weaker hand. Without the Champenois, there was no way he could supply Berlin with the champagne it expected. For its part, Berlin was not about to spend resources putting down civil unrest in France. It needed every soldier for the catastrophe unfolding on the Russian front.

Klaebisch, fearing *he* might end up on the Russian front, backed down. De Vogüé's death sentence was postponed, and the strike finally ended, but not before nearly every champagne house was heavily fined. Moët & Chandon suffered the worst. It was put under direct German control, and all its top managers were imprisoned.

By mid-1944, especially after D-day, the Germans knew their days were numbered and began cracking down even harder. Arrests, deportations, and executions increased sharply. That July, Otto Klaebisch placed a huge order for champagne, then, three weeks later, abruptly canceled it and returned to Germany. Millions of francs of unpaid bills were left behind.

In Épernay, the Germans stockpiled a great quantity of dynamite, the plan being to blow up the city's cellars and bridges if they had to evacuate. The city was spared when the U.S. Third Army, under General George Patton, swept into Épernay on August 28, taking the enemy completely by surprise.

From that point on, Allied bombing of the province intensified. One of the targets was Rilly, a tiny village of vignerons on the northern slopes of the Montagne de Reims. At first, no one could understand why the Allies were bombing it so determinedly. Only after the liberation did it become known that the Germans had been using the railway tunnel there to hide its V2 rockets.

In the spring of 1945, the city of Reims gained a prominent resident. General Dwight D. Eisenhower, Supreme Commander of the Allied Expeditionary Force, had moved his headquarters there to oversee final operations and await Germany's unconditional surrender. "It was appropriate the surrender should happen here," a resident said, "in a city the Germans had caused so much suffering only thirty years earlier."

The signing took place at 2:41 A.M. on May 7 in the city's technical college. "Well," said Eisenhower afterward, "I guess this calls for champagne." Someone produced a bottle and opened it. It was flat. Eisenhower went home to bed.

By 8:30, he was up again, walking down Boulevard Lundy toward his office. Upon arriving, the first thing he did was send one of his men to fetch six cases of champagne, seventy-two bottles in all, for a proper celebration. The champagne was something special: it was Pommery & Greno from the widely acclaimed 1934 vintage.

As one historian later said, the last explosions of the war were the popping of champagne corks.

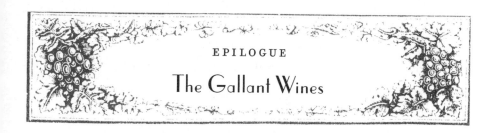

The Gallant Wines

It had been a long journey, one that began at Attila's campsite, took us to tiny vineyard villages where riots in 1911 nearly
plunged France into civil war, led us to the trenches of World
War I, and finally to the battlefields of World War II. All along
the way, we felt as if we were accompanied by an army of
ghosts.

There was Marcel Savonnet, our World War I friend who died
just after celebrating his 106th birthday. There was also Dom
Pierre Pérignon, no longer a myth to us but someone real who
had labored in the very vineyards we traipsed. There was also
Albert Corpart, Pommery & Greno's vineyard manager, whose
spirit hovers over Champagne's vineyards to this day. When
Reims was evacuated before the second Battle of the Marne,
Corpart insisted on staying behind and watching over Pommery
as its caretaker. When a gas artillery shell struck the champagne
house and started a fire, he ran to put it out. Working with a gas
mask, however, was nearly impossible so he tore it off and extin-
guished the fire. A few months after being decorated by the gov-

ernment for his heroism during the war, Corpart died from the effects of the gas.

Robert-Jean de Vogüé was more fortunate. He survived the horrors of a Nazi death camp, but only barely. His son Ghislain told us that the family at first did not recognize the ill and wasted man who returned to them in 1945. De Vogüé eventually recovered and went on to turn Moët & Chandon into what, until 1962, was the largest family-owned business in France. The organization he founded, the CIVC, proved its mettle in the war and survives today as the governing body for the entire champagne industry.

So much about champagne is about survival, be it wars, bad weather, terrible harvests, maladies like phylloxera, or even boycotts. When Americans, for instance, boycotted French wines after France refused to join the war against Iraq, champagne was the exception. Not only was it unscathed by the protest, sales actually increased.

No matter what happens, champagne seems to go on, evolving, adapting to the times and defying the odds. Today, champagne is a multibillion-dollar industry, a far cry from what it was just a few years ago. While big doesn't necessarily mean bad, Pierre Lanson finds something a bit sad about it.

"Business is so different now," he told us over lunch, noting that Lanson was no longer a family business. Like many other champagne houses, it had been taken over by corporate giants, first by the conglomerate, LVMH, and later by Marne & Champagne, a firm that makes more than two hundred brands of champagne. "In a way, we are victims of our own success," his wife, Elaine, said. "We couldn't afford to keep our own business."

"So much of what champagne is today is about money," Pierre added. "In my father's day, it was about people." Pierre's father, Victor, had guided the champagne house through the dark days of World War II. "That's my father there," Pierre said, pointing to a photograph on the wall. "He made a point of walking through the vineyards and cellars twice a week so he would never lose contact with the workers."

Before we could ask a question, Pierre launched into a story about his father. "He was always elegant and never old, even though he lived to be ninety-eight." Victor had been an artillery officer in World War I and survived eighteen months at Verdun. "But let me tell you how he died," Pierre said. He smiled as he recalled the moment.

"It was in 1967 when his doctor paid him a house call. My father, as always, was dressed in a beautifully tailored suit. He ushered the doctor in, served him a glass of champagne and poured one for himself. They chatted for a few moments while sipping their champagne. And then my father said, 'I'm sorry, Doctor, but I fear I'm going to bother you now.' With that, he died, still holding his glass of champagne.

"Isn't that a wonderful story?" Pierre asked.

We had to agree, but then we had heard so many wonderful stories in Champagne, some heartwarming, others heartrending. Memories die hard there, we found. Monuments, traditions, and cemeteries help keep them alive. So too do the wines themselves, especially those made during the Great War.

There is something magical, almost supernatural, about champagnes made under such horrific conditions. "Never were wines so gallantly made," said one writer. "They were blessed by heaven."

Perhaps the best epitaph for those wines and the people who made them was written by Patrick Forbes, who worked for many years in Champagne. "So great was their love of the vine, so strong their determination to save something for those who returned, that day in, day out, they risked—and sometimes gave—their lives for the vines."

Living long after their makers are gone, those wartime vintages reach out and grip the souls of people who are privileged to taste them. Such was the 1914 that Maurice Pol-Roger made, "the wine of victory," as he called it, which was "drinking beautifully" when the Armistice was signed.

Thirty years later, when Champagne was again liberated, Maurice uncorked another bottle. "Superb golden color," he wrote in his notebook. "Only a trace of mousse remains but an irresistible nose of coffee and vanilla; unctuous and creamy in the mouth with an astonishing vinosity and enduring flavors of orange, toast, and rum."

The bracing acidity of the grapes had enabled the 1914 to evolve into one of the greatest, most long-lived champagnes ever made, one that was still drawing raves in 1998, more than eighty years after it had been made. "The greatest wine experience of my life," said Richard Juhlin, one of the world's foremost experts on champagne. "The color was deep and shining like a golden pagoda. The taste was chewy and tremendously sweet."[1]

We had the privilege of tasting that legendary champagne ourselves when Christian Pol-Roger surprised us by opening a bottle for us. It was still golden and chewy as Juhlin described it, but no longer "tremendously sweet." Much of the fruit had faded in the seven years that had passed. Nevertheless, it was a revelation, like going to Mount Olympus. Who's going to complain if not all of the gods were at home?

While many consider the 1914 to be the greatest champagne of the twentieth century, 1915 is close behind, and it is that champagne Claude Taittinger remembers. It was the first champagne he had ever tasted. His father, who had been a soldier in World War I, served it at a lunch to celebrate Claude's first communion.

"My father always made a little speech on special family occasions," Claude said. "I remember him reminding us that we must never forget this champagne had been harvested under the bombs, and that many people lost their lives so the grapes could be brought in. He said that it had the blood of France running through it.

"I had the feeling this was true, that it actually contained some drops of blood. I am seventy-nine now, and have drunk a bit of champagne every day of my life since then, but the 1915 is the one that stays with me. I have never forgotten its taste."

Every spring in Champagne, the vines begin to weep. The French call it "les pleures" (the time of tears), when sap begins flowing from the wounds inflicted by pruning.

Throughout the centuries, Champagne and its vines have had good reason to weep, given so many wars and other traumas. But the tears the vines shed are a symbol of hope, a sign the vines have survived another winter and that another season of growth is ahead.

It was during one of those springs, as the vines were weeping, that we realized we still had one more stop to make on our journey. We had never taken time to visit the vast number of cemeteries that dot the landscape, or come to grips with the fact that within a fifty-mile radius of Reims, there are more than half a million graves.

It made us think of Alan Seeger, the young American poet who was killed on the Somme and buried in a mass grave near Belloy-en-Santerre.

At the Oise-Aisne American Cemetery, near Reims, where more than 6,012 men are buried, we visited the grave of another poet, Joyce Kilmer. For the first time, his words, "I think that I shall never see / A poem lovely as a tree," struck us as incredibly moving and poignant. As we stood by Kilmer's grave, a heavy fog began rolling in, obscuring the white marble crosses and Stars of David, and turning the plane trees surrounding the cemetery into ghostly images.

A few minutes later, we walked to a small chapel where the names of 241 American soldiers whose remains were never recovered are carved in marble. While reading the names, the chimes of the carillon began playing "Auld Lang Syne." The music brought to mind the words of another writer who visited this same cemetery fifty years earlier:

> When the battles are over and the soldiers have all gone, the real heroes of the Great War—the dead—will reassemble under the moon in the vast cemeteries, whose crosses look like nothing so much as vines that have never borne fruit. And there, champagne will be celebrated once again.[2]

It was time for us to go home.

NOTES

Introduction

1. The story of Attila is cited by several sources including Patrick Forbes, *Champagne: The Wine, the Land and the People* (London: Victor Gollancz, 1985), 83–84.
2. Untitled document, CIVC (Comité Interprofessionnel du Vin de Champagne) archives, 51.
3. From Frederick S. Wildman, *A Wine Tour of France* (New York: Vintage Books, 1976), 42.
4. Forbes, *Champagne*, 92–93.
5. The story of Clovis is from Robert Tomes, *The Champagne Country* (New York: Hurd and Houghton, 1867), 49.
6. Leonard Smith, Stéphane Audoin-Rouzeau, and Annette Becker, *France and the Great War* (Cambridge: Cambridge University Press, 2003), 181.
7. Correlli Barnett. *The Great War* (London: BBC Worldwide, 2003), 87.
8. Ibid., 9.

Chapter 1: The Monarch and the Monk

1. Patrick Forbes, *Champagne: The Wine, the Land and the People* (London: Victor Gollancz, 1985), 90.

2. Henry McNulty, *Champagne* (London: William Collins Sons & Co., Ltd., 1987), 30.

3. Forbes, *Champagne*, 98.

4. Villagers' quotes from untitled documents, CIVC archives, 60–63.

5. For Dom Pérignon, main sources were François Bonal, *Dom Pérignon: vérité et légende* (Langres: Editions Dominique Guéniot, 1995) and René Gandilhon, *Naissance du champagne* (Paris: Hachette, 1968).

6. Bonal, *Dom Pérignon*, 34.

7. René Gandilhon, *Naissance du champagne*, 30.

8. Several sources including Bonal, *Dom Pérignon*, 59–60.

9. Primary sources for the life and health of Louis XIV were accounts by various doctors in *Journal de santé de Louis XIV*, Stanis Perez, ed. (Grenoble: Editions Jérôme Millon, 2004), Prince Michael's biography *Louis XIV: The Other Side of the Sun* (London: Orbis Publishing, 1983), and Nancy Mitford's *The Sun King: Louis XIV at Versailles* (London: Sphere Books Limited, 1966).

10. Prince Michael of Greece, *Louis XIV*, 9.

11. Ibid., 141.

12. Forbes, *Champagne*, 94.

13. The story of Vatel is from Frederick S. Wildman, *A Wine Tour of France* (New York: Vintage Books, 1976), 34.

14. Prince Michael of Greece, *Louis XIV*, 214.

15. Ibid., 184.

16. The quotes from Jean-Baptiste de Salins and Pierre Le Pescheur are from *Journal de santé de Louis XIV*, 430–34.

17. The description of the "war of words" is from *Journal de santé de Louis XIV*, 430–34; and Eric Glatre, *Chronique des vins de Champagne* (Chassigny: Castor & Pollux, 2001), 66–98.

18. Gandilhon, *Naissance du champagne*, 7.

19. Ibid., 12.
20. Ibid., 11.

Chapter 2: The Men in the Iron Masks

1. Information about de Troy and his painting is based on conversations with Christophe Leribault, curator of the Musée Carnevalet in Paris, and Nicole Garnier-Pelle, curator of the Musée Condé in Chantilly.

2. The description of the Regency and petits soupers is from Colin Jones, *The Great Nation: France from Louis XIV to Napoleon* (London: Penguin Books, 2002), 36–73; and Patrick Forbes, *Champagne: The Wine, the Land and the People* (London: Victor Gollancz, 1985), 131.

3. Hugh Johnson, *The Story of Wine* (London: Mitchell Beazley, 1989), 218–19.

4. Claude Taittinger, *Champagne by Taittinger* (Paris: Stock, 1996), 32.

5. Hugh Johnson, *Story of Wine*, 219.

6. The King Frederick and bubbles story is from several sources, including Serena Sutcliffe, *A Celebration of Champagne* (London: Mitchell Beazley, 1988), 14.

7. The description of Catharine the Great and the Russian court is in ibid., 14–15.

8. Hugh Johnson, *Story of Wine*, 219.

9. Ibid., 217.

10. André Simon, *The History of Champagne* (London: Octopus Books, 1971), 58–61.

11. The problems with exploding bottles are described in numerous sources, including: Forbes, *Champagne*, 152; Johnson, *Story of Wine*, 338; Eric Glatre, *Chronique des vins de Champagne* (Chassigny, Castor & Pollux, 2001), 100; and Cynthia Parzych and John Turner, *Pol Roger & Co.* (London: Cynthia Parzych Publishing, 1999), 17.

12. Claude Moët's trips to Versailles are described in Forbes, *Champagne*, 415.

13. Tom Stevenson, *Champagne* (London: Sotheby's Publications, 1986), 235.

14. Nancy Mitford, *Madame de Pompadour* (London: Sphere Books Limited, 1954), 40.

15. The conversation between Louis XV and Madame de Pompadour is assembled from quotes in Nancy Mitford, *The Sun King: Louis XIV at Versailles* (London: Sphere Books Limited, 1966).

16. Forbes, *Champagne*, 132.

17. Colin Jones, *France* (Cambridge: Cambridge University Press, 1994) 175.

18. Ibid., 181–82.

19. The story of tribunals drinking champagne while sentencing people to the guillotine is from Glatre, *Chronique*, 115.

20. The capture of the royal family is described in Forbes, *Champagne*, 141; and Glatre, *Chronique*, 110–11.

21. Jones, *France*, 187.

22. Glatre, *Chronique*, 112.

23. Johnson, *Story of Wine*, 334.

24. Napoleon's childhood and student days were described in Gilbert Martineau, *Madame Mère* (Paris: France-Empire, 1980); and Felix Markham, *Napoleon* (New York: New American Library, 1963).

25. The story of Jean-Rémy's becoming the head of Moët is from Stevenson, *Champagne*, 235.

26. Glatre, *Chronique*, 110.

27. Ibid., 119.

28. The dinner conversation between Jérôme Bonaparte and Jean-Rémy Moët is from Forbes, *Champagne*, 418.

29. Ibid., 144.

30. The story of Bavarian soldiers breaking into Jacquesson is from Robert Tomes, *The Champagne Country* (New York: Hurd and Houghton, 1867).

31. Napoleon's last visit to Moët on March 17 is described in Forbes, *Champagne*, 145.

32. Ibid., 146.

33. Georges Clause and Eric Glatre, *Le champagne: Trois siècles d'histoire* (Paris: Stock, 2002), 106.

Chapter 3: On the Top of Golden Hours

1. The description of Tomes's arrival in Champagne comes from his memoir, *The Champagne Country* (New York: Hurd and Houghton, 1867), 1–5.
2. Ibid., 25.
3. Ibid., chapter 3.
4. Ibid.
5. Ibid., 109.
6. Colin Jones, *France* (Cambridge: Cambridge University Press, 1994), 215.
7. Ibid., 176.
8. The story of Veuve Clicquot and the invention of remuage is from several sources, among them Hugh Johnson, *The Story of Wine* (London: Mitchell-Beazley, 1989), 336–37.
9. Patrick Forbes, *Champagne: The Wine, the Land and the People* (London: Victor Gollancz, 1985), 143.
10. Eric Glatre, *Chronique des vins de Champagne* (Chassigny: Castor & Pollux, 2001), 122.
11. Tomes, *Champagne Country*.
12. Georges Clause and Eric Glatre, *Le champagne: Trois siècles d'histoire* (Paris: Stock, 2002), 88–89.
13. The story of Bohne's salesmanship in Russia is from ibid., 85–86.
14. Glatre, *Chronique*, 144.
15. The story of Champagne Charlie in the United States is from the Heidsieck family archives.
16. All news quotes cited in Eric Glatre and Jacqueline Roubinet, *Charles Heidsieck: Un pionnier et un homme d'honneur* (Paris: Stock, 1955), 33.
17. Tomes, *Champagne Country*, 60–61.
18. Ibid., 68.
19. Ibid., 115.

Chapter 4: All That Glitters

1. The material on Pommery is from the archives of Pommery & Greno.

2. The account of the Franco-Prussian War is from Geoffrey Wawro, *The Franco-Prussian War: The German Conquest of France in 1870–1871* (Cambridge: Cambridge University Press, 2003).

3. Ibid., 221.

4. Ibid., 213.

5. Ibid.

6. All Hohenloe quotes are from the Pommery & Greno archives.

7. The menu for the 99th Day of the Siege is courtesy of Claude Terrail and his restaurant, La Tour d'Argent.

8. Colin Jones, *Cambridge Illustrated History of France* (Cambridge: Cambridge University Press, 1994), 217.

9. André Simon, *The History of Champagne* (London: Octopus Books, 1971), 96.

10. The "funeral" at Maxims is described in François Bonal, *Le livre d'or du Champagne* (Lausanne: Editions du Grand-Pont, 1984), 167.

11. Patrick Forbes, *Champagne: The Wine, the Land and the People* (London: Victor Gollancz, 1985), 160–61.

12. Ibid.

13. The story of porters carrying champagne to British soldiers in Lagos, Nigeria, is from the archives of Moët & Chandon.

14. *Folklore de Champagne*, no. 75 (1981).

15. Ibid.

16. The history of Universal Expositions and the popularity of champagne is from Johannes Willms, *Paris, Capital of Europe: From the Revolution to the Belle Époque* (New York: Holmes & Meier, 1997), 337.

17. The story of Mercier and his balloon is from the archives of Mercier.

18. Forbes, *Champagne*, 157.

19. Eric Glatre, *Chronique des vins de Champagne* (Chassigny: Castor & Pollux, 2001), 274–75.

20. The use of false names for champagne-making, including the bootmaker, is described in Robert Tomes, *The Champagne Country* (New York: Hurd and Houghton, 1867), 82–83.

21. The story of the false Pommery is described in Forbes, *Champagne*, 197.

22. Hervé Luxardo, *Le Peuple Français, Edition 5, Premier Trimestre*, 25.

23. Louis Estienne, *Au jour le jour: Journal, 1909–1914* (Landreville: La Maison Pour Tous, 1961), 8–9.

24. Willms, *Paris, Capital of Europe*, 338.

Chapter 5: When the Marne Drank Champagne

This chapter is based largely on interviews with local residents and three volumes of *Folklore de Champagne*, nos. 67, 75, and 78. Some material was also gleaned from Cyril Ray, *Bollinger: Tradition of a Champagne Family* (London: Heinemann-Kingswood, 1971), 67–87; and from several articles by François Bonal, particularly his brief biography of Gaston Cheque that appeared in *Figures champenoises d'Autrefois*. Historical background is also from Jean Nollevalle, *1911: L'agitation dans le vignoble Champenois* (Épernay: La Champagne viticole, 1961) and the diary of Louis Estienne, *Au jour le jour: Journal, 1909–1914* (Landreville: La Maison Pour Tous, 1961).

Chapter 6: Up the Bloody Slopes

1. All material about Pommery, including Outin's diary, came from the Pommery archives.

2. Cynthia Parzych and John Turner, *Pol Roger & Co.* (London: Cynthia Parzych Publishing, 1999), 90.

3. Ibid., 91.

4. The story of Gallieni and the taxis of the Marne is from Colin Jones, *France* (Cambridge: Cambridge University Press, 1994), 244.

5. C. Moreau-Berillon, *Au pays du Champagne: Le vignoble, le vin* (Reims: L. Michaud, 1924), 285–86.

6. Ibid.

7. Ibid.

8. The account of Charles Walfard is from Rob Robinson and Paula Jarzabkowski, *Champagne 1914: A Great Wine at the Start of the Great War* (unpublished manuscript).

9. The accounts of the destruction of Reims Cathedral and of Fathers Andrieux and Thinot are from the Pommery archives.

10. The story of Pol-Roger's 1914 harvest is from Parzych and Turner, *Pol Roger*, 92–95.

11. Leonard Smith, Stéphane Audoin-Rouzeau, and Annette Becker, *France and the Great War: 1914–1918* (Cambridge: Cambridge University Press, 2003), 89.

12. Ibid., 110–11; also described by Nathalie Simon in "Soudain, un arbre de Noël," *Le Figaro* (December 10, 2004), 28.

Chapter 7: Underground, Under Fire

1. The description of opera in the crayères is from Patrick Forbes, *Champagne: The Wine, the Land and the People* (London: Victor Gollancz, 1985) 182.

2. Other details on life underground comes largely from the Pommery archives.

3. François Bonal, *Le livre d'or du Champagne* (Lausanne: Editions du Grand-Pont, 1984), 174.

4. Albert Chatelle, *Reims, ville des sacres: Notes diplomatiques et secretes et récits inédits* (Paris: Téqui, 1951).

5. The story of Paul Poiret is from François Bonal, *Le livre d'or*, 174.

6. C. Moreau-Berillon, *Au pays du Champagne: Le vignoble, le vin* (Reims, L. Michaud, 1924), 288.

7. François Bonal, *La chronique de François Bonal* (Épernay, 1984).

8. The departure of Hermann von Mumm is recounted in Eric Glatre, *Chronique des vins du Champagne* (Chassigny: Castor & Pollux, 2001), 301.

9. Cynthia Parzych and John Turner, *Pol Roger & Co.* (London: Cynthia Parzych Publishing, 1999), 98.

10. The account of Pol-Roger's duel with the Marne préfet is taken from the Pol Roger archives.

11. Patriotic cuvées noted are in François Bonal, *Le livre d'or*, 175.

12. The story of the fake funeral in the cellars of Mumm is recounted in Forbes, *Champagne*, 185.

13. The use of champagne as a morale-booster is explained in Bonal, *Le livre d'or*, 175.

14. The story of Alan Seeger is based on his letters, poems, and diary.

15. The destruction of Pommery & Greno and the story of Corpart come from the Pommery archives.

Chapter 8: No Drums, No Trumpets

1. Leonard V. Smith, Stéphane Audoin-Rouzeau, and Annette Becker, *France and the Great War: 1914–1918* (Cambridge: Cambridge University Press, 2003), 116.

2. Richard N. Current, T. Harry Williams, and Frank Friedel, *American History: A Survey* (New York: Alfred A. Knopf, 1961), 646–57.

3. Russia's connection to Champagne and Roederer is based on interviews.

4. Correlli Barnett, *The Great War*, rev. ed. (London: BBC Worldwide Ltd., 2003), 87.

5. The account of the French National Assembly voting to give soldiers champagne is recounted in Eric Glatre, *Chronique des vin de Champagne* (Chassigny: Castor & Pollux, 2001), 306.

6. Pétain's defeatest attitude and replacement is described in Smith, Audoin-Rouzeau, and Becker, *France and the Great War*, 149–50.

7. Albert Chatelle, *Reims, ville des sacres: Notes diplimatiques et secretes et recits inédits* (Paris: Téqui, 1951), 146.

8. The evacuation of Reims is described in ibid., 241.

9. The story of confident Germans having trains standing by to haul champagne was reported in *Reims à Paris,* December 18, 1918.

10. The account of colonial troops being promised champagne if they

protect Reims is in François Bonal, *Le livre d'or du Champagne* (Lausanne: Editions du Grand-Pont, 1984), 175.

11. Barnett, *The Great War,* 178.

12. Ibid., 179.

13. Ibid., 209–10.

14. Smith, Audoin-Rouzeau, and Becker, *France and the Great War,* 158.

15. The description of Charlotte singing is from Chatelle, *Reims, ville des sacres,* 253.

16. The accounts of President Wilson's visit to Reims and the city's reconstruction come from the local newspaper, *Reims à Paris.*

17. The devastation caused by phylloxera is described by a number of sources, including Christy Campbell, *Phylloxera: How Wine Was Saved for the World* (London: HarperCollins, 2004), 177–78, 204 (anecdote about circus), 238–41; and Patrick Forbes, *Champagne: The Wine, the Land and the People* (London: Victor Gollancz, 1985), 165–70.

18. Campbell, *Phylloxera,* 204–5.

19. Ibid.

20. The story of Pol-Roger and "the wine to drink with victory" is taken from Maurice Pol-Roger's personal notes.

Chapter 9: When the Bubbles Burst

1. Patrick Forbes, *Champagne: The Wine, the Land and the People* (London: Victor Gollancz, 1985), 191.

2. The story of President Wilson banishing alcohol from the White House is in François Bonal, *Le livre d'or du Champagne* (Lausanne: Editions du Grand-Pont, 1984), 171.

3. Cynthia Parzych and John Turner, *Pol Roger & Co.* (London: Cynthia Parzych Publishing, 1999), 103.

4. Accounts of smuggling are from Forbes, *Champagne,* 190; C. Moreau-Berillon, *Au pays du Champagne: Le vignoble, le vin* (Reims: L. Michaud, 1924), 296; and, concerning St. Pierre and

Miquelon, Eric Glatre, *Chronique des vins du Champagne* (Chassigny: Castor & Pollux, 2001), 303.

5. The story of Warner Allen and the Prince of Wales is in H. Warner Allen, *A Contemplation of Wine* (London: Michael Joseph, 1951), 186–87.

6. The story of Pommery's smuggling champagne to Al Capone was related in a personal interview with Xavier de Polignac.

7. Gaston Derys, *Mon docteur le vin* (Paris: Draeger, 1936), sec. 17.

8. Allen, *Contemplation of Wine*, 187.

9. The erratic behavior of Western economies is cited in Colin Jones, *Cambridge Illustrated History of France* (Cambridge: Cambridge University Press, 1994), 259–60; and Richard N. Current, T. Harry Williams, and Frank Friedel, *American History: A Survey* (New York: Alfred A. Knopf, 1961), 709–27.

10. Forbes, *Champagne*, 192.

11. Ibid., 193.

12. Glatre, *Chronique*, 329.

13. Untitled documents, CIVC archives, 78.

14. The two-hundredth and two-hundred-fiftieth anniversaries of Dom Pérignon are related in François Bonal, *Dom Pérignon: vérité et légende* (Langres: Editions Dominique Guéniot, 1995), 176; and Glatre, *Chronique*, 332.

15. The story of the founding of the Commission de Châlons is described in William I. Kaufman, *Champagne* (New York: Park Lane, 1973), 132.

16. Paul Johnson, *Modern Times: The World from the Twenties to the Eighties* (New York: Harper & Row, 1983), 26.

17. Ibid., 343.

18. Robert O. Paxton, *Vichy France: Old Guard and New Order, 1940–1944* (New York: Columbia University Press, 1982), 12.

19. Ibid.

20. The story of Laurent Perrier's use of a statue to hide his champagne is from a personal interview with Bernard de Nonancourt.

21. Glatre, *Chronique*, 347.

22. The description of the takeover of the champagne industry is based on personal interviews conducted for Don and Petie Kladstrup, *Wine & War: The French, the Nazis, and the Battle for France's Greatest Treasure* (New York: Broadway Books, 2001).

Epilogue: The Gallant Wines

1. Richard Juhlin, *4,000 Champagnes* (Paris: Flammarion, 2004), 314.
2. Untitled document from CIVC archives, 51.

BIBLIOGRAPHY

"1914–1918: Memoires d'une Sale Guerre." Special issue. *En Champagne-Ardenne*, no. 9 (2001). Reims, 2001.

Allen, H. Warner. *A Contemplation of Wine.* London: Michael Joseph, 1951.

Alsop, Susan Mary. *Yankees at the Court: The First Americans in Paris.* Garden City, N.Y.: Doubleday & Company, 1982.

Arlott, John. *Krug, House of Champagne.* London: Davis-Poynter, Ltd., 1976.

Barnett, Correlli. *The Great War.* Rev. ed. London: BBC Worldwide Limited, 2003.

Barzini, Luigi. *The Europeans.* New York: Simon & Schuster, 1983.

Beaugé, Bénédict. *Champagne: images et imaginaire.* Paris: Hazan, 1998.

Bonal, François. *Dom Pérignon: vérité et légende.* Langres: Editions Dominique Guéniot, 1995.

———. *La chronique de François Bonal.* Épernay: September, 1984.

———. *Le livre d'or du Champagne.* Lausanne: Editions du Grand-Pont, 1984.

———. *Anthologie du Champagne.* Langres: Editions Dominique Guéniot, 1995.

Bosser, Jacques. *Champagne! L'histoire et l'art du Champagne*. Paris: Editions Hermé, 2004.

Bourguignon, Philippe. *L'Accord parfait*. Paris: Editions du Chêne, 1997.

Calvert, Catherine, ed. *The Heart of France: A Journey of Discovery*. New York: Sterling Publishing, 2000.

Campbell, Christy. *Phylloxera: How Wine Was Saved for the World*. London: HarperCollins, 2004.

Chatelle, Albert. *Reims, ville des sacres: Notes diplomatiques secretes et récits inédits*. Paris: Téqui, 1951.

Clause, Georges, and Eric Glatre. *Le Champagne: Trois siècles d'histoire*. Paris: Stock, 1997.

Coutant, Catherine, Benoît de la Brosse, and Jean-Marie Lecomte. *Saint-Vincent en Champagne ou la tradition à nouveau partagée*. Louvergny: Editions Noires Terres, 2003.

Current, Richard N., T. Harry Williams, and Frank Freidel. *American History: A Survey*. New York: Alfred A. Knopf, 1961.

Derys, Gaston. *Mon docteur le vin*. Paris: Draeger, 1936. Translated by Benjamin Ivry, with an introduction by Paul Lukacs. New Haven: Yale University Press, 2003.

Duijker, Hubrecht. *The Wines of the Loire, Alsace and Champagne*. London: Mitchell Beazley, 1983.

Estienne, Louis. *Au jour le jour: Journal, 1909–1914*. Landreville: La Maison Pour Tous, 1961.

Folklore de Champagne nos. 67 (1979), 75 (1981), 78 (1982).

Foote, Shelby. *The Civil War: A Narrative. Vol. 1: Fort Sumter to Perryville*. New York: Random House, 1958.

Forbes, Patrick. *Champagne: The Wine, the Land and the People*. London: Victor Gollancz Ltd., 1985.

Gale, George. "Phylloxera Vastatrix, Devastator of Vines." *The World of Fine Wine*, no. 2 (2004).

Gandilhon, René. *Naissance du champagne: Dom Pierre Pérignon*. Paris: Hachette, 1968.

Garnier-Pelle, Nicole. *The Painting Collection at Chantilly: Masterpieces of the Condé Museum*. Paris: Art Lys, 2000.

——. *Chantilly, Musée Condé: Peintures du XVIIIe siècle*. Paris: Editions des Réunion des Musées Nationaux, 1995.

Glatre, Eric. *Chronique des vins de Champagne*. Chassigny: Castor & Pollux, 2001.

——. *Champagne: Le guide de l'amateur*. Geneva: Minerva, 1999.

——and Jacqueline Roubinet. *Charles Heidsieck: Un pionnier et un homme d'honneur*. Paris: Stock, 1995.

Hart, James A. "Alan Seeger," *Dictionary of Literary Biography*. New York.

Heidsieck, Marcel, and Patrick Heidsieck. *Vie de Charles Heidsieck: souvenirs recueillis et composés par Marcel et Patrick Heidsieck d'après des documents de famille*. Reims: Société Charles Heidsieck, 1962.

Jarzabkowski, Paula, and Rob Robinson. *Champagne 1914: A Great Wine at the Start of the Great War*. Unpublished manuscript.

Jefford, Andrew. *The New France: A Complete Guide to Contemporary French Wine*. London: Mitchell Beazley, 2002.

Johnson, Hugh. *The Story of Wine*. London: Mitchell Beazley, 1989.

Johnson, Hugh, and Jancis Robinson. *The World Atlas of Wine*. 5th Edition. London: Mitchell Beazley, 2001.

Johnson, Paul. *Modern Times: The World from the Twenties to the Eighties*. New York: Harper & Row, 1983.

Jones, Colin. *The Great Nation: France from Louis XV to Napoleon*. London: Penguin Books, 2002.

——. *Cambridge Illustrated History of France*. Cambridge: Cambridge University Press, 1994.

Juhlin, Richard. *4000 Champagnes*. Paris: Flammarion, 2004.

——. *2000 Champagnes*. Solna: Methusalem, 1999.

Kaufman, William I. *Champagne*. New York: Park Lane, 1973.

Keegan, John. *The First World War*. London: Hutchinson, 1998.

Kladstrup, Don, and Petie Kladstrup. *Wine & War: The French, the Nazis, and the Battle for France's Greatest Treasure*. New York: Broadway Books, 2001.

Le Page, Louis. *Épernay pendant la guerre*. Paris: Imprimerie perfecta, 1921.

Lichine, Alexis. *Alexis Lichine's New Encyclopedia of Wines & Spirits*. 7th ed. London: Cassell Publishers, 1987.

Liger-Belair, Gérard. *La physique des bulles de champagne*. Paris: Académie Morim, 2004.

Mambret, Jacques. *Champagne!* Reims: Editions Dominique Fradet, 2002.

Markham, Felix. *Napoleon*. New York: New American Library, 1963.

Martineau, Gilbert. *Madame Mère*. Paris: France-Empire, 1980.

Mathieson, Neil. *Champagne*. Edison, N.J.: Chartwell Books, 1999.

McInnes, Ian. *Painter, King & Pompadour: François Boucher at the Court of Louis XV*. London: Frederick Muller Limited, 1965.

McNie, Maggie. *Champagne*. London: Faber and Faber, 1999.

McNulty, Henry. *Champagne*. London: William Collins Sons & Co., Ltd, 1987.

Médiathèque d'Épernay. *Mémoires de la table: Vins de Champagne et d'ailleurs*. Ex. Cat. Paris FFCB, 2000.

Michael, Prince of Greece. *Louis XIV: The Other Side of the Sun*. London: Orbis Publishing, 1983.

Mitford, Nancy. *The Sun King: Louis XIV at Versailles*. London: Sphere Books Limited, 1966.

———. *Madame de Pompadour*. London: Sphere Books Limited, 1954.

Moreau-Berillon, C. *Au pays du Champagne: Le vignoble, le vin*. Reims: L. Michaud, 1924.

Nollevalle, Jean. *1911: L'agitation dans le vignoble champenois*. Épernay: La Champagne Viticole, 1961.

Norton, Lucy, ed. *Saint-Simon at Versailles*. London: Harnish Hamilton, 1980.

Parzych, Cynthia, and John Turner. *Pol Roger & Co*. London: Cynthia Parzych Publishing, 1999.

Paxton, Robert O. *Vichy France: Old Guard and New Order 1940–1944.* New York: Columbia University Press, 1982.

Perez, Stanis, ed. *Journal de santé de Louis XIV.* Grenoble: Editions Jérôme Millon, 2004.

Pinkney, David H. *Napoleon III and the Rebuilding of Paris.* Princeton: Princeton University Press, 1958.

Piper, David, general editor. *The Random House Library of Painting & Sculpture.* 4 vols. New York: Random House, 1981.

Poems of the Great War: 1914–1918. St. Ives: Penguin Books, 1998.

Ray, Cyril. *Bollinger: Tradition of a Champagne Family.* London: Heinemann-Kingswood, 1971.

Reims à Paris. 1918 editions.

Rigaux, Jacky, and Christian Bon. *Les nouveaux vignerons: Le réveil des terroirs.* Messigny-et-Vantoux: Editions de Bourgogne, 2002.

Seeger, Alan. *Letters and Diary of Alan Seeger.* New York: C. Scribner's Sons, 1917.

———. *Poems.* New York: C. Scribner's Sons, 1916.

Seward, Desmond. *Monks and Wine.* London: Mitchell Beazley, 1979.

Simon, André. *The History of Champagne.* London: Octopus Books, 1971.

Simon, Nathalie. "Soudain, un arbre de Noël," *Le Figaro* (December 10, 2004), 23.

Smith, Leonard V., Stéphane Audoin-Rouzeau, and Annette Becker. *France and the Great War 1914–1918.* Cambridge: Cambridge University Press, 2003.

Stevenson, Tom. *Champagne.* London: Sotheby's Publications, 1986.

Sutcliffe, Serena. *A Celebration of Champagne.* London: Mitchell Beazley, 1988.

Taittinger, Claude. *Champagne by Taittinger.* Paris: Stock, 1996.

Thibault, Michel. *Reims: Mémoire en Images.* Saint-Cyr-sur-Loire: Editions Alan Sutton, 2002.

Tomes, Robert. *The Champagne Country.* New York: Hurd and Houghton, 1867.

Wawro, Geoffrey. *The Franco-Prussian War: The German Conquest of*

France in 1870–1871. Cambridge: Cambridge University Press, 2003.

Wildman, Frederick S. *A Wine Tour of France*. New York: Vintage Books, 1976.

Willms, Johannes. *Paris: From the Revolution to the Belle Époque*, New York: Holmes & Meier, 1997.

ACKNOWLEDGMENTS

When one has been as fortunate as we've been in having help from so many people, it's hard to know where to begin, so let's begin at the beginning.

One of the first people we contacted for this book was Claude Taittinger. Claude refers to himself as a "Sunday historian," and there seems to be nothing he does not know about champagne and Champagne. He's written several books himself and generously agreed to review some of our early drafts, making corrections and offering helpful suggestions along the way. By inviting us to tastings and introducing us to other knowledgeable Champenois, he helped us understand how the world of champagne has changed, and continues to change. His enthusiasm and attention to detail go a long way to explain why he makes such great champagne, and why we feel so privileged to have had the benefit of his counsel and friendship. Thank you, Claude.

Thanks as well to Christian Pol-Roger. Christian is the heart and soul of his champagne house, a man whose effervescent personality and warm hospitality are legendary. No one conveys the spirit and joy of champagne better than he does, as we discovered on a cold winter's day while we were taking part in a book signing in Épernay. Suddenly, in popped Christian, carrying a couple of bottles of his 1996 *rosé*. "Something to warm you up," he said, then added, "How about coming home with me for lunch?" How could we refuse? There, in front of a crackling fire, we listened as he and his wife Danielle described what life is like in Champagne. These are two of the busiest people we have ever known, jetting around the world, hosting events and promoting their champagne. Yet they always make visitors feel welcome, as though you were just the people they wanted to see. On one occasion, when our energy and incentive were flagging, Christian gave us the best pep talk we could have had. He pointed out that there is a clear connection between good writing and fine champagne. "Actually," he said, "it's something Maurice Druon of the Académie Française—you know his books, *Les Rois Maudits*—told me a few weeks ago. He said that both require the same dedication and willingness to make sacrifices for quality."

Prince Alain de Polignac, former chief oenlogist at Pommery & Greno, is another person to whom we are deeply indebted. He is a descendant of Louise Pommery, and it was our good fortune to meet him while he was working to preserve the Pommery archives. Records, old photographs, whatever he came across was generously shared with us. As much as anyone, Prince Alain made World War I come alive. Escorting us to the top of one of Pommery's towers, he showed us how close the champagne house had been to the front line. "We had at least twenty graves there," Prince Alain said, pointing toward one of the vineyards, "graves of soldiers and some of our workers who were killed in the bombardments. We wanted to keep them and build a memorial, but at the end of the war the government decided to establish war cemeteries so the bodies were removed. In memory of them, we erected this plaque with their names." At the top was the name of Prince Alain's grandfather.

Pierre and Elaine Lanson shared their family's history with us as well. They not only brought out fascinating stories from the past but also raised important points about Champagne's future—all of this over some terrific food and champagne at their home.

Daniel Lorson, director of communications at the CIVC, is another person whose help was indispensable. Had it not been for him, we would never have "met" Robert Tomes. "I have this little book you might find interesting," Lorson told us, "if I can find it. It's somewhere in my library." Much to our delight, a small package arrived in our mail a few weeks later. It was the charming and sometimes caustic memoir Tomes had written during his sojourn in Champagne in the 1860s.

Brigitte Batonnet, the CIVC archivist, was equally generous with her time, answering our endless questions and frequently sending us articles she thought might be helpful, which they certainly were.

It was purely by accident that we met Christian Schopphoven, a picture-archivist at the Médiathèque d'Épernay. We had gone to Champagne to observe events marking the eighty-fifth anniversary of the end of World War I. As we were passing through the village of Avenay Val d'Or, we noticed there was an exhibit of old photographs, cartoons, and drawings from the trenches. It had been put together by Schopphoven and was based on his personal collection. He was there when we walked in. When we told him what we were doing, Schopphoven offered to help any way he could. And did he ever, supplying us with more pictures than we ever dreamed of. He also introduced us to his boss, Annie de Sainte Marèville, director of the Médiathèque. She, too, shared her personal collection of old pictures with us and opened up the library's archive of newspapers from the early 1900s.

Two other archivists deserve special thanks as well. Madame Colette Cortet of Les Amis de Vieux Reims at the Musée Verger, and Francis Leroy at the Municipal Archives of Épernay.

Admittedly, some of our "research" went straight to our heads, and for that we must thank Nicole Snozzi-Arroyo of Champagne Laurent-Perrier. What a delight she is, and what a pleasure it always is to share a bottle of champagne with her. Plus, she seems to know everyone. "Whom should we talk to about this?" we would ask, or, "What about that?" Nicole always had an answer.

One person she urged us to meet was Marie-France Beck at Champagne Charles Heidsieck. Marie-France, who is in charge of public relations, is like a barely contained tornado, whirling about her office and juggling half a dozen things at once. Catching her at the right moment is the challenge. Happily for us, we managed to do that and came away with invaluable accounts of Champagne Charlie's life and exploits.

Mary Roche at Louis Roederer Champagne is completely different. She is soft-spoken, gentle, but like Marie-France, incredibly helpful. Although she's American, Mary knows as much about Champagne as most Champenois. Thanks to her, we got a close-up look at Roederer's connections to the Russian royal court.

Thanks also to Rémy Krug who had to put up with Petie's upset stomach during an interview (NOT, we emphasize, caused by his outstanding champagne). Krug described his grandmother's heroism during the war and the dangers she faced.

Count Xavier de Polignac also brought out some family stories, notably one about his grandfather's arrest in Chicago during Prohibition.

One of the most fascinating parts of our research involved the Riots of 1911. Françoise Weinling provided us with an intimate glimpse of that period by describing how her grandfather, who owned a small vineyard, helped organize demonstrations. Her poignant tribute to him, written in a small historical journal, was what first drew our attention to the suffering of vignerons during that time. Françoise's grandfather died in poverty after a series of terrible harvests in the 1930s.

Françoise also introduced us to François Chaussin, mayor of Landreville in the Aube, who presented us with a copy of the diary which his great-uncle, Louis Estienne, kept during the riots. Chaussin also showed us how his great-uncle had celebrated the harvest of 1893 by scrawling the date on his barn wall with wine (the date was still visible) and had written a postcard with wine as ink to a friend.

In the Midi, the Comité Interprofessionnel du Vin de Languedoc-Roussillon provided us with information about the 1907 winegrowers' uprising there.

Throughout our writing, there was one telephone number we

dialed repeatedly. It belonged to Eric Glatre. He was never too busy to take our calls and field our questions. His books are essential road maps to Champagne's long and complicated history.

When we ventured into the art world, there were two people who were especially helpful: Nicole Garnier-Pelle, chief curator of the Musée Condé at the Château de Chantilly, and Christophe Leribault, chief curator of the Musée Carnavalet in Paris. Garnier-Pelle gave us a private showing of the paintings by de Troy and Lancret. Leribault, the world's leading authority on de Troy, helped us to understand why de Troy painted a picture featuring a champagne cork bursting from its bottle. We were amused when Leribault volunteered that he doesn't drink champagne.

In helping us obtain additional information and pictures for our book, we want to thank Magali Lapié of Moët & Chandon, Raphaëlle Cartier at the Réunion des Musées Nationaux, Marion Muzi-Falconi at Veuve Clicquot, photographer Michel Jolyot, and Madame Mathieu-Rosten of Champagne Lanson.

In a very special category, we also want to extend our gratitude to Roger Savonnet who introduced us to his father Marcel and, as a result, provided us with one of our most moving experiences.

The writer Catherine Coutant also helped bring the past into the present. We were at "literary luncheon" organized by Danielle Pol-Roger when Catherine remarked, "Did you know that the bones of Saint Helena have been stolen again?" The bones, originally spirited away from Rome by the monk Teutgise, had been resting at the Abbey of Hautvillers for centuries. When we replied that we hadn't heard about the recent theft, Catherine added, "What's strange is that whoever stole them left behind the reliquary which was made out of gold and decorated with gemstones." Perhaps there really is magic in those old bones.

Occasionally, we called upon people from our *Wine & War* days. Among them, Ghislain de Vogüé, who described how his father, Robert-Jean, stood up to the weinführer during World War II and kept the Champenois united. There were also Monsieur and Madame Claude Terrail who own the famed Paris restaurant, La Tour d'Argent. One of their treasures is a collection of antique menus including that of the Christmas dinner served during the Siege of Paris. The Terrails graciously provided us with a copy.

Inevitably, we also leaned on family and friends. Don's father, another Don, helped track down information about "Rheims, New York." Anne and David Jacobs provided us with additional details of how sparkling winemakers there sought to take advantage of champagne's reputation.

In this category of family and friends, we also include our agent Robert Shepard who has become such a good friend that he's almost like family. His calming influence, good judgment, and frankness helped us through more than one tough spot. It was a treat having his company on one of our trips to Champagne.

There is another friend we would like to thank as well, a new one, and that's our editor Mauro DiPreta. Mauro, assisted by associate editor Joelle Yudin, paid us the ultimate compliment of leaving us alone while we worked on the manuscript, then probably regretted it when we missed our initial deadline. Nevertheless, he exercised the patience of Job until we finally completed the book. His vision and insightfulness were invaluable. Before

we began writing, Mauro suggested we expand the focus of the
project beyond World War I, putting the traumas Champagne has
suffered in a larger context. It was a deft call, and we are extremely grateful to him for that and for everything else he has
done.

As always, our deepest gratitude goes to our daughters, Regan
and Kwan-li, who helped and supported us in more ways than
they will ever know.